Beyond Kinship

Beyond Kinship

Social and Material Reproduction in House Societies

Edited by

ROSEMARY A. JOYCE and SUSAN D. GILLESPIE

Foreword by Clark E. Cunningham

PENN

University of Pennsylvania Press

Philadelphia

Publication of this volume was supported by grants from the Committee on Research, University of California, Berkeley, and the Research Board, University of Illinois, Urbana-Champaign.

10 9 8 7 6 5 4 3 2 1

Published by
University of Pennsylvania Press
Philadelphia, Pennsylvania 19104-4011

Library of Congress Cataloging-in-Publication Data
Beyond kinship : social and material reproduction in house societies / edited by
Rosemary A. Joyce and Susan D. Gillespie ; foreword by Clark E. Cunningham.
    p.   cm.
Includes bibliographical references and index.
ISBN 0-8122-3547-9 (cloth, alk. paper) — ISBN 0-8122-1723-3 (pbk., alk. paper)
1. Dwellings.   2. Vernacular architecture.   3. Kinship.   4. Material culture.
I. Joyce, Rosemary A., 1956–   .   II. Gillespie, Susan D., 1952–
GN414.B49   2000
307.3'36—dc21   00-021501

Contents

Foreword
Clark E. Cunningham   vii

Preface   xi

1. Beyond Kinship: An Introduction
Susan D. Gillespie   1

2. Lévi-Strauss: *Maison* and *Société à Maisons*
Susan D. Gillespie   22

3. Toponymic Groups and House Organization: The
Nahuas of Northern Veracruz, Mexico
Alan R. Sandstrom   53

4. Transformations of Nuu-chah-nulth Houses
Yvonne Marshall   73

5. Temples as "Holy Houses": The Transformation of Ritual
Architecture in Traditional Polynesian Societies
Patrick V. Kirch   103

6. The Continuous House: A View from the Deep Past
Ruth Tringham   115

7. Maya "Nested Houses": The Ritual Construction of Place
Susan D. Gillespie   135

8. The Tanimbarese *Tavu*: The Ideology of Growth and the Material
Configurations of Houses and Hierarchy in an Indonesian Society
Susan McKinnon   161

9. House, Place, and Memory in Tana Toraja (Indonesia)
Roxana Waterson   177

10. Heirlooms and Houses: Materiality and Social Memory
Rosemary A. Joyce   189

Notes   213

References   225

List of Contributors   261

Index   263

Foreword

Clark E. Cunningham

My first research in eastern Indonesia, on Timor in the late 1950s and early 1960s, involved demonstrating, in a modest fashion, the relationship between the house as a physical, symbolic, and social model of order and the system of kinship and marriage in that society (Cunningham 1964). For that reason I was particularly pleased to serve as a discussant at a symposium, "Opening up the House: A Dialogue Across the Discipline," organized by my colleague at the University of Illinois, Susan Gillespie (an ethnohistorian), and one of our former students, Rosemary Joyce (an archaeologist), and held at the American Anthropological Association annual meeting in 1996. And I am very glad that they were able to build upon that nicely integrated symposium to prepare this creative book which brings together archaeologists, cultural anthropologists, and ethnohistorians to consider, from their various perspectives, the usefulness and complex meanings which might be attached to the notion of the "house society" as introduced by Claude Lévi-Strauss (1984).

One might say that for some decades now the focus in cultural anthropology has been on "words" rather than "things." This book is an excellent contribution to a recently returning concern with the study of material things in all their complexity, one which I applaud, and the book is unique in the way in which it brings together specialists in these three approaches to anthropology to focus upon a single topic.

Some forty years ago, in spring 1958, at the end of my first year of study at the Institute of Social Anthropology at Oxford University, our written examination included an item on which we were to write an essay. It was a simple quotation from Emile Durkheim: "Society is people and things." British social anthropology has often been viewed as highly sociological in nature, but our training then also included learning about "things" and understanding them in their cultural and technological contexts. Durkheim's comment was taken seriously, and our essay answers were to reflect the fact that we understood these complex relationships.

We learned anthropological lessons about society at the Institute, but for our instruction about things we went across to the Pitt-Rivers Museum, where we did hands-on work with artifacts of diverse sorts from around the world. We made drawings of items such as clothing, decoration, tools, baskets, and ritual paraphernalia while learning about their use and the materials from which they were made. Few could forget going out back of the museum to see the diminutive Miss Beatrice Blackwood demonstrate the aboriginal Australian bull-roarer, swinging it in great circles over her head and making it begin to roar (and leading us to fear she might take off from the parking lot). Our final exam included a session at the museum in which we had to identify about ten selected objects and describe their making and their meaning. At that time, not surprisingly, we studied the art and craft items of largely preliterate societies, the stuff of that museum. We were not concerned with modern things which were and had been making impacts on most such societies for decades, such as bicycles and trucks, injection syringes (about which I was to write later in 1970), or guns.

At the Institute we were reading Marcel Mauss's *The Gift* and learning about notions of exchange and prestation, and we were being introduced by Rodney Needham to the ideas of Lévi-Strauss about marriage exchange and affinal alliance that were embodied in his book, *The Elementary Structures of Kinship*, of which Needham had become particularly aware during his earlier study at Leiden University. Needham was also tutoring me about the ways many of Lévi-Strauss's notions had already been developed in Dutch anthropology on the basis of research in Indonesia, eastern Indonesia in particular. The work of van Wouden in 1935 was particularly influential, and Needham was to complete his translation and publication of it in English in 1968 (van Wouden 1968 [1935]). Needham said that the house might embody symbolism and usages associated with systems of descent and affinal alliance, and he had sought to demonstrate this in brief fashion in his first article to describe a "prescriptive marriage system," that of the Purum (Needham 1958).

Under his guidance I went to eastern Indonesia for doctoral field research, to Timor, to study a society with such a descent and alliance system, and I sought to describe (among other things) the ways in which the organization and conceptual order of the princedom, the local village, the house, and the system of descent and alliance are congruent in complex ways, as van Wouden had indicated. Since that time a number of other students of Needham—and later some of their students—have been joined by others from diverse countries for research on eastern Indonesia, and their writings have been rich and theoretically challenging. And we now have a complex body of ethnography on Austronesia generally that deals with the house both as a physical and symbolic structure and as an ordering principle for (as well as metaphor of) social organization (Fox, ed. 1993). We also have a richer understanding of the complexities of kinship and marriage alliance, as well as symbolic usages and patterns and heirlooms and estates. Attention to these topics has grown in many parts of the world, as this volume attests, and was stimulated by the attention given to the notion of "house societies" by Lévi-Strauss.

Interest in material things and their complex and changing cultural and social contexts and meanings has grown in directions other than the house. Some diverse examples would be the proliferation of rich studies of textiles (such as that by Barnes 1989); consideration of indigenous arts and crafts, which are in jeopardy owing to diverse impacts of contemporary events and forces (Taylor 1994); subtle discussions of personal narrative and individual biography as seen through objects (Hoskins 1998); or what Plath calls "car culture," which he studied in industrialized Japan (Plath 1990).

Whether one can speak appropriately of "house societies" as a particular category is something which this book explores, and which is rightfully debated; but the notion is certainly proving fruitful in stimulating new ways of viewing research in several parts of the world, as this book so well demonstrates. Some older assumptions about the nature and functioning of kinship are also brought into question with this research from several disciplinary directions. And, more important, it is proving to be a notion ethnohistorians, archaeologists, and cultural/social anthropologists can share in discussing, and they can learn from this new common focus. In certain parallel respects, the great attention given by anthropologists recently to that other place in which we dwell, the human body, has also served to link cultural, biological, and linguistic anthropologists in fruitful communication and sometimes collaboration.

The past decade in American anthropology has been one of serious debate over whether the subdisciplines of the field—cultural, archaeological, biological, linguistic—are now so separate and hold such different theoretical aims and approaches that they should continue to remain together in either the intellectual or organizational form which Franz Boas set down in the early days of the field. This book presents ample evidence that when cultural anthropologists, ethnohistorians, and archaeologists, for example, work together on common areas of continuing interest, such as kinship and the material and conceptual ordering of place and space, the collaboration can be highly fruitful in providing new insights into such longstanding issues, as well as into particular regional problems that are clarified through comparative perspectives.

Preface

This book began to take shape, as one part of a long-term collaboration between the editors, with a symposium organized by Rosemary Joyce and Susan Gillespie entitled "Opening Up the House: A Dialogue Across the Discipline" at the 95th Annual Meeting of the American Anthropological Association in San Francisco, California, in 1996. Having applied the concept of house societies to ancient Mesoamerica in a number of papers (e.g., Gillespie 1994, 1995, 1999; Gillespie and Joyce 1997; Joyce 1996, 1999), we were convinced that it could provide an important site of reconnection between archaeologists and ethnographers. The symposium was particularly concerned to draw out common interests between multiple subdisciplines of anthropology and to expand the geographic range of use of the "house" concept. With the exception of Yvonne Marshall, all the contributors to this volume were part of this symposium.

Based on the highly positive response by participants and members of the audience to the symposium, we developed the proposal for this book. The themes of material reproduction and social memory guided the final selection of participants in the publication from the broader range of symposium presentations. Ian Kuijt, Adrienne J. Lazazzera, Pia-Kristina Anderson, Roger C. Green, and John D. Monaghan also contributed important papers to the symposium that are not included here solely because of the refinement of the focus of the volume. We deeply appreciate their participation in the symposium itself.

Because of the central place the Northwest Coast had in the original formulation of the house model by Claude Lévi-Strauss, we had searched unsuccessfully for an archaeologist working in that region to take part in the symposium. We were delighted when Ruth Tringham brought Yvonne Marshall's highly pertinent research to our attention, so that it could be included in the present volume.

We would like to acknowledge the support of our respective universities while we were developing the symposium and the book. Susan Gillespie is grateful for a leave from the Department of Anthropology at the University of Illinois that allowed her to write the introductory chapters. We would also like to thank the reviewers of this volume for the University of Pennsylvania Press, John Chance and Julia Hendon, for their careful readings of the manuscript.

1

Beyond Kinship
An Introduction

Susan D. Gillespie

The anthropological study of kinship has been dominated by two central issues: 1) the relationships linking families to larger kinship groups that incorporate multiple families and endure longer than a single family; and 2) the relationships between kin ties and locality, that is, between "blood" and "soil"
(Kuper 1982:72). Since the founding of anthropology in the nineteenth century,
abstract models and classificatory types have been offered to account for these
relationships from comparative and evolutionary perspectives, but they have
generally failed to live up to expectations. Ethnographic descriptions have
dispelled the notion that prescriptive and proscriptive kinship "rules" govern
social life. Kin ties are acknowledged to be optative and mutable rather than
established at birth or marriage, and "fictive" relationships can be considered
just as legitimate as "biological" ones. Indeed, even the presumed irreducible,
natural component of kinship—a link between persons resulting from procrea-
tive acts—has been exposed as a Western notion that misleadingly privileges
one construction of social relationships over potential others (Schneider 1972,
1984).

A more useful perspective assumes a processual rather than a classificatory approach to kinship, focusing on the practices and understandings by
which relationships are constructed in everyday social life, rather than on
abstract or idealized rules. One such approach specifically examines how, in
certain societies, people conceive and enact kin or "kin-like" relationships as
a group by virtue of their joint localization to a "house."[1] The house as a social group, as characterized by Claude Lévi-Strauss (1982, 1987), is much
more than a household. Groups referred to by the term "house" are corporate
bodies, sometimes quite large, organized by their shared residence, subsistence, means of production, origin, ritual actions, or metaphysical essence, all

of which entail a commitment to a corpus of house property, which in turn can be said to materialize the social group. Houses define and socially reproduce themselves by the actions involved with the preservation of their joint property, as a form of material reproduction that objectifies their existence as a group and serves to configure their status vis-à-vis other houses within the larger society.

Examining social organization from the focal point of the house, where this unit is applicable, can help to explicate both long-lived extra-familial relationships and the link between kinship and locality within this dynamic and processual perspective. Studies of "house societies" are especially concerned with how local life—the actions and structural integrations of groups and their members within particular political and economic contexts—is intertwined with genealogy, that is, kinship through time (Lévi-Strauss 1982:171). Diachronic investigations of houses emphasize the differential success of long-term strategies for acquiring, keeping, or replacing resources that are the basis for status and power, strategies whose outcomes constitute hierarchy and result in historical change.

In addition to overcoming some of the obstinate problems of kinship analysis, studies of house societies reflect growing interdisciplinary interests in material culture (e.g., Miller and Tilley 1996) and in the construction of place—the "cultural processes and practices through which places are rendered meaningful" (Feld and Basso 1996:7; see also Forth 1991; Hirsch and O'Hanlon 1995; Waterson 1997). Houses link social groups with architectural units that facilitate their physical delimitation and position in society, thereby integrating the social with the material life in its pragmatic and semiotic aspects.[2] In turn, the interpretation of enduring social formations as mediated by substantial material constructions, such as houses, allows for the incorporation of archaeological information, vastly increasing the time depth available to understand the variability and evolutionary trajectories of specific social systems. These efforts contribute to the ongoing disciplinary convergence sometimes called the "historicization of anthropology," providing a critically important historical dimension to ethnography (Ohnuki-Tierney 1990:1). This convergence can also help to erase the artificial boundary separating the sociotemporal periods labeled "prehistory" and "history," as anthropologists, historians, and archaeologists find themselves engaged in comparative studies of societies once considered incomparable, each discipline enriching and, where necessary, correcting the results of the others.

The essays in this volume bring together, for the first time, the concerns of ethnography, archaeology, and history in a cross-cultural, cross-temporal comparative study (Figure 1-1) centered on the house as an enduring social group that is materially represented by a physical structure and the objects that go with it—furnishings, curated heirlooms, and graves—within a designated locus in the landscape. In highlighting the material dimensions of house societies, the authors emphasize not just the objects themselves but the "person-object" relationships that emerge from the various uses by actors of tangible (and also intangible) phenomena "to constitute crucial parts of the self and world" (Mc-Cracken 1988:75). Their concerns are with the politico-economic factors that constitute resources and constraints with which houses must contend, as well as with the meaning systems engaged in the construction and continued maintenance and embellishment of houses or house-locales and related objects. These meaning systems are subject to contestation and ultimately serve to differentiate social groups, especially in terms of hierarchical differences; thus, they are necessarily pragmatic and functional, and not merely representational (e.g., Hodder 1991a:154). Because the phenomena that act as the focal point for group identity often outlive the specific individuals who first created or used them, they are constantly subjected to resignification, and the portable objects and even houses may be moved about in the process.

Analysis of the material dimension of house societies thus entails a consideration of the temporal and spatial dimensions as well; indeed, a key function of houses is to anchor people in space and to link them in time. The temporal dimension includes the domestic cycle of individual house groups, the life history of the structures, the continuity and changes experienced by social houses over generations, and the time depth inherent in the ideology of the house or its valued heirlooms that serves to embody a collective memory about the past, a reference to origins that often forms a salient bond uniting house members. The spatial dimension includes the arrangement of individual furnishings or features and people within the house, the definition of the spatial boundaries of a house (which may extend far beyond a single building), the disposition of houses and their properties within a community whereby the relationships that they signify become naturalized along with other features in the landscape, and the sociopolitical and economic relationships between house societies and their neighbors on a regional level. Time, space, and material come together at the maximal scale in considering the different trajectories of house configurations within and between regions over many centuries.

These essays refer to the specific conceptualization of "house" and "house societies" first proposed by Claude Lévi-Strauss in the 1970s (Lévi-Strauss 1979a, b). His explication of house societies has been heavily scrutinized, even disparaged, resulting in significant criticisms and clarifications (e.g., Carsten and Hugh-Jones, eds. 1995; Macdonald, ed. 1987; Waterson 1990). The analyses presented here acknowledge this critique, but in highlighting the material

Alaska
Tlingit
Nuu chah nulth
Kwakiutl
British Columbia
Washington State
Yurok
California
NORTHWEST COAST

Hawaii

POLYNESIA

MEXICO
Nahua
Maya
GUATEMALA
BELIZE
HONDURAS
COSTA RICA
MESOAMERICA

RAPANUI
(EASTER ISLAND)

COUNTRY NAMES
State and Province Names
Cultures and CULTURE AREAS

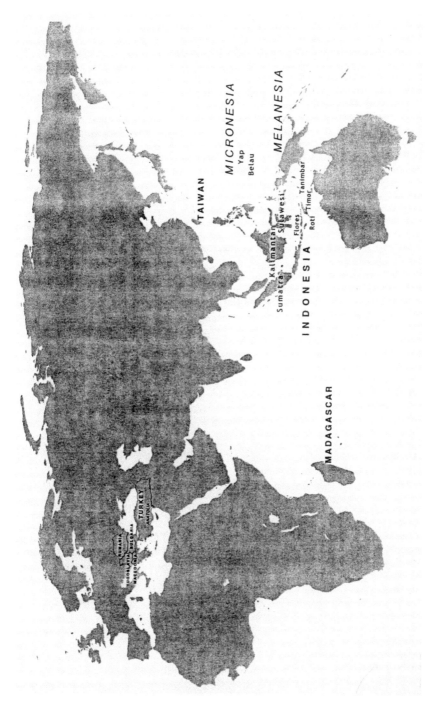

Figure 1-1. Regions, countries, and peoples discussed in this book.

dimensions of house societies, they deviate from some current research trends and also go beyond Lévi-Strauss's minimal attention to the most prominent aspect of house societies, namely, the houses themselves. The major characteristics of his model and how they are utilized by the authors in this volume are briefly reviewed in this chapter. Distinguishing the full heuristic value of the house as originally envisioned by Lévi-Strauss requires a more lengthy review of his work on the subject with a discussion of how other scholars have modified or refined his ideas; this is presented in the following chapter.

THE HOUSE AS A SOCIAL UNIT

The "house" emerged as an important analytical concept in anthropology and related social sciences beginning in the 1970s, the result of independent scholarship that examined many different societies in various parts of the world (Carsten and Hugh-Jones 1995; Macdonald 1987). This development resulted, in part, from the increasing realization that the established analytical vocabulary of kinship failed to adequately characterize social units (e.g., Kuper 1982; Schneider 1965, 1972, 1984), and the concomitant recognition of the heuristic significance of indigenous concepts and terms (e.g., Bourdieu 1977; Lévi-Strauss 1979a, b). This epistemological shift contributed to the revelation that in many societies the word for "house" also refers to a group of people associated with some spatial locus, one that most often includes a dwelling or other structure. In practical discourse and action the house may represent social, economic, political, and ritual relationships among various individuals, who may form a permanent or temporary collectivity.

Examples of this continuing scholarship include studies of societies in South America (Gudeman and Rivera 1990:1–2), Micronesia (Parmentier 1984), early modern Germany (Sabean 1990), ancient central Mexico (Carrasco 1976; Chance 1996), nineteenth-century Northwest Coast of North America (Ames 1995), and most especially Africa (Gottlieb 1992:50; Gray and Gulliver 1964; Grinker 1996; Kuper 1993; Şaul 1991) and Southeast Asia. In these last two areas especially, ethnographers were recognizing that the term usually translated as "clan" is the word for "house" (Fox, ed. 1980; Gottlieb 1992:50), and in Southeast Asia it has become common practice to adopt this indigenous usage, referring to localized kin groups as houses rather than imposing an etic classificatory term (e.g., Barraud 1979; Fox, ed. 1980; Traube 1986). This has become even more frequent as ethnographers have adopted the Lévi-Straussian concept of the house (e.g., Boon 1990b; Carsten and Hugh-

Jones, eds. 1995; Errington 1989; Macdonald, ed. 1987; McKinnon 1991; Waterson 1990). At this same time, significant studies were also beginning to appear concerning the physical house as a meaningfully constituted architectural unit around and within which people organize their behaviors (e.g., Bourdieu 1973, 1977; Cuisenier 1991; Cunningham 1964; Ellen 1986; Fox, ed. 1993; Kent, ed. 1990; Rapoport 1969; Ruan 1996; Samson 1990; Vom Bruck 1997; Waterson 1988, 1990).

Despite the growing attention to the house as an important cultural category found across the globe, only one scholar—Claude Lévi-Strauss—developed the idea of the "house" (*maison*) as a specific analytical category of comparative utility that coincides with a recurrent indigenous concept (Lévi-Strauss 1982). He introduced the notion of house as a "type of social structure" (Lévi-Strauss 1987:151) to be added alongside the familiar taxa of family, lineage, and clan, with the following definition: "a corporate body [*personne morale*] holding an estate made up of both material and immaterial wealth, which perpetuates itself through the transmission of its name, its goods, and its titles down a real or imaginary line, considered legitimate as long as this continuity can express itself in the language of kinship or of affinity and, most often, of both" (Lévi-Strauss 1982:174).

The differences between a house and a unilineal descent group are somewhat subtle and must be drawn out from the various examples Lévi-Strauss (1982, 1987) gave of *sociétés "à maisons,"* "house" societies. In characterizing societies as divided into lineages or clans, anthropologists classify them into presumably distinct types (e.g., patrilineal, matrilineal) in which a singular form of social relationship—descent—is primary. The primacy of descent is expressed as "rules" of succession, inheritance, marriage partners, and often postmarital residence. Furthermore, every member of society is equivalently impacted by these governing principles; that is, everyone belongs to one specific lineage or clan within societies that, due to exogamy rules, must include multiple descent groups. Houses turn all these classificatory assumptions on their head. Although houses, like clans and lineages, are long-lived corporate entities to which persons belong and from which they construct their identities and configure their social interactions, there is no singular form of affiliation. Descent and inheritance may flow through either or both parents depending on circumstances; endogamy and exogamy may coexist; postmarital residence is contingent on a number of factors; and marriage patterns, exchange relations, co-residence, or shared labor may be the primary determinants of social relationships, rather than their outcomes.

A significant factor in Lévi-Strauss's crystallization of the house as a long-lived property-owning social unit is that this term is actually used in the various societies that were organized into houses—they recognized the overlap between the house as a dwelling that shelters a social group and/or its property and the group itself. Even more important is the source of his information on house societies. Lévi-Strauss drew his examples from a wide range of societal complexity, from hunter-gatherer peoples such as the Kwakiutl and Yurok of North America, to the extremely varied mixed-subsistence and agricultural societies of Austronesia and Africa, to the noble houses of medieval Europe and Japan (1982, 1983, 1987). With these last examples he explicitly sought to show the organizational similarities between Western and non-Western peoples and to demonstrate the utility of historical documentation for long-term studies.[3]

In his cross-cultural comparative analysis, Lévi-Strauss (1987) further argued that, by emphasizing descent principles to classify societal types, some anthropologists were ignoring other kinds of relationships, especially marriage alliance. Alliance and descent are cross-cutting relationships that give rise to conflicting tendencies and loyalties among persons and groups, all of which come together in the house. The conjugal couple that establishes a house unites the wife-giving and wife-taking groups that provided each spouse, and produces children who express certain relationships to both paternal and maternal kinsmen as well as affines. The house therefore projects an outward façade of unity, one that masks these underlying tensions and conflicting loyalties. Lévi-Strauss thus considered the house a "fetish" in the Marxist sense, as the representation of a relationship between allied (wife-giving and wife-taking) houses (1987:155–56).

Moreover, house membership usually does not impact everyone equivalently. There are societies in which some persons may belong to more than one house simultaneously, or some persons may not belong to any house, or all persons may be considered members of a single house. Hierarchy is generally present both within and between houses, such that there are high-ranked and low-ranked houses (the latter may be attached to high-ranked houses, and thus may not actually be considered as houses), whose members express their relationships with one another and with other houses quite differently. It is "the language of kinship or of affinity, or most often, of both" that makes the house what it is. In many societies only some groups are able to strategically utilize and stabilize certain relationships—manifested as kinship and marriage ties—in order to maintain their connection to an estate (and thereby to each other and to other houses) over generations, while other groups are not able to do so. This is a basis for social hierarchy, which may be experienced as considerable differences in prestige, wealth, and ritual and political power, both within and between houses. In the process, rules are often ignored and kinship itself is "subverted" (Lévi-Strauss 1987:152).

A focus on the house can thus enable anthropologists to move beyond kinship as a "natural" and hence privileged component of human relationships. Houses are concerned with locale, subsistence, production, religion, gender, rank, wealth, and power, which, in certain societies, are expressed in principles and strategies of consanguinity and affinity. Furthermore, the continued existence of a house is dependent on the successful execution of strategies for maintaining its estate and reproducing its members over multiple generations, a process that is best observed with the long time span available to historical pursuits (Lévi-Strauss 1983, 1987). Studies of house societies thus require the addition of a historical or diachronic dimension to ethnography.

THE DIACHRONIC PERSPECTIVE

Ethnographic studies concerned with the house model have tended to concentrate on the symbolism of the house and the everyday behaviors out of which house members enact and reify relationships (especially in Carsten and Hugh-Jones, eds. 1995; see also Barraud 1979; Fox, ed. 1980; Howell 1990; Lewis 1988). This is a largely synchronic and idealized within-house viewpoint that considers all houses as essentially equivalent. It is especially pertinent in more egalitarian situations in which there are no substantial differences among individual houses or in which the entire community is envisioned as a single house, and from perspectives in which economic and political factors are held stable. Janet Carsten and Stephen Hugh-Jones (1995:46) proposed even more such studies to provide "a strong, ethnographically-based view of the house understood in holistic terms which takes account of processes of living that may be said to be universal."

In contrast with this approach, the houses in Lévi-Strauss's examples become most visible in the context of competitive between-house interactions that are inherently asymmetrical and shift over time. All houses are not the same. No two houses will incorporate exactly the same estate; each will have its own names, heirlooms, ritual privileges, and material property that serve to differentiate houses and form a basis for ranking them. Houses are also differentiated in the context of their interactions with each other. For example, for some marriage alliance relationships a specific house stands as (usually superordinate) wife-giver, while for others the same house will be (usually subordinate) wife-taker. These permutations of rank and difference may be relatively enduring, but they can succumb to the exigencies of external factors and the failure of internal strategies to maintain the house or its estate, especially in the face of competition from attached groups or junior branches that aspire to household. Within-house and between-house rivalries may intensify, and house statuses may fluctuate due to unstable economic or political factors, as new sources of wealth become available or interactions with other societies change the local dynamics.

These two contrasting approaches to the study of the house thus constitute more than a difference in orientation—within-house versus between-house relationships—since both must come into play in understanding a total social system. Investigating the house of Lévi-Strauss entails an enlargement of the temporal and spatial fields. The disjunction between these two approaches is well illustrated in Thomas Gibson's (1995) study of the elaborate house rituals in Ara, a Makassarese village in South Sulawesi. He determined that these rituals function to highlight the unity of sibling sets *within* each individual house. This conclusion led him to dismiss Lévi-Strauss's characterization of the house, because its emphasis on the conflicting relations of alliance and descent did not seem to apply to this case (1995:146).

In an aside to these conclusions, however, Gibson noted that in terms of *between*-house relationships, these same rituals *in the past* once functioned to promulgate status differences among nobles, commoners, and slaves. He further suggested that in "pragmatic" rather than "symbolic" terms, the house of Lévi-Strauss did become apparent when these processes were viewed over a period of time. Relationships among houses were accentuated in competitive rituals, honors and titles were accumulated and inherited, and achieved status was sometimes converted into ascribed status as social differences were naturalized by interhouse dynamics: "One of the purposes of rituals was to push claims to higher status. If a house was allowed to get away with using certain symbols, its new rank would be secured. In this respect, Ara in the nineteenth century would have looked very like one of Lévi-Strauss's ranked societies where the 'rules' seem made to be broken" (Gibson 1995:147–48). In other words, when the analyst's attention turns away from the ideology of kinship and idealized shared living and working arrangements within the individual house, toward competition for rank and status on the societal or supra-societal political level over a period of generations, then the house in the Lévi-Straussian sense may suddenly reveal itself. Thus Gibson (1995:148) remarked, "It is perhaps at this more 'historical' level that we should look for the relevance of Lévi-Strauss's argument, for it is here that his concern with myth and history, kinship and class, is located."

This same opinion had previously been emphasized by Lévi-Strauss himself (1983, 1987:158, 193–94) in his preference for historical materials over ethnographic (short-term) descriptions of societies in order to conceptualize the house as a cross-cultural category. He suggested that the long view of history is essential to understand the mechanisms of consolidation and eventual dissolution of houses, because by definition they are perpetual bodies that outlive individuals. To be certain of the existence of houses in a *société à maisons* (houses plural), one must discern the cumulative outcome of strategic choices made by generations of individuals from the alternatives available to them, based on what they believed would improve or at least maintain their status and property rights (Lévi-Strauss 1983:1225), outcomes that would, inevitably, result in difference over time (as historical change) rather than the sameness that derives from timeless universal processes.

Despite this diachronic emphasis in Lévi-Strauss's own discussions and his own recourse to historically known societies, few after him have looked to the documentary record to reveal the operation of houses in various world regions, so the potential for understanding house societies from this perspective has generally been unrealized.[4] However, although the outcomes of maneuvering for status and position are best seen over the long run, historical documentation is not absolutely requisite to investigating the temporal component of house societies. As Waterson (this volume) points out, all our data—ethnographic, documentary, archaeological—are historical and contingent to local situations.

The dimension of time within house ideology has been abundantly attested by ethnographic description. One important component of temporal depth available to anthropologists is the life cycle of houses as lived through their members, which is observable and accessible through long-term observation and by recourse to memories (Sandstrom, this volume). Marriage alliances between various houses, when they are repeated over generations, form another common reference to time. These are not simply an expression of social structural "rules" within the time frame of the present, but are exegetically explained as instances of following an established precedent, referencing a timeline going back many generations. Alliances between Indonesian houses, for example, are often predicated on the notion that an original brother-sister pair, separated by the departure of one sibling from the natal house to marry into another house, is continually reunited in the subsequent marriages of their cross-sex descendants (their replacements) generations later; this is the symbolic basis for the well-known Indonesian asymmetric connubium first detailed by F. A. E. van Wouden (1968 [1935]; see, e.g., Barraud 1990; Boon 1990b; Errington 1989; Fox 1980; Howell 1990; McKinnon 1991).

The Objectification of Perpetuity

In house societies (and in some non-house societies as well), perpetuity—the maintenance of links between past and present that are requisite to the notion of precedence—is a fundamental value even if, though publicly claimed, it may have little basis in fact, as may happen when persons attempt to create a higher status. The legitimacy and status of the house qua house often derives from the acknowledgment of ties to illustrious founders, usually house ancestors; ancestor veneration itself is a "historicist" means for "implementing dynamic options in social life" (Boon 1977:89). Authority for actions in the present is based on precedence extending back into a legendary or even primordial past. Descent in the biological sense is only one component of a larger concern for shared origin, which serves to localize and bind a social group (Fox 1987:172, 1980:12).

The allusion to origins and its linkage to the living may be expressed in various ways. For example, house members may own (as immaterial property) and perform origin narratives. These include "elaborate accounts of the emergence and/or the arrival of predecessors; traditions of the migration and journeying of groups and individuals; tales of the founding of settlements, of houses, or of ancestral shrines; accounts of contests to establish priority, to secure the rightful transmission of ancestral relics, to assert the often disputed ordering of succession to office or, in some areas, to establish precedence in affinal relations" (Fox 1993:16). Such narratives are frequently signified by material objects—features in the landscape, the house itself, and the curated heirlooms that are a focus for social memory and "provide physical evidence of a specific continuity with the past" (Fox 1993:1; see Joyce, McKinnon, Waterson, this volume). They represent yet another objectification or fetishization of a relationship among house members, a relationship through time.

In Lévi-Strauss's definition, houses are dependent for their continued existence on the maintenance of linkages of members to these objectifying phenomena, both material and immaterial, through various kinds of ongoing actions. Intangible property, such as names or titles, is continually embodied by living persons, often in a cycle of generations, as when grandchildren take the names, and hence the identities, of their grandparents (Lévi-Strauss 1982:175; see also Hugh-Jones 1993:115; Kan 1989:71). As noted above, other inherited immaterial property that refers to the past may include dances, songs, and ritual performances, the ancestral spirits themselves, and claims to potential spouses in allied houses. Objects that are acquired in the context of marriage exchanges also serve as mnemonics for alliance relationships linking houses, representing a kind of social history. These and the other inherited heirlooms are often kept in a special area within the house, an action that may thereby sacralize that structure.

The physical house itself may be an icon of origins and a material witness to critical episodes in the life history of the social group. The "living" house, as it is enlarged, modified, and embellished over generations, objectifies the changes that signify longevity and accrued value (Waterson 1993, this volume). Other physical manifestations of continuity within the house may be the incorporated portions of previous structures that had once stood in the same place (Tringham, this volume), as well as the literal remains of the ancestors themselves, as subfloor burials or curated bones (Gillespie, Kirch, McKinnon, this volume).

Carsten and Hugh-Jones (1995:36–37) argued for a processual view of kinship in which people and the houses they occupy are viewed in the same analytical terms—both are living, spirit-inhabited phenomena that "build" and maintain each other (see Chapter 2, this volume). But from the perspective of house perpetuity, there is an important distinction between people and the structures upon which house relationships are constituted. The physical house (or temple or shrine), heirlooms, ancestral relics, and immaterial property represent a concentration of value, which is the key component to the standing of the house as an institution and its prestige in relation to other houses. The house so objectified signifies stability over time, although it is often rebuilt or even moved as part of the aging process (e.g., Carsten 1995a). In contrast, the individual members of the house as a social group cycle through the house, their own existences much shorter in duration. They represent perpetuity only as they conscientiously and legitimately—through the language of kinship and affinity—replace and metaphysically embody their forebears, the sum of their life spans contributing to the status of the house as a *personne morale*. Susan McKinnon (1991, this volume) explains this contrast as the ideal of generalization and concentration of value in the house versus its particularization (in the actions of specific individuals) and partial dispersal of value (e.g., in marriage exchanges).

The dialectic of stability and change reflected in the relationships maintained between property and people has been dichotomized in more general terms according to a concentric spatial model of "center" versus "periphery" in Shelly Errington's (1989) characterization of Southeast Asian house societies (see also McKinnon 1991:177–78):

I suggest that Houses in this part of the world are profoundly centered entities, consisting of a center and a serving group. The center is often a stable object, such as a temple, a palace, or a set of regalia. The center is often regarded as the descendant or visible remains of an ancestral "root" or "'source." . . . Because the center does not reproduce or die (it often consists of leavings of the dead, or of objects called "inanimate" in Euro-American cosmology), it lasts through long periods. The center is retained by the serving group. . . .

The serving group, or caretakers, or worship community, of the center consists of humans. Humans do die, and consequently they must recruit more humans to the service group if the central object is to be served in the future. . . . The service grouping forms the periphery around its central objects; because it consists of humans who die and breathe and move around, the periphery is metaphorically and usually literally more mobile than its center. What is central (if I may so put it) to the House in island Southeast Asia—what defines the service grouping as an entity—is not the periphery, the "social group," but the center. (Errington 1989:239)

Perpetuity is thus manifested in concrete form in the ongoing activities of persons with respect to localizing phenomena, as a medium for enacting relationships with one another. By the same token, the permanent form of these objects and structures (which may actually require their replacement) facilitates the perpetuation of the *personne morale*, as long as an ethos of preservation, rather than dispersal, of the estate is maintained.

THE HOUSE IN THE PRESENT AND PAST

Integrating the concern for the materialization of the house over time, as a consequence of ongoing group practices, at a societal or regional perspective and with an accompanying interest in sociocultural change, should open up the study of the house beyond the temporal limitations of ethnography and even of history to the vast time span accessible via archaeology. The house can serve as a nexus for the meaningful convergence of ethnography and archaeology (and related social historical disciplines), with ethnographers fleshing out the rich contextual details of the immaterial aspects of life not immediately accessible to archaeologists as well as providing examples of the diversity of cultural forms, while archaeologists supplement the recent past with knowledge of configurations no longer extant, enlarge on the life histories of physical houses, and detail the sequential progression and transformation of house societies in various world areas. Both fields of endeavor are needed to write the "biographies of built forms" (Waterson, this volume).

In the spirit of such a cooperative interdisciplinary enterprise, this collection of essays engages ethnographers and archaeologists to delineate the material dimensions of houses and house societies, emphasizing the actions and strategies that they manifest. The tenor and perspective of these papers are necessarily different from the few previous published anthologies on the house and house societies (see Chapter 2). While the authors acknowledge the important contributions made in earlier attempts to refine Lévi-Strauss's house, they highlight certain aspects of his model and pay correspondingly less attention to issues that have been well studied by others. For example, there is little discussion of idealized kinship principles and practices, and greater concern for practical and especially long-term relationships enacted among the individuals who form houses, between people and physical houses, and between houses.

Moreover, unlike some previous attempts to determine the definitional criteria whereby societies could be properly classified as house societies or not (e.g., Macdonald, ed. 1987), the emphasis here is on the heuristic utility of the concept of the house, especially its dynamic and processual aspects, rather than its classificatory status. The essays therefore vary in their emphasis on specific aspects of the house model, and not all of these case studies involve bona fide "houses" in the Lévi-Straussian sense. The inclusion of this range of variation allows consideration of the degree to which his model can be useful in various kinds of ethnographic and archaeological situations, and to prevent it being seen as a universal proposal or a panacea for the ills plaguing traditional kinship studies.

Indeed, the nature of the archaeological record generally prevents prehistorians from dealing with such intangible issues as kinship relations or metaphorical representations of the house as a fetish. Archaeologists cannot, except in some instances of historic archaeology, determine whether ties of descent or affinity were strategies used by particular individuals to maintain the integrity of an estate; in fact, they cannot identify the actions of specific individuals except in extraordinary circumstances. However, they can examine the outcomes of group actions that have enduring material components, especially those that occurred repeatedly within long time frames. Utilizing the house model eliminates the problem of trying to interpret what configuration of kin or descent group occupied physical houses or house compounds, with the understanding that the house is an institution that used multiple strategies to recruit members whose everyday practices integrated kinship, economics, religion, and politics.

The most comprehensive archaeological interpretations of house societies will probably be those aided by the continuity of archaeologically known practices into the more recent historical past and the ethnographic present (e.g., Gillespie, Joyce, Kirch, Marshall, this volume). Nevertheless, even for those investigating the deep past, the house model has value for understanding such mundane practices as the continued rebuilding of houses in the same location. In many parts of the world, houses were rebuilt (after being destroyed by natural or intentional means) in the same place, either continuously or following slight temporal gaps, sometimes with the remains of the old houses incorporated into new ones. Interpreting this rebuilding as part of a complex ideology that serves to localize a social group and, in effect, organize kin-like relationships in the process, provides a far richer context than seeing it merely as the outcome of some unexamined custom or the consequence of presumed social or ecological constraints on house location.

The continuity of house location must have been socially meaningful, as Ruth Tringham demonstrates in her chapter on Neolithic houses of southeast Europe. Most of the houses in that space-time were made of clay, a cheap and relatively ubiquitous material, and they were frequently burned as part of the life cycle of individual dwellings. Far from being a simple act of destruction, however, the burning of clay houses is what transformed them into enduring phenomena, as it also facilitated their incorporation into the new structure that replaced the old at the same location. Tringham's comparison of Neolithic house continuity patterns in Southeast Europe and Southwest Asia reveals an unwarranted bias in the common evolutionary assumption that Southwest Asia was more precocious in its advancement toward urbanism. She suggests that instead of experiencing evolutionary differences, the peoples of these two regions developed different trajectories in siting their houses—manipulating the built environment—to construct a continuity of place.

Identification with a specific house, against the panoply of other houses, therefore "offers people a kind of immortality" (Waterson, this volume). It lengthens the temporal span of their individual identities because the house itself is a reference to the past, as social and historical memories are focused on houses or empty places where houses once stood (see Tringham, Marshall, Joyce, Waterson, this volume). Roxana Waterson explores this theme in some detail in her examination of the elaborate "origin houses" in Tana Toraja, South Sulawesi, Indonesia. She demonstrates the interconnection of Sa'dan Toraja people and houses, as they are ritually linked not just to their own dwellings but to certain highly elaborated noble houses, whose physical and spiritual components—the heirlooms, bones, and spirits of the dead as well as the placentas of the newly born—anchor people to place and to ancestral origins. Houses are what the Toraja refer to when they talk about their interrelationships, in effect, seeing themselves through the biographies of the houses through which they trace connections to each other and to the landscape. Waterson's explicitly diachronic perspective demonstrates how meanings of "place" are dependent on the changes that occur over time, opening the way for a direct connection between ethnographic and archaeological investigations.

Susan McKinnon's chapter takes us into the house to observe how a single crafted object can quintessentially symbolize the unity of contradictions that Lévi-Strauss originally suggested the house should fetishistically represent. Her discussion of the beautifully carved wooden ancestral altars (*tavu*) that once graced the noble houses of Tanimbar, Eastern Indonesia, reveals how links to ancestors and house history are embedded in the physical form of this altar and enacted in the practical behaviors associated with it. The ancestors are the "base" or "root" (*tavun*) of the house as a social unit; this is a common botanic metaphor. They are represented by the *tavu*, which is given the form of an abstract standing human figure with upraised arms that originally reached from its base on the floor to a shelf on the roof support that housed ancestral relics and heirlooms. On certain ceremonial occasions the head of the noble house sat upon the bench at the foot of the *tavu*, representing thereby the "tip" that developed out of its ancestral "base." The *tavu* thus served as a material bridge between ancestral spirits of the past and their descendants in the present. A hard, enduring object that abstracts the human form rather than representing any particular individual, the *tavu* also manifested the ability of the noble houses to generalize and objectify the house value that signifies their high standing, something that the Tanimbarese commoners are unable to accomplish. It further represented the tension inherent within any house between the obligation to concentrate value and the contrary strategic desire to control its dispersal, as an investment in the form of marriage alliances, to ensure the social reproduction of the house.

The ancestral altars of the Maya peoples of Mexico and Guatemala, as discussed by Susan Gillespie, have a similar function as a material focus for contacting the souls of the house's ancestral dead, and in the prehispanic era the dead were actually buried under these altars or similar forms. The altars were built and sometimes used in the same manner as benches or beds, so that, as in Tanimbar, the metaphysical link to the past was maintained in a practical manner by sitting upon the objects that served as a bridge to the ancestors. The Maya altars are not meant to depict a human being, however, but are considered smaller versions of houses. This is a meaningful alternative representation in that houses and people are co-identified; houses are personified and persons (bodies) are objectified (Carsten and Hugh-Jones 1995:43). Gillespie draws on Lévi-Strauss's discussion of the fetishized house as a microcosm, as well as notions of the house and body as parallel conceptual models (e.g., Carsten and Hugh-Jones, eds. 1995), to explore the various levels of Maya "houses" that served as containers for house spirits, multi-family groups, communities, and ultimately the entire cosmos in a concentric spatial arrangement. In enclosing and thus unifying diverse elements, the house is a means of creating "place" within the landscape. Significantly, specific ritual actions are required to create and activate these nested houses, actions undertaken by those who thereby define themselves as a group with a common stake in the house.

As both a social and a physical place, the house locates persons within a complex web of categories and relationships (Forth 1991:56) that can be mapped against materially defined spaces, as Alan Sandstrom explains in his chapter on the Nahua village of Amatlan in central Mexico. Amatlan exhibits many, if not all, of the characteristics of a house society, and its inhabitants were, until recently, distributed among various named cleared areas in the forest that they called "houses" and that played a significant role in their social identities. Sandstrom highlights the salient features of these "embryonic" houses and discusses the economic factors, primarily the scarcity of agricultural land, that impede the maintenance of house estates. He further demonstrates the changing residential patterns over individual life spans, as married men acquire the wherewithal to move out of their fathers' dwellings and build their own (usually nearby). His mapping of the movement of siblings to their own or spouses' houses within the local landscape revealed that married sisters and brothers continued to live close to and interact with one another across their respective households. This proxemic analysis demonstrates in a pragmatic form the latent and long-term significance of cross-sex sibling ties that is masked by the discursive emphasis on agnatic male relationships. Sandstrom (and also Waterson and Gillespie) points out that the "house" as a spatial locus may encompass more than a single structure, and its investigation requires examining the interactive relationships of various kinds revealed in the spatial orientation of structure groupings with their surrounding or associated cleared areas. An archaeological example of this scenario is provided by Patrick Kirch's (this volume) explanation of the Polynesian *marae* as a set-aside "open" space.

The long-term perspective of archaeology and documentary history makes it possible to trace the life history of individual structures—to determine their stages of enlargement and elaboration; to account for the decline and demise of the house, possibly as a result of the growth of rival houses; and to demonstrate, where applicable, the transformative changes to houses that materially encode the correlative changes to the social groups associated with them. Yvonne Marshall accomplishes this last feat with her historical overview of the changes to the Nuu-chah-nulth (Nootka) houses since the last century. Her examination of a Northwest Coast people, one of Lévi-Strauss's original exemplars of house societies, fills in important missing details from his defining work by concentrating on the physical structure of the houses, as well as by tracing them through time in concert with the demographic and economic changes that transformed Nuu-chah-nulth society. Between the nineteenth and twentieth centuries, the Nuu-chah-nulth dwelling underwent a rapid metamorphosis from an externally undifferentiated residence, housing people, to an externally elaborated but essentially vacant building, housing paraphernalia and symbolizing the increased wealth of the social group that maintained its ritual and representative functions. In a matter of decades, even this form disappeared as the social houses gave way to a new socioeconomic configuration based on wage labor and a cash economy.

Comparative and cumulative studies can allow for more general conclusions involving larger regions and more extensive time spans. Drawing on ethnographically-described Tikopia as a type case for a Polynesian house society, Patrick Kirch interprets his archaeologically-derived data from that island to provide a more complete picture of Tikopia, past and present. He begins with a review of Raymond Firth's ethnographic findings here to argue that the Tikopian *paito*, "house," fits the criteria of Lévi-Strauss's house, and as such has significant utility for interpreting the island's archaeological remains. Kirch further demonstrates that the well-known Polynesian temple complex evolved out of an older and more widespread Austronesian pattern whereby ordinary dwellings were sacralized over time by the interment of the ancestral dead within their walls, becoming thereby "holy houses" or cult centers. Significantly, the transformation from holy house to temple in eastern Oceania, but not in the western half of this world area, provides archaeological evidence for regional transformations of social configurations, like those that ethnographers have determined for living house societies (see Chapter 2).

The interpretation of archaeological structures as Lévi-Straussian social houses is made stronger by such practices as burial under or around houses or the curation of skeletal remains, which may be evidence of ancestral veneration or more generally a desire to maintain perpetuated links to deceased members within the house (see Kirch, Waterson, McKinnon, Gillespie, this volume). A related convention that is archaeologically visible is the caching of objects within houses or their associated tombs, some of them having been curated for centuries prior to their deposition. Viewing these objects as the materialization of historical memory of the house, and not merely as proof of one's wealth or economic status, adds a new dimension to understanding their value. Rosemary Joyce locates the prehispanic Maya practice of ritually depositing valuable goods within this social context. Those that have endured through the ages are primarily costume ornaments of stone or shell, and they have been recovered archaeologically from special locations—under house or temple floors, in tombs, and in sacred natural features. Joyce demonstrates that these were not simply wealth objects taken out of circulation for ritual purposes; they were curated heirlooms, virtually all of which were deposited long after they were first made as markers of house prestige. Maya hieroglyphic inscriptions were frequently added to the objects to identify their "owners," allowing for a tentative start to writing the biography of Maya noble houses by way of the valuables that preserved the house in social memory, from their manufacture to their final deposition centuries later.

Joyce's closing chapter further reiterates the major themes of this book, beginning with the critique of traditional kinship theories and the multiple ways that the house of Lévi-Strauss can resolve the difficulties embedded in traditional taxonomic approaches and incorporate more contemporary processual and practice-oriented concerns in social anthropology. Her in-depth examination of the Yurok of California fills a major gap in the literature on the house. Lévi-Strauss (1982) considered the Yurok pivotal to his understanding of the house, but he never provided enough information on them to explain why they held the key to house societies. Joyce draws on the rich details from Alfred Kroeber's original ethnographic field work to illustrate how the Yurok were an exemplary house society, as their houses represented continuity and identity, localized social relationships within the larger community, and were maintained by group actions and negotiations for status.

Joyce's discussion emphasizes the material dimensions of the house and its manifest utility for linking interdisciplinary research on culture and society. Her explicitly comparative approach, especially when added to previous studies, reveals how the same symbolic and pragmatic concepts reappear in house societies: the requirement of group actions invested in the house estate to continually and actively define the membership of the social house; the abiding emphasis on ancestral origins and precedence; the importance of naming as a way to assign value and permanence to people, places, and other phenomena; and the mapping of social relations across a landscape by the identification of people with houses or house locations, an identification maintained by social memories materialized in concrete signs.

The essays in this volume also highlight the value of research among existing ethnographic and historic archives and museum holdings to obtain the long-term perspective needed to realize the emergence, operation, and transformation of house societies. This brings up a final point: all these studies, not just the archaeological and historical cases, deal with the past. The ethnographic descriptions of house societies, here and in the published literature, refer to societal configurations and house materializations no longer extant or else on the verge of extinction, as modernizing forces sweep the entire globe. These include the imposition of colonialism and capitalism, religious missionization displacing the ancestors, and political marginalization preventing the accumulation of wealth or achievement of rank, with an accompanying rearrangement of economic and social structures. In particular, the contractual relationships inherent in the wage-based, cash economy of modern class society supersede the legitimacy of social relationships that draw upon the "language of kinship and affinity," as Lévi-Strauss (1982:186–87) himself noted (see Chapter 2). "House societies" are disappearing, although "houses" are more resilient; witness the popularity of fraternity/sorority houses and similar fraternal organizations that maintain a long-term actively engaged investment in a corpus of material and nonmaterial property, using "the language of kinship" to link house members.

In this sense the house per se—a phenomenon belonging to a time when virtually all social ties were still referenced in terms of kinship, however defined—may not appear to have much significance for contemporary sociocultural anthropology, although the value of kinship analysis to the study of past societies has recently been reiterated (Godelier et al. 1998:3). However, the many aspects of the temporal and material dimensions of houses explored in this collection transcend the boundaries of house societies in the Lévi-Straussian sense. These topics include: 1) a focus on material objects, structures, and landscapes for enacting and maintaining relationships among persons, even over generations as the objects or their physical signs outlive individuals; 2) the objectification of social difference as hierarchy; 3) the house as a localizing force within a physical landscape and a multidimensional social network; 4) the imbuing of social memory in fixed features and in portable, transactable goods; 5) the active negotiation of the boundaries and obligations of persons and social groupings organized around a common investment in property; 6) and the historical changes, as well as evolutionary trajectories, that can be traced in societal configurations. All these issues can inform our understandings of all societies, present and past. Out of these shared concerns, ethnographers, historians, and archaeologists can recognize their common interest in the house.

This chapter has been greatly improved by discussions with Clark E. Cunningham, Susan McKinnon, Rosemary A. Joyce, David C. Grove, and Edward M. Bruner. I thank them for their earnest comments, suggestions, and criticisms.

2

Lévi-Strauss
Maison and *Société à Maisons*

Susan D. Gillespie

The definition and descriptions of "house" and "house society" introduced by Claude Lévi-Strauss are not as straightforward and unproblematic as he might have believed, as subsequent scholarship has shown. His failure to develop this model in any detailed case study left nagging questions unresolved. Furthermore, his intention to utilize the house as a new social structural "type" alongside clan, lineage, and family reveals a notable flaw in his conception, for in his own discussions he eschews the simple classification of societies according to rules that arrange people into corporate descent groups, and the "house" is considered too variable a category to serve classification purposes. Nevertheless, aspects of his notions of house and house societies have proved so intriguing as to tempt other ethnographers to develop and clarify them. In the process, his definition of the house as an organizational institution found in some societies at a certain level of political-economic complexity has increasingly been abandoned, while the symbolic or fetishistic portions of his model have been highlighted in studies that see in the house a new means for elucidating social group relations that may have universal applications. These critiques and the subsequent reconceptualizing of the Lévi-Straussian house are reviewed in this chapter, but it concludes with a call to return to his original formulation (although not the static notion of a classificatory type). Lévi-Strauss's definition and characterization emphasized the materiality, locality, and duration of the house along with the use of the "language of kinship and affinity" to bind its members and to perpetuate the estate from which their identity was derived. In addition to focusing on kinship in terms of practice, discourse, and negotiation rather than as rules to be obeyed, and on the long-term outcomes of strategic decisions and actions rather than on idealized characterizations of social groupings, Lévi-Strauss recognized in the house a societal configuration

probably common in the past but now on the verge of extinction. This distinc-
tion should not be lost; indeed, comparing the role of kinship past and present
adds immeasurably to our understanding of social organization.

The "house" has become a key analytical unit in anthropology and related
social sciences, but, as noted in Chapter 1, only one scholar—Claude Lévi-
Strauss—developed a model of the house as a specific kinship category of
considerable comparative utility that simultaneously coincides with indigenous terminology (Lévi-Strauss 1982). Lévi-Strauss explored the role houses
(*maisons*) play in house societies (*sociétés "à maisons"*) in a course of lectures
from 1976 to 1982 at the Collège de France (Lévi-Strauss 1984). An expanded
version of his earliest exposition on this topic was published in a 1979 essay
(1979b) entitled "Nobles sauvages," which was reprinted as a chapter in his
revised edition of *La Voie des masques* (1979a). This book became available in
English translation (1982), as did his 1976–82 lecture synopses on house societies (1987), and a brief review of this construct appears as a dictionary entry
(1991).

In all these publications, Lévi-Strauss's definition of house has remained
unchanged since his 1976–77 course, but its singular characteristics and
cross-cultural variability were further elaborated by his subsequent inclusion
of additional ethnographic examples (Lévi-Strauss 1984, 1987). His studies of
house societies relate to his other work on structuralist analysis, alliance theory, and a dichotomy between "elementary" and "complex" societies that
centered on marriage practices and carried with it certain evolutionary implications. His discussions on this topic should also be seen in the context of
the contemporary critique of kinship theory. Lévi-Strauss's general intent was
to demonstrate how adopting the house as a social structural type would clarify
ambiguities inherent in anthropologists' struggles to map their classificatory
kinship schemes onto rather intransigent indigenous principles and practices.
An important consequence of this scholarship was the revelation that the
house can transcend the traditional problem-riddled taxonomic approach to
kinship and social structure, which was coming under serious attack (e.g.,
Kuper 1982; Schneider 1972, 1984). The house also bridges the analytical
divisions between literate and nonliterate societies, and thus the distinction
typically maintained between the concerns of history and those of anthropology (Lévi-Strauss 1983), with all that such a division implies in terms of the
conceptualizing of the "other."

Despite his intention to clarify the study of kinship practices, Lévi-Strauss
instead garnered a great deal of criticism on virtually every point. His definition of the house has been ignored or rewritten. His characterization of the

house as a fetishization of marriage alliance has been considered inappropriate or simplistic, although the fetishistic or representational aspect of the house has been carried even further. He has been reprimanded for having ignored what should have been a major object of inquiry—the physical house itself—and rebuked for treating the house as a new classificatory type within an outmoded evolutionary trajectory. Finally, he has been criticized for failing to rise above the naive conceptions of kinship that he himself argued against. This chapter considers all these developments, but concludes that there is still much to be gained from the original vision of the house of Lévi-Strauss.

THE HOUSE AS A *PERSONNE MORALE*

Lévi-Strauss (1979a, b, 1982) introduced the house firmly within the context of kinship studies, specifically with regard to problems encountered by ethnographers attempting to classify societies according to their dominant kinship principles. He began with Franz Boas's unsuccessful efforts to explain the social organization of the Kwakiutl of the Northwest Coast of North America as the result of some historical chain of events in concert with those of neighboring societies. The Kwakiutl had a patrilineal orientation that contrasted with that of their matrilineal neighbors to the north, but certain of their practices did not strictly align with patrilineality and, Boas believed, indicated a possible shift towards matrilineality.

For example, authority over a gens was inherited by a son from his father, yet, among the Kwakiutl aristocrats, certain types of property were passed from father to daughter, and sons also inherited from their mothers. Moreover, affinal relations seemed to be substitutable for descent. Husbands could acquire the property and affiliation belonging to their wives, and, if no marriageable daughters were available, men seeking an alliance with another family would "marry" a son instead, or a part of their future father-in-law's body, or even a piece of furniture, in order to claim some access to that family's property. Boas eventually gave up trying to account for Kwakiutl practices in terms of presumed historical ties with their neighbors to the north and south. Being unable to explain the Kwakiutl descent group as either an agnatic gens or a matrilineal clan left him with only the indigenous term, *numaym* (*numayma*), to refer to their principal kinship unit, a culture-specific name that had no known counterparts and hence no utility for comparison and explanation (Lévi-Strauss 1982:163–170).

Lévi-Strauss then compared the travails of Boas with those of Alfred Kroeber, who had similarly failed to find a good match between the analytical terminology of ethnology and the kinship practices of the Yurok of California. Unexpectedly, the patrilineal Yurok did not capitalize on that descent principle to divide themselves into circumscribed groups "capable of constituted social action." Instead, kinship operated bilaterally and diffusely, with kindred-like ties extending out in all directions incorporating innumerable other persons. Kroeber actually reached the unlikely conclusion that the Yurok lacked social organization in the anthropological sense, although the populace did live in distinct settlements in which they formed individual households occupying substantial dwellings (Lévi-Strauss 1982:172; see Joyce, this volume).[1]

These two pioneering anthropologists failed to understand the nature of social relationships among certain North American peoples because their "institutional arsenal" was incomplete, limited as it was to such modeling concepts as tribe, village, clan, lineage, and family (Lévi-Strauss 1982:173–74). They could thus do little other than characterize Kwakiutl and Yurok kinship organization in negative terms, explaining which principles and types of units were absent without adequately accounting for what was present. Yet the answer had been before them all along, and is still available in their accounts, for both the Yurok and the Kwakiutl had described to the anthropologists their relationships with one another in terms of their various "houses." "Voilà le mot lâché"—"At last, the word is out" (Lévi-Strauss 1979b:46, 1982:172). They had talked about their houses as named, perpetual establishments that served as the principal "jural entities" (*personnes morales*). The houses, rather than individuals or families, were the actual subjects of rights and duties, and houses engaged in long-term exchange and debt relationships with one another. The anthropologists, however, took this word to refer only to the dwellings, nothing more (Lévi-Strauss 1982:172–73, 1987:151).

The Yurok house was defined less by kinship ties among its members—for it was composed of hereditary occupants, their close agnates and cognates, more distant relatives and affines, and even non-related clients—than by its operation as a corporate body focused on a physical structure (Lévi-Strauss 1987:152). Yurok houses were, in principle, long-lived entities with distinct names deriving from their location, the decoration of the physical house façade, or ceremonial functions that were carried out at the house. Kwakiutl houses were named for ancestral or mythic founders and for real or legendary places of origin.

The "aristocratic" or "chiefly" houses also owned or controlled considerable property, consisting of both immaterial and material components. For the Kwakiutl, the immaterial portion included such hereditary prerogatives as names or titles, mottoes, dances, offices in secret societies, and the right to make and use certain emblems. The material portion was quite substantial, composed of hunting, gathering, and fishing territories as well as the house itself and its portable contents—the well-known masks, costumes, canoes, boxes, ceremonial dishes, and so forth. In societies such as the Kwakiutl, in which houses were ranked and individual house members were hierarchically ordered, marriage was necessarily anisogamic and was an important strategy for perpetuating and increasing the house estate. Both exogamy and endogamy were practiced concurrently, one to increase access to property and the other to prevent portions of the estate from leaving the house in marriage (Lévi-Strauss 1982:167–83).[2]

To understand the house as a social category, and not merely an architectural form or the locus of a household, Lévi-Strauss then turned to medieval and early modern Europe (1982:174ff) and feudal Japan (1983), a far cry from the hunter-gatherer Kwakiutl and Yurok, who typified the more traditional focus of anthropological inquiry. Here was an important breach of the conceptual division commonly maintained (including by Lévi-Strauss himself) between complex literate societies and those considered "primitive" or "archaic"; the distinction between "our" form of society and the "other," and thus also between the concerns of history and those of anthropology. As Lévi-Strauss explained, "modes of social life and types of organization well attested in our history can throw light on those of other societies, where they appear less distinct and as if blurred, because [they are] poorly documented and observed for periods that are too short" (1982:194, see also Lévi-Strauss 1983).

Historians, in their characterization of the noble houses of Europe, had described the same kind of unit that had confounded Boas and Kroeber in North America, but the historians had the advantage of the lengthy temporal span of record-keeping and a long-term view of social process. The documentary information revealed that, despite a patrilineal bias, strict lineage rules for succession and inheritance did not apply to the noble European house, nor was house continuity dictated by the biology of reproduction. Indeed, the medieval house has been characterized by one historian (Schmid 1957:56–57) as something quite different from a family or lineage, consisting instead of a " 'spiritual and material heritage, comprising dignity, origins, kinship, names and symbols, position, power and wealth' " (in Lévi-Strauss 1982:174). Such a description, Lévi-Strauss noted, is comparable to Boas's conclusion that the Kwakiutl numaym is best understood by disregarding the living individuals as constituting a kin-based group, and considering instead that the numaym was composed of "a certain number of positions to each of which belong a name, a 'seat' or 'standing place,' that means rank, and privileges. Their number is limited, and they form a ranked nobility" (Lévi-Strauss 1982:169).[3]

In these diverse societies, seemingly noncomparable on many dimensions, the same institution was present, which in every instance was referred to indigenously as a house. On this basis Lévi-Strauss established a definition of the house as a social unit that succinctly encompassed the key common features he observed. The definition remains the same in his various publications, except that in his 1991 encyclopedia entry for "maison," given here, he numbered for clarity the six features that characterize a house and, in his words, thereby distinguish it from a clan or lineage:

La maison est 1) une personne morale, 2) détentrice d'un domaine 3) composé à la fois de biens matériels et immatériels, et qui 4) se perpétue par la transmission de son nom, de sa fortune et de ses titres en ligne réelle ou fictive, 5) tenue pour légitime à la condition que cette continuité puisse se traduire dans le langage de la parenté ou de l'alliance, ou 6) le plus souvent les deux ensemble. (Lévi-Strauss 1991:435)

The two published English translations of his studies of house societies (1982: 174, 1987:152), on which much subsequent scholarship has relied, present slightly differing versions of this definition of the house as "a corporate body [moral person] holding an estate made up of both material and immaterial wealth, which perpetuates itself through the transmission of its name, its goods, and its titles down a real or imaginary [descent] line, considered legitimate as long as this continuity can express itself in the language of kinship [descent] or of affinity [alliance] and [or], most often, of both" (1982:174) (bracketed words are from the 1987 translation).

This definition emphasizes the perpetuation of, and the maintenance of an estate by, a *personne morale*, a long-lived entity subject to rights and obligations. The "language" of kinship and/or affinity is employed to achieve these twinned goals by providing the means to legitimate the intact transfer of the estate across generations of house members. As for the people who must maintain the house, they assume a physical and social "place"—they are given an identity for themselves and a framework for interacting with others—by their membership within, or attachment to, a house (Claudine Berthe-Friedberg in Rousseau 1987:182; see Forth 1991).

Further Applications of the House Model

Having established a definition of the house, in later lectures Lévi-Strauss (1984, 1987) turned his attention to other possible *sociétés "à maisons"* (variously and ambiguously translated as "house societies," "societies with houses," and "house-based societies") elsewhere in the world. It is important to note that while his original exposition of the house concerned "patrilineal" societies, his subsequent lectures concentrated on cognatic societies (1987:185) especially those of Austronesia. Cognatic kinship systems—also known as bilateral and undifferentiated, terms to replace the negative-sounding "nonunilinear"—had long confounded anthropological classification in this part of the world (Davenport 1959; Goodenough 1955:72; Murdock 1960). The absence of the unilineal principle, as it had been explicated by African descent theorists, should have precluded the formation of African-like long-lived corporate groups in this region; yet they did exist (Barnes 1962). Shared territory was posited as a substitute for the descent principle as a means of limiting group membership; territory or residence had simmered in the background for some time as an alternative to the priority ascribed to descent (e.g., Kroeber 1938; Leach 1968; Lewis 1965). Combining descent and residence gave rise to the idea of "localized" descent groups that were acknowledged to include members not related by descent, a solution that nevertheless retained the primacy of the descent principle (Scheffler 1973:774–75). However, these various attempts alternatively to privilege descent, inheritance, residence rules, or some combination of them all to explain the emergence and operation of cognatic kin groups had still proven unsatisfactory (Lévi-Strauss 1987:154).

In addition, Lévi-Strauss briefly examined social systems in Africa, "generally considered by anthropologists as the favourite domain of unilineal institutions" (Lévi-Strauss 1987:185). But even in Africa, ethnographic accounts from many areas suggested that the segmentary model was inadequate in the face of the latent (or even explicit) operation of undifferentiated filiation, and patrilineages were found to include many non-agnates among their members. Furthermore, despite the overarching importance given to abstract lineage models, African lineages were actually difficult to distinguish from residential units, indicating some of the same overlapping of kinship and territorial principles as that operating in Austronesia (1987:186). Lévi-Strauss's purpose in reviewing this literature was to demonstrate that the anthropologists' analytical distinctions themselves are misleading, and thus the source of these problems lies in our constructs and terminology, not with recalcitrant societies: "One is therefore led to question whether, when anthropologists multiply labels by which to distinguish each shade of difference in systems called patrilineal (but with matrilineal aspects), matrilineal (but with patrilineal aspects), bilineal, double descent, cognatic, etc., they are not the victims of an illusion. These subtle qualifications often belong more to the particular perspective of each observer than to intrinsic properties of the societies themselves" (1987:187). Similar conclusions were being reached in other anthropological critiques of kinship at this time (e.g., Bourdieu 1977; Keesing 1970; Kuper 1982; Leach 1968; Schneider 1965, 1972, 1984).

In proposing that his characterization of the house be applied to all these societies, Lévi-Strauss further demonstrated how the problems encountered by anthropologists resulted not just from some incomplete set of structural types but, more fundamentally, from a non-workable substantivist or essentialist orientation to social organization. A major source of difficulty, he suggested, was the assumption that the social phenomenon under investigation—to be defined and explained according to principles such as descent or residence— was a "corporate group." This is a jural unit derived from English juridical applications that, as he noted, does not match exactly its French equivalent, *personne morale*. Marcel Mauss (1985[1938]:18–19), for example, had characterized the *personne morale* as an entity with a moral and legal personality in the sense of being autonomous and responsible, possessor of rights and subject to obligations, but the notion of a *personne* is first defined by its roles and relationships to other such entities and to the larger society. Lévi-Strauss observed that in Anglo-American anthropology, with its emphasis on assigning people to specific corporate groups, it had become axiomatic to "cut up social reality" into groups with bounded and mutually exclusive membership and to classify various kinship practices into types based on the specific principles (e.g., descent or residence) followed in any single society to delimit such a group (Lévi-Strauss 1987:153–54; see also Errington 1989:234–35). Thus the cognatic societies of the Pacific region presented a problem, because the peoples there appeared to organize themselves into corporate groups despite the absence of consistently applied "rules" of descent, inheritance, and residence. Furthermore, group boundaries were unexpectedly indefinite and porous, all of which called into question their function as jural entities as well as the presumed fixity of kin-based social identity.

Lévi-Strauss therefore suggested that attention should shift away from bounded groups as "constitutive of the social order and considered as legal persons" (1987:155). In the first place, there is a certain optative aspect to group membership. Individuals may often choose what group to join based on various criteria and strategies, and groups may choose who shall be their members; the latter is particularly evident at funerary rites when rival claims are made for the corpse (Lévi-Strauss 1987:179–80; see also Fox 1987:175; Waterson 1995b:207). More important, an overemphasis on the principles used to delimit group membership undervalues the relationships established and maintained *between* groups. According to Lévi-Strauss's understanding of what he was calling house societies, houses are most visible in their interactions with other houses. The house as a social institution "is a dynamic formation that cannot be defined in itself, but only in relation to others of the same kind, situated in their historical context" (Lévi-Strauss 1987:178).

Not unexpectedly, Lévi-Strauss considered marriage alliance to be the most important relationship linking houses. Alliance was at the core of his earlier theory of kinship in *Elementary Structures of Kinship* (1969[1949]) (Carsten and Hugh-Jones 1995:9; Gibson 1995:130) and was a major component of his critique of Anglo-American anthropology with its overriding emphasis on descent (Errington 1989:236). In his examples of interhouse alliances, Lévi-Strauss concentrated on eastern Indonesian societies that ritually recognize the important social relationship maintained between wife-giving and wife-taking groups, groups that are often referred to by the indigenous term for house. These alliances, and especially the exchange systems that are tied to them, are what create or reiterate an asymmetrical relationship between houses (e.g., Barraud 1979:88; 1990; Errington 1989:234; Fox, ed. 1980; McKinnon 1991).

More fundamentally, Lévi-Strauss noted that the basis of any house—the family itself—was established in an act of alliance represented most saliently by the conjugal couple. Their marriage creates a union of conflicting tendencies—virilocality and uxorilocality, patrilineality and matrilineality—that are played out in various ways (Lévi-Strauss 1987:155). Thus, he demonstrated how the Anglo-American emphasis on delimiting the principles of social group membership was the wrong approach: "Anthropologists have therefore been mistaken in seeking, in this type of institution, a substratum which they have variously thought to find in descent, property and residence. We believe, to the contrary, that it is necessary to move on from the idea of *objective substratum* to that of *objectification of a relation*: the unstable relation of alliance which, as an institution, the role of the house is to solidify, if only in an illusory form" (1987:155, emphasis in original).[4]

On this subject Lévi-Strauss then added another level of understanding to the house that has subsequently received much attention: the house is a "fetish" in the Marxist sense. It is the representation of a relation (between wife-givers and wife-takers) perceived as a thing "objectified in the house" but which, "as a relation, cannot be the substratum of any attribute" (Lévi-Strauss 1987:155–56). The house projects an outward face of unity—exemplified by the marriage of husband and wife—but this unity is "greatly fictitious" and masks underlying tensions that threaten to fragment it. The house is the hypostatization of the opposition of wife-takers and wife-givers, of the conflicting obligations of filiation and alliance, and of the tangible antagonisms resulting from the differential claims on members of the new family made by the exogamous groups who contributed the spouses (1987:157–58, 1982:185). The family is therefore not a substantive phenomenon of unproblematical definition; it is the objectification of contested perspectives and contrary expectations: "the father, as wife-taker, sees in his son a privileged member of his lineage, just as the maternal grandfather, as wife-giver, sees in his grandson a full member of his own. It is at the intersection of these antithetical perspectives that the house is situated, and perhaps is formed" (Lévi-Strauss 1982:186).

Moreover, the physical house itself may materially represent the fetishized aspect of the house as the juxaposition of relationships that constitute person and society. Lévi-Strauss briefly mentioned in this context the elaborately decorated dwellings of the Karo Batak of Sumatra and the Atoni of Timor, whose architectural layout and corresponding distribution of activities "make of the house a veritable microcosm reflecting in its smallest details an image of the universe and of the whole system of social relations" (1987:156). Other material phenomena that make up the house estate, or immaterial property such as names or claims to potential spouses in allied houses, may also objectify the house, represent its longevity, and serve as a central pivot for the construction of social memories grounded in the house (Boon 1990a:136–37; Errington 1983b; Lévi-Strauss 1987:160; McKinnon 1991).

The notion that kinship and affinal relations were hypostatized as a house contributes to a broader understanding of how the ties that people perceive among themselves emerge from practical action, what Pierre Bourdieu (1977: 37) called "practical" as opposed to "official" kinship (see also Waterson 1995b), from the perspective of "strategies" rather than "rules" (Bourdieu 1977:9). Lévi-Strauss (1987:180) similarly observed that with regard to the house, concepts of descent, marriage, inheritance, residence, etc., are not "ideal rules, static by definition," but rather "the strategies elaborated and put into practice, not by individuals, but by moral persons assured of a lifetime longer than those of the individuals composing them"; this is a departure from his earlier "deterministic, rule-bound version" of structuralism (Carsten and Hugh-Jones 1995:9). Indeed, although he spoke of the house as a "type" of social structure, Lévi-Strauss proposed to see the house as emergent in the negotiated outcomes of strategic choices made by groups and individuals against a backdrop of collective constraints and demands (Lévi-Strauss 1983:1229–30).[5]

Although Lévi-Strauss intended the house to be an addition to the classificatory terminology of social structure, as the objectification of a relation it cannot easily be added alongside lineage and clan. Neither does it fit with existing concepts in terms of scale. Family, lineage, clan, and tribe or caste can be arranged in a linear scheme based on increasing size, complexity, and inclusivity, but the house may exist at all these levels, expressing this entire range of variability (Lévi-Strauss 1987:160). An example is the Balinese *dadia* described by Hildred and Clifford Geertz (1975). As Lévi-Strauss (1987:158) noted, "When they [Geertz and Geertz] encounter it in an aristocratic context, the word 'house' comes spontaneously and with justification to their pen; but in the village context they no longer know what definition to choose, and hesitate inconclusively between lineage, caste, cultural association and faction. It is 'a little of all these, and even sometimes a political party', as Boon [1977:145] acutely comments" (see also Boon 1990b:217).

In sum, Lévi-Strauss concluded that the house as a social category confounds the usual classificatory efforts of anthropologists, in that: 1) it is a "moral person" but not a corporate group delimited by rules of descent, inheritance, or residence; 2) it is better perceived in operation as the objectification of relations rather than as a substantive phenomenon; 3) it can exist at what we recognize as various societal levels; 4) it unites what anthropologists consider to be antithetical and mutually exclusive principles of kinship, marriage, residence, and succession, principles which themselves are actually illusory; and 5) it thereby transcends the categorical distinctions among different types of societies that have been distinguished using those principles. He emphasized its differences from traditional classificatory units and principles as follows:

On all levels of social life, from the family to the state, the house is therefore an institutional creation that permits compounding forces which, everywhere else, seem only destined to mutual exclusion because of their contradictory bends. Patrilineal descent and matrilineal descent, filiation and residence, hypergamy and hypogamy, close marriage and distant marriage, heredity and election: all these notions, which usually allow anthropologists to distinguish the various known types of society, are reunited in the house, as if . . . this institution expressed an effort to transcend, in all spheres of collective life, theoretically incompatible principles. (1982:184)

The Protean Quality of Houses and House Societies

Despite his stated interest in process, Lévi-Strauss's description of the house as a unity of oppositions has been considered static and thus limited in its utility (Carsten and Hugh-Jones 1995:36–37). His published lecture summaries provide general descriptions of social organization drawn from a cross-cultural survey, but there is no in-depth examination of the everyday interactions and processes by which the tensions of conflicting rights and obligations—the within-house and between-house relationships—were manifested and negotiated to present some "outward face of unity." On the other hand, Lévi-Strauss was more concerned with the long-term perspective, believing it extremely difficult, if not impossible, to discover the distinctive characteristics of the house solely from short-term ethnographic observation (Lévi-Strauss 1983, 1987:158, 193–94). He considered historical documentation, where available, a better source of information to understand the operation of the house over time as the result of strategic decision-making whose goal was to reproduce a corporate body linked to a perpetual estate, as if the house becomes most visible only in retrospect. He never published a detailed study on this topic; instead, he illustrated his discussions with various but brief examples from the works of others.

It is from the long-term perspective that Lévi-Strauss saw the house as a dynamic institution and house societies as permutating rather than fixed in the number and ranking of their constituent houses. Houses, *personnes morales*, are the agents of historical change, especially in reference to the between-house relations Lévi-Strauss most emphasized (Lévi-Strauss 1987:180). They "come into being and fade away" (1987:148) because they require consistent success in negotiations and manipulations to maintain themselves in the face of competition from other houses and the aspirations of low-ranked or non-house groups that desire to elevate their status.

The actual historical trajectories of house societies will therefore vary. Houses may continually rise and fall in rank and power relative to one another over a period of generations (Boon 1990b:216–17). Some houses may manage to exist (at least in name) over centuries, as in the case of certain noble houses of Europe. In other societies their number may be permanently fixed by societal consensus, such that it would be inconceivable for a house to cease to exist (e.g., Barraud 1979:88). In some cases, even when a house did perish, its name and the place where the physical house once stood would be remembered and referred to in special contexts (Waterson 1988:42), and it could be resurrected later (Waterson 1995b:203). Under certain conditions entire societies might transform themselves into *sociétés à maisons*, only later to become less "housy" (Boon 1990b:214).

This dynamic, even transitory (in the long run) quality of houses and house societies raised the question as to why houses have appeared in only some societies and at certain time periods. In response, Lévi-Strauss noted the presence of noble, aristocratic, chiefly—that is, higher-ranked—houses in many of these societies: Northwest Coast, Yurok, medieval Europe, feudal Japan, Bali. The high-ranking houses were the ones most likely to successfully preserve their property, perpetuate their estates over generations, make strategic marriage alliances, and substitute affinity for descent and descent for affinity. Lévi-Strauss suggested these societies had achieved a certain degree of complexity in which kinship was becoming no longer sufficient to organize political and economic life, but in which class-, contract-, or market-based relationships were not yet dominant. These societies, at these particular points in time, might be considered instances of a transitional situation between kin-based and class-based organization, "where political and economic interests, on the verge of invading the social field, have not yet overstepped the 'old ties of blood,' as Marx and Engels used to say. In order to express and propagate themselves, these interests must inevitably borrow the language of kinship, though it is foreign to them, for none other is available. And inevitably too, they borrow it only to subvert it" (1982:186–87).

Once again, his leading example was the Kwakiutl. For historical reasons (namely, the introduction of European trade), new forms of property arrangements were governing Kwakiutl economic and political relationships, leading them to "disguise all sorts of sociopolitical maneuvers under the veneer of kinship" (Lévi-Strauss 1982:171). In contrast to this "transitional" situation, the house should not exist or will do so in only an embryonic form in societies not at a level of complexity that involves the accumulation of wealth and expressions of rank and power, and especially those in which marriage alliance does not have a strategic economic and political importance for the perpetuation of an estate (Lévi-Strauss 1991:436). And conversely, as noted in Chapter 1, houses, as the basis for sociopolitical/economic organization, are superseded in class-based societies, particularly the capitalist formations of the modern era.

ABOUT AND BEYOND THE HOUSE

Lévi-Strauss's definition and further characterization of the house as an analytic unit of cross-cultural utility have been subjected to critical review by scholars applying this concept to some of the same societies he examined, as well as to many others (for reviews of his model, see, e.g., Boon 1990b:213–15; Carsten and Hugh-Jones 1995; Errington 1989:233–38; Macdonald 1987; Waterson 1990:138–39). On the one hand, he meant to clarify several thorny issues that have impeded scholarship on the nature and variety of kinship practices. He moved beyond the usual assumption that kinship is an isolable feature of simpler societies, and he incorporated into the house such factors as "wealth, power and status, normally associated with literate and class-based societies" (Carsten and Hugh-Jones 1995:9). On the other hand, his discussion was founded on certain traditional understandings of kinship principles, and he failed to advance his ideas sufficiently beyond them to adequately replace them. Lévi-Strauss has thus been blamed for moving too far away from those understandings (by scholars trying to maintain conventional classificatory nomenclature) as well as for sticking too closely to them (by scholars seeking to surpass the limitations of older kinship theories).

As a result of this critique, Lévi-Strauss's definition of the house, from which he never wavered, became detached from his characterization of the house as an objectification of the conflicting obligations of descent and alliance. His definition of the house has been attacked as both too specific and too ambiguous to adequately serve as a social type, although its ambiguity has also been credited with providing the opportunity for other scholars to refine it by applying this concept to more detailed case studies (e.g., Waterson 1990, 1995a; Sandstrom, this volume). However, attention has generally not been focused on his definition of the house; instead, the emphasis he gave to marriage alliance and the related notion of the house as a fetish have received the most criticism and have undergone the most revision.

Lévi-Strauss's ideas have taken hold primarily among scholars working in Southeast Asia (Carsten and Hugh-Jones, eds. 1995; Macdonald, ed. 1987; Waterson 1990) and secondarily in Amazonia (Hugh-Jones 1993, 1995; Lea 1995; Rivière 1993, 1995), large regions where cognatic kinship principles are not infrequent and where the "house" was already becoming well recognized as an indigenous referent for a socio-residential unit (see Chapter 1). In their attempts to apply his model to detailed case studies of specific communities, anthropologists encountered recurring problems that begged the question as to how, or even whether, Lévi-Strauss's notion of the house and house societies should be utilized analytically and cross-culturally. Their concerns have appeared in a number of individual studies as well as in several anthologies dedicated to examining the Lévi-Straussian house (e.g., Carsten and Hugh-Jones, eds. 1995; Macdonald, ed. 1987).[6] What has happened to the house of Lévi-Strauss is that it has been both adopted with some success and rejected for its lack of any heuristic utility (e.g., compare Waterson 1990 to Rousseau 1987). Where adopted, it has frequently been stripped of its original conceptualization and merged with, if not replaced by, various other indigenous and analytical usages of the term "house." Despite these criticisms, most scholars have continued to see value, although not always the same value, in Lévi-Strauss's proposal to employ a house-centered focus in the study of social organization.

When Is the House a "House"?

An early attempt was made to refine Lévi-Strauss's house model by applying it to more detailed ethnographic studies in a cross-cultural investigation that could better delimit the parameters of house societies. This project was undertaken in 1985–86 by a group of scholars associated with the Centre National de la Recherche Scientifique in Paris who had conducted fieldwork in western Island Southeast Asia. The outcome of their comparative study is aptly named

De la hutte au palais: sociétés "à maison" en Asie du Sud-Est insulaire (Macdonald, ed. 1987), for it proposed that within this area of the world the house as a *personne morale* is clearly associated with hierarchy, and the more hierarchical the society (up to the level of kings in their palaces), the greater the likelihood of discerning houses meeting the criteria established by Lévi-Strauss and functioning as residential, economic, ritual, and political units (Macdonald 1987:7–8; Sellato 1987b:34–35).

Because there is a great deal of variation within the region, with societies ranging from highly stratified to egalitarian, these scholars considered it essential to distinguish the different manifestations of house societies. For example, there are variable forms even among the hierarchical societies. Some have only a single royal house, while others are composed of competing noble houses. A "vertical" situation in which one ruling house holds sway over commoners (who are not themselves organized into houses) was classified as distinct from a "horizontal" configuration in which virtually everyone is organized in this way, and social interaction is conducted within the framework of houses as *personnes morales* (Sellato 1987a:204).

Furthermore, houses of a different sort were observed in the more egalitarian societies in this region, for, as noted above, "house" is a common indigenous term for a social unit in Southeast Asia. Importantly, these usages were included within Lévi-Strauss's house model by divorcing his definition from his later characterization of the house as a unifying image of certain relationships, treating these as two separable concepts. In his introduction to the CNRS volume, Charles Macdonald suggested that these two views of the house represented distinct forms which seemed to exist in different types of societies, and that they must have become conflated due to an evolution in Lévi-Strauss's own thinking when he had to apply his original abstract definition to diverse societies. Macdonald framed this as a dichotomy between the house as a "concrete group," the *personne morale* of Lévi-Strauss's definition, which he termed the *maison-institution*; and the house, not as a concrete group but as an ideal representation, the *maison-fétiche* (Macdonald 1987:5; although Sellato 1987a:202 in the same volume disagreed as to whether the *maison-fétiche* should be considered a house).

As a minor modification to Macdonald's revision, Stephen Headley (1987: 214), another CNRS researcher, suggested that the house-institution/house-fetish dichotomy be considered endpoints on a comparative spectrum of house societies ranging from "strong" to "weak," which corresponds roughly to a scale of hierarchy from stratified to egalitarian. In this perspective the house remains a useful concept even where it is "weak" (i.e., it fails to meet the definitional criteria set by Lévi-Strauss), for example, in peasant rice-growing societies of Java and Malaysia. In these societies an idiom of consanguinity (expressed as "siblingship") maintains the identity of a house as a kin group and allows it to be extended far beyond the household. Rather than considering the house as absent in these societies, Headley proposed that it was present only in a fetishized form—"the projection of unity through the extension of the idiom of siblingship to virtually everyone" (Headley 1987:217).[7]

The CNRS scholars were not alone in detaching Lévi-Strauss's definition from his characterization of the house, and this has become a critical issue in subsequent attempts to deal with the concept. The simultaneity of the house as both institution and fetish, assumed in Lévi-Strauss's discussion, has often been split asunder and considered to refer to two different versions of the house in different types of societies. Furthermore, the more frequent criticisms of the Lévi-Straussian house refer to his characterization, ignoring his definition. A common complaint is that he highlighted marriage alliance in the hypostatization of the house as fetish to the exclusion of other key signifiers of house unity, especially the unity of the sibling group in Southeast Asia and Oceania, which itself is intimately related to the predominant cognatic kinship systems in those regions (e.g., Marshall, ed. 1981; see critiques in Carsten 1995a, b; Gibson 1995; Headley 1987; Howell 1995; Hugh-Jones 1995; Janowski 1995). The fetishized house that may result from sibling ties extends itself outward through siblingship rather than downwards through descent (Carsten 1987:166), and the temporal dimension (perpetuity) associated with descent is therefore moot.[8] In any event, marriage alliance is often transformed into, or conceived as, consanguinity rather than affinity, with a husband-wife pair conceptualized as a brother-sister pair (Barraud 1990; Howell 1990).

Another criticism is that marriage alliance, producing conflicting obligations between wife-taking and wife-giving groups that must be mediated within the house, is not universally relevant to house societies because exogamy is not always a preferred strategy. James Boon (1990a, b) and Shelly Errington (1987, 1989) tinkered with Lévi-Strauss's ideas to adapt them to societies of western and central Indonesia in which high-ranked houses practice endogamy rather than exogamy as a means of preserving an estate. Other scholars have taken issue with Lévi-Strauss's emphasis on descent, the counterpart to alliance. Austronesian societies display a strong emphasis on origins and the maintenance of continuity with the past, which is "essential for social identity and social differentiation," but this is not the same concept as descent (Fox 1993:16–17).

The original rationale for proposing "institution" and "fetish" as separate manifestations of the house, a dichotomy that also maintains taxonomic sociopolitical distinctions based on hierarchy, was to modify the Lévi-Straussian house so as to make sense of virtually all societal variability in Southeast Asia (Macdonald 1987:8). The house would thereby retain some heuristic value even in societies that lack bona fide houses (Headley 1987:217). Nevertheless, this attempt to expand Lévi-Strauss's notion of the house to match the empirical studies of Southeast Asian peoples revealed a fundamental problem. Given that anthropologists working in various parts of the world were increasingly aware of the "house" as a common indigenous label for a social group and a useful focus for interpreting kin-based, economic, religious, and political organizations, Macdonald (1987:4) asked quite simply whether what ethnographers *and* what indigenous persons call the "house" correspond to Lévi-Strauss's concept of the house. Perhaps these multiple kinds of houses are founded on a single underlying principle, but this need not necessarily be so; and even if they are, Lévi-Strauss has not necessarily provided us with that all-encompassing principle. In other words, when is the "house" as it appears in native language and emerges out of native practice a "house" in the Lévi-Straussian sense? From the perspective adopted by Macdonald and Headley, the house as defined by Lévi-Strauss ("institution," "strong") seemed to be only one manifestation within a much larger spectrum of possible forms.

Other scholars bypassed Lévi-Strauss's definition of the house, although they acknowledged his contribution to house-centered studies, and maintained the notion of the house as the metaphorical encompassment of many persons united by fictive and real kin ties and/or economic or ritual relationships. Janet Carsten's (1995a, b) studies of the Malays of Pulau Langkawi emphasized the centrality of houses, women, and siblingship in understanding social organization at the household level and beyond. In his ethnography from a quite different area of the world, a Mixtec community in Mexico, John Monaghan (1995:245) described the entire community as a "great house" à la Lévi-Strauss, because the acts of commensality that relate community members to one another are the same as those that relate members of a household (see Sandstrom, this volume). Adam Kuper (1993) added Lévi-Strauss's notions to the indigenous concept of the house already being recognized in African studies. He demonstrated the conceptual and organizational links between the homestead and the entire polity as a "royal house writ large" in nineteenth-century Zulu society (1993:486). Stripped of all its distinguishing qualities, the house of Lévi-Strauss has reached the point where it is used to refer to any corporate kin group in the generic sense of a convenient all-encompassing rubric (Helms 1999:57–58).

These various applications of the house concept based on Lévi-Strauss's inspiration, but in the absence of the "institutional" house, ultimately question the status of the house as a type of social structure, as Lévi-Strauss had proposed. As Roxana Waterson (1993:224, 1995a:50–53) noted, the key issue that confronts scholars is whether his definition should be broadened to encompass all the instances where "houses" have been observed. Should it be extended to more egalitarian societies and those that lack critical house signifiers, such as perpetuity in the maintenance of an estate using the strategic "language" of marriage alliance and kinship? At the other end of the political scale, should it include stratified societies in which the polity is conceived only ideologically as a single house to which everyone—noble and commoner— is attached by different kinds of links? Or, should it be limited only to those usually hierarchical societies that exhibit most or all of the characteristic features laid out by Lévi-Strauss?

Is the House a Type of Social Structure?

At the heart of the subsequent critique and clarification is precisely the analytical utility of both house and house society, as promulgated by Lévi-Strauss, as a new classificatory type. The lack of fit of the house to the taxonomic status of existing terms (family, clan, lineage) referring to corporate bodies was especially troublesome, for it meant that the house could not be accommodated within standard kinship classification. For someone seeking to understand the organization of kin-based groups, this presumably single institution could not account for the many different manifestations of the house even within one region, such as Austronesia, where the "house" as an indigenous concept may encompass a household, a lineage, a clan, a village, or an entire polity (Fox 1987: 172–73).[9] Moreover, if the house, in which patrilineal and matrilineal ties come together, can help to make sense of cognatic societies (and it was these that Lévi-Strauss emphasized in his later lectures at the Collège de France), then a priori this same institution should not also make sense of unilineal societies, if an analytical distinction is to be maintained between them (Howell 1995:153).

A further complication is the realization (alluded to by Lévi-Strauss) that unilineal societies never actually conform to the idealized model in which everyone is assigned at birth to a descent group for the purpose of organizing political or economic activities (Kuper 1982); Edmund Leach had previously suggested that the notion of a "structure of unilineal descent groups" may be a "*total* fiction" (1968:302, emphasis in original). As noted above, the imprecision in the application of "rules" of descent, inheritance, and group membership observed in Austronesia was being recognized as well in Africa, the heartland of British descent theorists. Here, too, the word translated as "lineage," for example, among the Nuer, often refers to the dwelling, with no immediate implications for biological ties (McKinnon 1991:29; see Evans-Pritchard 1940:195), and "kinship" ties are based as much on shared locality as on presumed descent linkages, forming the "duality of 'blood' and 'land'" (Lévi-Strauss 1987:181; Kuper 1982:71). These empirical observations seem to obviate any attempt to maintain a distinction between "house" and "lineage": lineages can be seen as houses and houses as lineages (Carsten and Hugh-Jones 1995:15–16).

Then there is the separate problem of moving from *maison* to a *société "à maisons,"* a society "of houses" (Macdonald 1987:5). *Société à maisons* was not defined by Lévi-Strauss but considered by him to be coincident with the existence of houses—where there are houses (plural), there is a house society—and he further speculated on the common conditions under which this specific "type" of social structure may have emerged. This raised the same taxonomic problem as did the house, for how could a single category encompass the diversity of cases that already had been classified into many different kinds of societies using various criteria, particularly the distinctions among stratified, ranked, and egalitarian systems (Bloch 1995b:71; Macdonald 1987:4; Sellato 1987a:195)? It seemed to Macdonald (1987:4) an "audacious" act to place the Iban *bilek* (longhouse) of Borneo in the same sociopolitical category as the House of Savoy. In other words, cognitive difficulties arose due to the lack of fit of "house society" within the existing taxonomy used to divide societies into different types.

Lévi-Strauss's proposal "to introduce into anthropological terminology the notion of 'house' (in the sense in which one speaks of a 'noble house'), and therefore . . . *a type of social structure* hitherto associated with complex societies . . . also to be found in non-literate societies" (1987:151, emphasis added) became a major focus in the debate over the utility of his concept. As his discussions demonstrated, he was borrowing a social structural characterization better known to historians, but his own work revealed that the house could *not* serve as a new type added to existing terminology. Given his stated intention (1983, 1987:151) for the house to blur traditional but now indefensible kinship categories, such as matrilineality and patrilineality, and to span what is actually a continuum from unilineal to cognatic principles, then his new type of social structure, especially as it has been modified by subsequent work, would encompass most of the world's known societies (Carsten and Hugh-Jones 1995:18–19). Lévi-Strauss's examples of house societies are so diverse, representing such great variation in social, political, and economic organization, that the privileging of the house as the common factor in all of them, and thereby treating them all as a single type, is a "disservice" (Howell 1995:150) to the field, rather than the hoped-for improvement over previous approaches to social organization.

The great conceptual dilemma exposed here is the taxonomic orientation to social structure, in which societies and their constituent units are classified into what are presumed to be mutually exclusive essentialist types, defined on the basis of one or a constellation of features, to be compared and contrasted on that basis. The failure of observed actions to be mapped onto these types has become a paradox in anthropology, out of which an entire "meta-discourse concerning the relation between the ideal and the real, structure and practice" (McKinnon 1995:171; 1991:29) has developed. Although the assumption that people divide and interrelate themselves on the basis of idealized kin types and rules was proving not to be a productive strategy and was beginning to be abandoned (e.g., Carsten and Hugh-Jones 1995:2; Errington 1989:238; McKinnon 1995:171–72; Waterson 1993:225), it is nevertheless difficult to escape from this epistemological "straitjacket" (McKinnon 1995:263n).

Thus, Lévi-Strauss spoke of the house as an alternative to traditional kinship analyses while still adhering to an orientation that not only privileged kinship as the most fundamental social relationship, but also derived from the very essentialist approaches he criticized. One reason why his characterization of the house as combining mutually incompatible principles—such as patriliny and matriliny or consanguinity and affinity—is considered vague and problematical, is because these are still treated as artificial kinship types that are expected a priori to be consistent and generalizable and to compose antithetical pairings (Errington 1989:238; see also McKinnon 1995:172). In the end Lévi-Strauss was unable to move beyond the limitations imposed by the concepts he used: "if the notion of 'house society' simultaneously attempts to resolve the problems of both descent-group and alliance models whilst still relying upon them . . . it seems unlikely that the invention of a new category, reliant on the old, will provide a new basis for a synthetic theory of kinship" (Carsten and Hugh-Jones 1995:19).

Transcending Types: Transformation and Process

Those who have found the Lévi-Straussian house most useful have ignored its proposed status as a classificatory type (and even Lévi-Strauss [1983:1227–29] suggested a cladistic or materialist approach to understanding social formulations to replace fixed taxonomies and essentialist types). On the contrary, the house "as a heuristic device . . . may allow us to get away from such types altogether" (Hugh-Jones 1993:116). Instead of simply adding more diverse configurations to a "house society type," scholars who utilize Lévi-Strauss's ideas tend to focus on processes and practices in which the house serves as an idiom for social groupings (Carsten and Hugh-Jones 1995:20; Hugh-Jones 1995:248). It has become more productive to examine the dynamic quality of kin-like, economic, ritual, and co-residential relations that are enacted within the physical and symbolic framework provided by the house.

While the house may ultimately present an outward face of unity, internally it represents and naturalizes hierarchy and divisions among its members (Carsten and Hugh-Jones 1995:11–12). It is not merely the locus for some unspecified union of mutually exclusive principles, but instead serves as the key arena for the "differential articulation of *mutually implicating* contrastive social forms" (McKinnon 1995:188, emphasis added). As Susan McKinnon (1995:172) observed, the variable forms that marriage, residence, or filiation may assume do not exist as isolable, mutually exclusive categories by which whole societies may be classified, but are principles that take their value from their interrelationship with one another in a single social system. Neither alliance nor descent nor any other principle has some "privileged ontological or epistemological status, but each derives its particular meaning in relation to the rest" (Howell 1995:165). Thus, a house-centered approach demonstrates the impossibility of maintaining traditional taxonomic distinctions. Lévi-Strauss saw the house as something "halfway between lineal and cognatic," but this does not imply three different types of societies (lineal—house—cognatic) as much as it characterizes a single society where the two opposed principles coexist and are mediated within the house (Hugh-Jones 1993:98).

Similarly, instead of classifying entire societies by type, it is better to investigate cultural extremes as evidence of the transformations of social principles (Boon 1990b:213). For example, Boon (1990b:439n.) indicated how the house is actually far more useful precisely when considered as something quite different from a type: "houses muddle conventional analytic distinctions of clan, lineage, guild, *warna, jati,* party, etc. . . . Paramount is the fact that 'house' can relate to 'house,' even across presumed boundaries of society, nation, or other construction" (Boon 1990b:439n.). Furthermore, the house can have great heuristic utility for comparative studies *especially* among diverse societies, a contribution to the analytical dialectic between "culture" and "society." Too much detail was being lost in reducing cross-cultural comparisons to their lowest common sociological denominator and then assuming that such labels as "unilineal" or "bilateral" adequately characterize social structure (Boon 1990b:212–13). Errington (1989:237–38) expressed the same misgivings: "Classifying societies by 'kinship type' obscures the very obvious fact that two Indonesian social organizations, only one of which is (for example) 'matrilineal,' have more in common than two 'matrilineal' social organizations, only one of which is Indonesian."

Other scholars have adopted the model of the house on the condition that it not be too rigidly defined (Rivière 1993:511) or serve as some "watertight typology" (Waterson 1995a:48). Waterson further suggested examining the differential functioning of the various principles of house societies as " 'variations on a theme' " (1995a:48). Rather than investigating the diversity of societies in Southeast Asia in order to discern which are and which are not house societies (cf. Macdonald, ed. 1987), she instead showed in detail how the ambiguities of kinship systems in Indonesia can be resolved by taking a house-centric perspective, despite the tremendous variation in the scale and complexity of these societies (Waterson 1990:138, 1995a:47). As also noted in the earlier comparative study (Macdonald, ed. 1987), houses, as indigenous constructs, run the gamut from the more egalitarian longhouse societies in which the house *is* the entire community, to those which exhibit a fluid social ranking of houses, to the more hierarchical societies in which the "'house' ideology is largely monopolized by the aristocracy," and finally to centralized states in which the "ideology of kingship . . . was grafted on to ideas about the house" (Waterson 1990:140; for this last category, see also Boon 1990a, 1990b; Errington 1989; Sellato 1987a). This wide range of sociopolitical difference cannot be accommodated by traditional classificatory conceptions that consider egalitarian, ranked, and hierarchical societies as noncomparable; yet, in an anti-taxonomic approach they all can be better comprehended by examining the role of the house as a central and fundamental organizing principle. The demonstration of variation among house societies is, in itself, a productive undertaking: "each application brings out ethnographic particulars that would remain masked without some concept of the house" (Grinker 1996:857). Thus, the broad applicability of the house in Lévi-Strauss's terms, which seemingly makes it "too all-embracing and unwieldy to be a truly incisive tool of investigation," has proven to be an advantage rather than a detriment in providing new insights into the study of Southeast Asian societies (Waterson 1995a:68).

Beyond simple variation, cross-cultural studies within a region, such as Indonesia, may ultimately show how entire societies are "transformations of each other whose common feature is the importance of the house as a focus of social organization" (Waterson 1995a:48). For example, Errington (1987, 1989) was able to include both major strategies of unity—alliance and sibling-ship, sometimes considered to be at odds with one another—under the rubric of the house by positing a major transformation in house societies across Island Southeast Asia. She contrasted the ideology and functioning of the house in certain societies concentrated in eastern Indonesia, in which alliance and exchange between multiple houses is a defining principle, and the "centrist"-oriented societies primarily in west-central Southeast Asia, in which a single endogamous house may be coterminous with society itself. The multiple permutations in other societal domains that are concordant with this key difference give the appearance of noncomparability among all these societies; yet from the house perspective, they can be viewed as transformations of each other (Errington 1987:405, 1989:207–9).

Regional studies may also begin to account for the presence or absence of house societies in terms of their *interactions with one another*, as well as in terms of ecological or sociohistorical conditions that advanced or impeded the development of substantial property, ascribed rank, and perpetuated estates. This endeavor goes far beyond the initial attempts to classify individual societies as house societies or to correlate house societies with certain isolated factors, such as hierarchy. An example is Albert Schrauwers's (1997) historical study of a South Sulawesi kingdom and its hinterland. The Bugis kingdom of Luwu' (Luwuq), on the southern coastal lowlands, exemplified a strongly hierarchical society in which the royal house, *kapolo*, was synonymous with the kingdom itself (Errington 1989; cf. Caldwell 1991). In the late nineteenth century, Luwu', in competition with neighboring kingdoms, was extending its reach into the highlands to the north and bringing other peoples under its suzerainty, including the more egalitarian To Pamona.

The To Pamona were not organized into houses, but Schrauwers describes how "proto-houses" tentatively emerged out of To Pamona interactions with the Luwu' kingdom, partly as the result of emulation (even veneration) of the royal center, but also in the more pragmatic context of trade in raw materials and exchanges of prestige goods. The proto-houses began as stem families within larger corporate entities (*santina*), which were ideally endogamous "occasional" kin groups that came together as a unit only in rituals of marriage and secondary funerals. On these occasions, elders competed for status and leadership within and between *santina*, seeking to incorporate more members through marriage alliance and to extend the generational depth of these proto-houses. However, these interactions required the exchange of prestige goods (obtained by trade with the southern lowland kingdoms) to affirm the kinship tie. Unlike true houses that keep some prestige goods out of circulation as inalienable wealth (Weiner 1992), the proto-houses of the To Pamona were unable to hold on to their valuables as a perpetual estate and to transform their unstable status into ascribed rank (Schrauwers 1997:365). Nevertheless, other highland societies did manage to achieve "household" through complex marital and economic interactions with the southern kingdoms in a period of rapid political change stimulated by major shifts in trade relations with the Dutch and Chinese (1997:374).[10]

In addition to examining the role of the house in the transformation of regional social systems over time, another way to realize the potential of Lévi-Strauss's concept of the house has been to move precisely in the opposite direction: to discover how individual social groups within a society create and enact house-centered relationships out of their mundane activities. This approach is part of the growing acceptance of earlier criticisms (e.g., Bourdieu 1977; Kuper 1982; Leach 1968; Schneider 1972) of the primacy assigned to kin-based links and identities as structural or natural givens, and it replaces kinship "rules" with a processual, multidimensional, quotidian, and "practical" (deriving from practice) framework for determining the various forms of interpersonal associations (Carsten and Hugh-Jones 1995:19).

Lévi-Strauss's discussions of Kwakiutl, Yurok, and medieval European societies indicated that people related themselves to one another not just in terms of what anthropologists understood as kinship ties among individuals, but also by the exchange relationships enacted and maintained over time between the houses to which they belonged. From this perspective, points that require more attention are 1) the relationship between physical houses as orienting loci and the social groups that identify themselves with, and are localized by, those houses (people-to-house); and 2) the various ways in which people actually trace their ties to each other to and through houses (house-to-house) (Waterson 1993:224). Individuals spell out their relationships via houses, not to create neatly bounded kin groups, but to respond to specific situations involving individuals or subsets of a larger collectivity, such as when property rights are challenged, bridewealth must be accumulated, or a consanguine is recast as a potential affine (Waterson 1986:92–93, 109, 1995b).

Moreover, houses are not always best considered as kinship or descent groups, a simplistic methodological refuge to which we too often revert (McKinnon 1991:29). Southeast Asian scholars noted that coherent and permanent social entities were better characterized as ritual and/or political units that may or may not coincide with kin-defined groups (e.g., Sellato 1987a:200). A house-like unity has also been explained as resulting primarily from economic factors (e.g., Gudeman and Rivera 1990; Leach 1968; Sabean 1990; see Joyce, Marshall, Sandstrom, this volume). In some cases the house (the social unit) is so fluid and ambiguous in its membership that as a *personne morale* it is best viewed as an abstraction that may not come into play except in certain contexts, its actual members fluctuating depending on the specific situation (Hugh-Jones 1993:110; Waterson 1995b).

Thus, Lévi-Strauss's claim (1982:187) that in house societies people use the "language of kinship . . . for none other is available" is belied by his own call for a focus on the house as the intersection of pragmatic concerns that overlap the artificially separated domains of kinship, economics, religion, and politics. As Carsten and Hugh-Jones (1995) observed, the answer to this conundrum should have been obvious to Lévi-Strauss, but he did not fully see it, trapped as he was in the older paradigm: "An alternative language is precisely that of the house. If the language of the house is 'about' kinship, it is no less 'about' economy and just as much about joint subsistence, production and consumption as it is about property. Crucially, this language is also about common spaces and about buildings which are palaces and temples as well as shelters and homes" (1995:19).

Their final sentence alludes to the ongoing scholarship on houses as pervasive structures that orient social identities and interactions as a consequence of the daily actions performed within and around them. The symbolic linkages of the house to the cosmos, society, and the body were being delineated by anthropologists in various world areas (see Chapter 1), especially in Southeast Asia, where house societies are also most recognized (e.g., Cunningham 1964; Ellen 1986; Waterson 1988, 1990). Indeed, a major shortcoming of Lévi-Strauss's explication of house societies was that he failed to examine the house itself, both as an architectural unit and as a locus for social interactions in multiple dimensions (Carsten and Hugh-Jones 1995:12).

This general critique, with its call for a dramatic broadening of the nature of house-centric investigations, was developed in a 1990 symposium at Cambridge University, published in 1995 with the revealing title, *About the House: Lévi-Strauss and Beyond* (Carsten and Hugh-Jones, eds. 1995). In their introduction to the volume, Carsten and Hugh-Jones (1995:2) proposed to go beyond Lévi-Strauss's concept and demonstrate the greater value of recognizing in the house an "anthropology of architecture which might take its theoretical place alongside the anthropology of the body," giving primacy to the orientations, behaviors, and ideas associated with the physical house.

In a "language of the house" (Carsten and Hugh-Jones 1995:19), the people and the physical house must be investigated on the same terms, not as analytically distinct phenomena. This requires examining the processes, which may be both cyclical and incremental, by which relationships between people, and between peoples and their houses, are enacted and transformed over the lifetime and beyond of a living individual. By the same token, houses must be viewed as living and developing entities just like the people who inhabit (or cohabit with) them. This view of the house is firmly grounded in indigenous conceptions. In much of the world houses are believed to be endowed with spirits or souls, and they are conceived as living beings whose different parts often are labeled by the same terms as those given to human body parts. Houses must be nourished to prevent their demise, and they are enlarged or modified to materialize the increased status that derives from senescence, often in concert with—and thus objectifying—the milestone events in the lives of their occupants (Carsten and Hugh-Jones 1995:37–38; Waterson 1990). This perspective proposed to bring together what Carsten and Hugh-Jones (1995:45) refer to as the two "sides" of the house, both the "ritual" construct emphasized by Lévi-Strauss, embodied in property and linked to ancestral origins, and the mundane aspect of household members engaged in quotidian activities, the actions that, while too often ignored by anthropologists, actually "build" the house.

OPENING UP THE HOUSE OF LÉVI-STRAUSS

The proposal to create a "language of the house" has great potential for uniting diverse perspectives to investigate houses and households that have, up to now, been treated as separable concerns. It will also highlight indigenous conceptions and practical actions that have too often been hidden under anthropologists' static analytical labels. Lévi-Strauss is credited with stimulating this broader conceptualizing of the house. However, something has been lost in the intellectual shifts away from his original model; namely, that in the *société à maisons* Lévi-Strauss had discriminated a specific social configuration that is *not* found in every society, although it has occurred in various parts of the world.

A common justification for either broadening or rejecting Lévi-Strauss's definition of the house has quite simply been that it did not match the particular society under investigation, despite the existence of indigenous conceptions of the house as a social unit (e.g., Carsten 1995a:126; Gibson 1995:129; Janowski 1995:85; Macdonald 1987; Rivière 1995:203; Rousseau 1987). The definitive answer to Macdonald's question (above) is that not every house, as this word appears in both indigenous and analytical usages to refer to a social group, is the house as defined by Lévi-Strauss.

Indeed, the "house" that socially and spatially locates a *personne morale* is often a residence but is not always shared by all house members, who may be dispersed among various dwellings, even in different localities. Rather than a domicile, it may be a shrine (e.g., Boon 1990b; Errington 1989; Howell 1995), or as a sacred place it may constitute a fusion of both functional categories (Waterson 1993; Kirch, this volume). In local usage the word "house" may signify a cleared or bounded space within which structures of various kinds are located, and not any specific building (Gillespie, Joyce, Sandstrom, this volume). As a material phenomenon about which persons are united, it may not be a building at all but a different object, such as a clan boat, fishing net, shield (Lévi-Strauss 1987:160), heraldic device (Boon 1990a:136–37), a box of feathers with flutes and trumpets (Hugh-Jones 1993:110), or a tomb (Bloch 1995b: 71; Waterson 1995b). The house need not even have a tangible form; it could be an abstraction represented, for example, as a named place of origin (Waterson 1995a:50), although it is often represented by material signs of its existence (Joyce, this volume). Furthermore, house membership need not govern one's domestic or economic activities; instead, it may be expressed primarily on ritual occasions (e.g. Hugh-Jones 1993; Traube 1986; Waterson 1995b). Studies of the meanings constituted in architecture or in habitual practice within a residence will not apply to all these instances of house in the sense in which Lévi-Strauss's definition applies.

Rather than try to subsume the house of Lévi-Strauss within the general rubric of a "language of the house," it is more productive to safeguard his definition. Lévi-Strauss never intended his definition of the house to apply to virtually every pre-modern society. Hence, he proposed it as a "type," a social structural formation distinguishable from other recurrent formations.

Returning to the house of Lévi-Strauss requires reconsidering the earlier proposal by some Southeast Asian scholars to separate his definition, as pertaining only to the institutional house, from his characterization of the conflicting tendencies of alliance and descent that are united in the house as a fetishization of relationships. As noted above, the latter idea has been subjected to further reconceptualization, but Lévi-Strauss's definition of the house has received less attention (cf. Hugh-Jones 1993; Sellato 1987b; Waterson 1990, 1995a). This is an important point, because his definition does not make reference to the fetishistic aspects of the house, to conflicting obligations of alliance and descent, or even to kinship groups, households, or physical houses. Waterson (1995a:48–50) remarked that, stripped down to its "irreducible features," it involves the ideal of continuity beyond the life span of individual members of a *personne morale*, a continuity objectified in the maintenance over generations of a corpus of valued material and immaterial property via a transference of its custodianship, accomplished by the "strategic exploitation of the 'language of kinship or affinity'" (Waterson 1995a:48–50).

As noted in Chapter 1, the materialization and perpetuity of the house over time are the characteristics that most discriminate house societies in the Lévi-Straussian sense (Sellato 1987b:34), but they have significant implications: "they must lead us to consider the relation of 'houses' both to systems of economic stratification and to hierarchies of status, prestige, or ritual power" (Waterson 1995a:51). There is a concentration of often considerable wealth or value at stake in the house, including rights to land and labor—the basis for subsistence. Unequal access to property and the variability in its quantity and quality necessarily differentiate houses from one another and from lower-ranked groups that do not constitute houses, or are attached to houses. This difference further entails the political or religious authority and privileges that high-ranking house members may have over individuals of subordinate status. For instance, the medieval noble house used by Lévi-Strauss as an exemplar, *maison* in French from the Latin *mansio*, refers not to the dwelling (Latin *domus*), but to all persons attached in service to that noble line, who were subject to the authority of their lord (Cuisenier 1991:31–32).

There are also hierarchical differences within houses; as Lévi-Strauss observed for the Kwakiutl, their version of the house (*numaym*) is better treated as a series of ranked positions than as a collection of kinsmen. Houses frequently include close and distant relatives as well as non-kin (Lévi-Strauss 1987:152; Joyce, Sandstrom, this volume), whose social standings are colored by these relational differences. Houses may also incorporate other houses within them or as part of their estate, often expressed as an elder/younger or senior/junior relationship (e.g., Carrasco 1976; Forth 1991:63; Fox 1980:12; McKinnon 1991:98, this volume; Traube 1980:295). Thus the definition of "house" inevitably leads to consideration of the constitution of "house societies" in which hierarchy is a paramount feature (Hugh-Jones 1993:116; Waterson 1995a). This fact should also motivate an investigation as to why some societies, or subsets within a complex political-economic system, fail to develop "houses" even as they may experience temporary "proto-houses" (Schrauwers 1997) or maintain "embryonic houses" (Sandstrom, this volume).

The continuity of the house from one living group of members to a replacement group—its social reproduction—is sanctioned via kinship (*parenté*) or marriage ties, or usually both, which allows for multiple mechanisms for perpetuation that may vary from one society to the next. For example, Maurice Bloch (1995b:72) noted at least two different socioideological means for achieving continuity in Asian societies: stem family systems in which a married pair sequentially succeeds and replaces its predecessor, and those in which houses are permanently associated with a founding ancestral couple that serves as a ritual focus for all their putative descendants.

Strategically manipulating the "language of kinship and affinity" involves more than just legitimately recruiting new members to reproduce the house; this language is often what expresses the mutually identifying relationships between the members of a house and the house's estate. For example, the origins of valuable house resources are often attributed to ancestors, and links between the ancestral past and the present generation are frequently objectified in various components of the house estate. These may include specific named heirlooms acquired by ancestors (Joyce, this volume); the reuse of names/titles that reference one's forebears (McKinnon, this volume); the house itself, especially as it may incorporate portions of an earlier structure or be relocated in the same spatial locus (Marshall, Tringham, this volume); or images that represent the ancestors (Barraud 1979:10–17; Howell 1990:253; McKinnon, this volume). Other objects symbolize enduring relations of marital alliance and are acquired as part of the exchange obligations that such alliances entail (Fox, ed. 1980; McKinnon 1991, this volume).

Furthermore, the "language of kinship" may be the legitimating ideology applied a posteriori to a quite different de facto motivation for group organization and delimitation, which is always enacted rather than given. What ultimately motivates the house as a social group is a common investment in the house estate (Joyce, Marshall, Sandstrom, this volume), a product of ongoing actions. As Yvonne Marshall (this volume) observed regarding the Northwest Coast Nuu-chah-nulth: "the corporate identity of a house must be performed into existence by a dwelling's inhabitants through their actions as co-residents. Narratives of kinship and descent draw together specific, contingent groups of house occupants by generating traditions of social connectedness rooted in a distant past, but they do not construct or define the house as social group, they follow from it." More generally, Alan Sandstrom (this volume) suggests replacing the "currency of descent (shared substance)" with the "currency of interaction" as the basis for house or house-like groups.

In sum, the "house" is not a helpful typological label; used merely as such, it explains little. Instead, recognition of the potential existence of houses in the more remote corners of today's world or in the "vast territory" of the human past (Godelier et al. 1998:3) should motivate an investigation of the interconnected pragmatic actions and strategic motivations that link persons over time to and through objects or places and thereby serve to define a social group, enable its relations with other persons and groups, and facilitate its social (and accompanying material) reproduction.

The Evolution of House Societies

The development of strategies of social reproduction to maintain the estate and transmit it intact to the next generation must have been a critical factor in the emergence of houses and house societies. The accumulation of highly valued objects and rights, often considered as sacra, would have contributed to the growth of ritual power that may have ultimately developed into political power (Sellato 1987a:199–201). A diachronic perspective, as discussed in Chapter 1, must accommodate a frank discussion of the evolution of house societies. Lévi-Strauss's own brief thoughts on the subject were presented in the context of social structural types, with the house as a kind of "hybrid" spanning the perceived chasm between societies based on kinship and those based on class and contract (Carsten and Hugh-Jones 1995:10) along some unilinear, progressivist trajectory. This is a universally discredited aspect of his work (e.g., Boon 1990b:439n; Carsten and Hugh-Jones 1995:10; Gibson 1993:130; McKinnon 1991:31, 1995:173; Schrauwers 1997:357).

However, there is no need to limit inquiry into the emergence of house societies to the outmoded framework of a single evolutionary sequence of social structural types, as Waterson (1995a:68) observed. While the rejection of the house society as some intermediate form is contingent upon the broader rejection of the notion of types, it does not follow that there are not general conditions under which *sociétés à maisons* may emerge as distinct, though quite variable, phenomena. This is especially the case when it is remembered that the house is *not* simply a corporate kinship group; indeed, it has been characterized as "a device whereby competition for wealth and power can be carried out under the cloak of innate differences in rank" (Gibson 1995:148), indicating its dynamic qualities.

Lévi-Strauss (1982:186–87) had noted that the requisite of differential status and wealth provides clues for the conditions under which house societies may take shape. As other scholars had observed, there is a striking correlation between house societies and hierarchy (Hugh-Jones 1993:116; Macdonald, ed. 1987). Waterson's (1995a) survey of Southeast Asian ethnography concluded that the house, as defined by Lévi-Strauss, was most apparent in those societies whose sociopolitical complexity placed them between the extremes of a continuum running from egalitarian to highly stratified (1995a:51, 68). These are sometimes referred to as "middle-range" societies in a broad spectrum that cannot adequately be characterized as a hierarchical/non-hierarchical opposition (Price and Feinman, eds. 1995). Rather than consider the house a "stage" in cultural evolution, it is more productive to investigate how the house plays a significant role in sociopolitical transformations: "Lévi-Strauss's writings about the house do raise the very interesting question of the ways in which the 'house', as institution and ideology, can be harnessed to the 'enterprises of the great' in societies which are in the throes of a political transition towards a greater concentration of power in the hands of a few, with a shift from kinship-based to more complex political, economic, and religious structures of organization" (Waterson 1995a:67).

As discussed in Chapter 1, and as the essays in this volume hope to demonstrate, such studies will require the combined efforts of ethnographers, archaeologists, and historians engaged in cross-cultural investigations over the long-term. This interdisciplinary undertaking should ultimately be able to answer questions concerning the conditions under which house societies emerge and disappear, even as they elucidate the historically contingent variation, and the chronological and regional transformations, of what were likely numerous and diverse *sociétés à maisons* within the grand course of human experience.

3

Toponymic Groups and House Organization

The Nahuas of Northern Veracruz, Mexico

Alan R. Sandstrom

Alan Sandstrom begins with the cogent observation that most studies of house societies have failed to examine the pragmatic factors that underlie this form of social organization. Amatlan, Mexico, does not constitute a house society, although its Nahua inhabitants were, until recently, spatially distributed among various toponymic groupings they called "houses," which played a significant role in their social identities. Drawing on long-term ethnographic research that allowed him to track the domestic cycles of Amatlan households, Sandstrom highlights the salient features of these "embryonic" houses and discusses the economic factors, primarily the scarcity of agricultural land, that precluded the maintenance and intact transmittal of house estates. His main concern is to demonstrate how understanding social relationships in terms of the house, as a relatively bounded group of individuals tied to a locus in space because of their common investment in land for subsistence needs, is superior to older ideas about kinship as the principal determinant of social organization, in that it allows for the interaction of economic, residential, kinship, and religious concerns to define a pragmatic unit that includes kin and non-kin. Furthermore, Nahua kinship relations are inherently contradictory because basic kin principles are subverted by the material conditions of life. The agricultural labor that house members agree to undertake cooperatively is the principal determinant of house membership. Sandstrom ultimately suggests replacing the "currency of descent (shared substance)" with the "currency of interaction" as the basis for house or house-like groups. He also cautions that, when considering the architectural dimensions of house societies, the house as a spatial locus may encompass more than a single structure, and in this case it refers better to a cleared space in the forest than to any building.

Studies of kinship and social organization are a distinguishing feature of most cross-cultural ethnographic reports. Anthropologists working in Mesoamerica, however, have paid little attention to kinship relative to other topics and even less to social organization beyond the domestic group in their studies of community life (Robichaux 1997a:149–50). A number of factors account for this lack of interest on the part of researchers, including widespread beliefs that kinship is not an important or interesting principle of organization in the culture area, that indigenous social organization has been largely replaced by the Spanish system, that most kinship systems in the region are bilateral and thus of limited interest to kinship theorists steeped in African unilineal descent systems, and that social structures lying between the domestic group and the larger community, region, and nation are unimportant in Mesoamerica (Hunt and Nash 1967:279). Nutini (1976), Robichaux (1997a, b), and Mulhare (1996) provide summaries of the factors that have led researchers away from studies of kinship and social organization in the region.[1]

One reason rarely mentioned for the lack of emphasis on kinship and social organization in anthropological studies in Mesoamerica is the seemingly chaotic situation faced by ethnographers in the field. Even in remote villages, field workers are easily overwhelmed by what appear to be contradictory rules regarding post-marital residence, inheritance, and household composition, along with practices that seem to be no more than pragmatic responses to a variety of contingencies. People themselves often stress the flexibility and fluidity of their kinship and social systems. It is easy to assume that system coherence has been lost in the brutal history of Mesoamerica following the Spanish invasion. In a previous publication (Sandstrom 1996), I attempted to explain variability in social structure beyond the domestic group in a Nahua village by proposing that many social structural elements in communities are latent, making their appearance only during crises. Coupled with this proposal is the idea that individuals attempt to manipulate their social circumstances for their own ends, thus producing variability in social forms. Intermediate social structures lying between the domestic group and the community, region, and state therefore appear to lack coherence to outsiders or temporary visitors, including ethnographers. Only through long-term field research can ethnographers be on hand to witness these latent social structures in action. While I continue to believe that this basic analysis is correct, it is incomplete because it does not directly address the seeming variability of domestic kinship arrangements.

The concept of house society promulgated by Claude Lévi-Strauss in a number of recent publications holds promise to clarify the kinship systems in both pre-Hispanic and contemporary Native American communities in Mesoamerica. The idea of house society is a departure from more standard descent-based theories of kinship that have dominated anthropological literature on the subject. However, there is no doubt that the standard approach to kinship in anthropology is in crisis. For example, David Schneider's 1984 book, *A Critique of the Study of Kinship,* and the work of other scholars, such as Jane Collier and Sylvia Yanagisako's *Gender and Kinship: Essays Toward a Unified Analysis* (1987), have called into question the validity of kinship studies undertaken by anthropologists over the past hundred years. Once the lifeblood of sociocultural anthropology, kinship has only recently reappeared as a symposium topic at the national meetings of the American Anthropological Association after nearly total absence of many years. In my view, the concept of house society has the capacity to revitalize studies of kinship not only in Mesoamerica but elsewhere as well, although probably not in the way that Lévi-Strauss might have imagined.

The crisis in kinship studies coincides with a widespread failure of confidence in the findings and theories of anthropology as a whole, exemplified by the postmodern attack on the scientific foundation of the discipline.[2] It is interesting to note that even during this period of turmoil and self-doubt it took a person of Lévi-Strauss's stature to suggest a new approach to kinship studies that has even a possibility of being accepted widely within the discipline. On the one hand, then, it is fortunate to have someone like Lévi-Strauss who is capable of commanding this respect. Perhaps it is his stance outside a strictly scientific anthropology that makes his idea of house society acceptable to so many contemporary practitioners. On the other hand, Lévi-Strauss's structuralist program departs so radically from empirical anthropology and the materialist wing of the discipline that his insights are limited by their degree of abstraction and the difficulties of verifying and replicating them in the field.

Lévi-Strauss developed the concept of house society in a series of lectures from 1976 to 1982 at the Collège de France. He models the concept on the noble houses in medieval Europe, where rules of kinship could not account for the activities of the nobility nor for the composition of aristocratic families. He reverses common wisdom by making the remarkable claim that anthropologists must look to European history with its extensive legacy of documents to better understand certain sociocultural features that are very difficult to isolate during field research in non-Western societies (Lévi-Strauss 1982:174, 1987:193–94). It is clear that over the years Lévi-Strauss's ideas about house societies were evolving as he applied them to widely scattered societies ranging from the Pacific Northwest through Africa to New Zealand. This evolution, coupled with Lévi-Strauss's penchant for obscure writing, has lent a certain ambiguity to the concept of house society. However, it is this very ambiguity that invites others to attempt to sharpen the concept and apply it to societies not considered by its originator.

The house society concept has been discussed in detail elsewhere (e.g., Carsten and Hugh-Jones 1995:1–46, see below; see also Chapter 2), so I will confine my summary to features most relevant to my work among the Nahuas of Mexico. According to Lévi-Strauss, houses in house societies are estates that are based on both material and nonmaterial wealth. Material wealth often includes land, while nonmaterial wealth may include a name or certain rights to symbols or rituals (Lévi-Strauss 1982:176). Houses are elements of social organization, but they are closely tied to physical structures with specific locations, a point emphasized by Carsten and Hugh-Jones (1995). More important, a house is a social nexus or focus of activity that integrates kinsmen and non-kinsmen. Non-kinsmen may be adopted or otherwise incorporated into the group using the language of kinship, even where rules of descent do not strictly apply. An example of this practice would be the use of ritual kinship. But the house is often a site of the contradictions in a kinship system and is therefore an institution that lacks stability and coherence. It is an institution based equally on descent and affinity, both patrilineal and matrilineal principles may be present, and endogamy and exogamy may operate simultaneously at different levels. House societies are often cognatic but individual houses may contain lineage-like structures antagonistic to cognatic principles. According to Lévi-Strauss, these contradictory attributes are encompassed and to a certain degree neutralized by the political nature of the house. House property is the focus of common interest for the inhabitants, and this property, whether material or nonmaterial, provides the motivation for people to insure that the house endures through the generations.

Just as Marx wrote about commodities taking on a life of their own, Lévi-Strauss asserts that in people's minds the house becomes fetishized (Lévi-Strauss 1987:155–56). The house may acquire a personality or spiritual presence and presumably become the subject of rituals. House fetishism is an illusion that creates a sense of reality and continuity for members of what is at heart an unstable social group. Lévi-Strauss makes a number of additional intriguing comments about the house. He writes that the marriage tie at the core of a house creates an alliance between two kin groups (or houses) but at the same time contains within it the antagonistic goals of each group. He suggests that house societies as social forms fall between kin-based and class-based societies in an evolutionary sequence (Lévi-Strauss 1982:186–87). He further implies that houses are ranked in this type of society based primarily on whether they are wife-givers (higher rank) or wife-takers (lower rank).

In typical fashion, Lévi-Strauss's ideas, suggestions, and implications outstrip the data presented and threaten to overwhelm the reader. He is convinced—and convincing—that the house society should be included as an analytical category in ethnographic research (Lévi-Strauss 1982:173–74, 1987: 193). Unfortunately, as noted below, attempts to sharpen the conception of the house are difficult, given the amorphous start provided by Lévi-Strauss. He does, however, give us a kind of summary of the house concept by "propos[ing] to see in it a *local* group resembling a *lineage*, disposing of a *domain*, and forming a unit . . . based solely on the principle of *succession*" (Lévi-Strauss 1987:192, emphasis in original). A somewhat clearer definition of the house is "a corporate body holding an estate made up of both material and immaterial wealth, which perpetuates itself through the transmission of its name, its goods, and its titles down a real or imaginary line, considered legitimate as long as this continuity can express itself in the language of kinship or of affinity and, most often, of both" (Lévi-Strauss 1982:174).

An example of the potential pitfalls that await ethnographers who use the concept in their work is evident in a recent book edited by Janet Carsten and Stephen Hugh-Jones entitled *About the House: Lévi-Strauss and Beyond* (1995). In it a number of anthropologists provide the reader with applications of Lévi-Strauss's idea of the house society. Unfortunately, the intricate and rich data they present from their field research are conveyed in a world of ideal forms. The semantic systems presented are abstract and so removed from real life that they constitute a kind of symbolic numerology that defies empirical application, not to mention critical evaluation. The reader learns about the complexities of indigenous categories without learning who holds these categories of meaning, who contests them, and how the ethnographer came up with them in the first place.

In these accounts, there is no mention of such down-to-earth factors as how people make their living. We hear nothing about ecological adaptation, productive activities, military threats, colonialism, acculturation, or competition over resources as factors that affect how kinship systems are constituted. Contributors do not mention the material context that gives rise to the various systems of meanings and relations. Despite their affinities to Lévi-Strauss's approach, these writers conclude that the concept of house society only partially explains their data and that it falls short of universal applicability. What is missing here is an etic analysis of people's behavior. This analytical perspective was largely lacking in the increasingly discredited traditional kinship studies as well. In my view, this missing element has proved fatal to the goal of providing explanations of people's behavior, because people do not follow abstract rules for long when these contradict their pragmatic necessities (Harris 1975). It is far easier to reinterpret, overlook, or rationalize away rules than to change material conditions. Insofar as analyses of house societies fall into the same mentalist cul-de-sac, they, too, will prove inadequate.

I do not mean to imply that mental, cognitive, or symbolic realms of a people are unimportant or that they exert no influence on behavior. On the contrary, understanding meaning is critical to anthropology. But analyzing meaning to the exclusion of the blood and sweat of real life is hopelessly incomplete. In my view, we should develop Lévi-Strauss's insight without falling victim to his own shortcomings or those of his symbolist followers. As Hugh-Jones states, "The solution is not to follow [Lévi-Strauss] to the letter . . . but rather to follow him in spirit by recognizing the significance of his more general insight" (1995:248). The concept of house society begs us to examine the pragmatic factors that lead people to live together in a house, with all of the contradictions and confusion these imply for preserving the tidiness of kinship rules. It also presents us with the challenge of identifying the ideological basis of house solidarity, given that rules of descent are inadequate to the task. Herein lies the strength and revolutionary potential of the concept.

HOUSE SOCIETY AMONG THE NAHUAS

I have been conducting anthropological research in a single Nahua village in northern Veracruz, Mexico, for over twenty-five years and, like many Mesoamerican ethnographers in their respective studies, I have encountered difficulties in clarifying the kinship system.[3] I will not detail my struggles in trying to sort out what appeared at first to be kinship relations completely lacking any discernible system. Perhaps my difficulties can best be summarized by relating that I seriously wondered if I had discovered the first people whose kinship system had undergone almost complete disintegration. In addition to problems characterizing a fluid and dynamic set of relations, the village fissioned twice during two and a half decades and, near the end of this period, people chose to disrupt and rearrange their living patterns to accommodate the promised introduction of electricity into the community. These ethnographic challenges, I believe, are becoming increasingly commonplace in the rapidly industrializing world.

Nahua men make their houses from local materials that are lashed together with strong vines collected in the tropical forest. They build the roof with a steep pitch and cover it with one of three different kinds of thatching material. They construct the floor by packing earth into a cement-like consistency. Houses are small by North American standards, measuring about 12 by 16 feet with the roof peak at 14 or 15 feet above the ground. Houses are used mainly for sleeping or eating, and most daily living occurs in the shade of the porch-like eave or in the area surrounding the house—a clearing carved out of the tropical forest. The orientation to life in the forest clearing rather than beneath the roof of a building may be important in understanding Nahua house society, as I discuss below. Little has been written about the symbolic aspects of contemporary Nahua houses (see, however, Cornejo Cabrera 1964; Lok 1987). We do know that the concept of house (*cali* or *calli*) plays a role in Nahua myth and ritual and that caves or springs, for example, are known as the houses of certain spirit entities. As discussed below, Nahua houses are conceived as having a sacred presence, and they are the object of significant ritual attention.

The Nahuas trace descent bilaterally, but they exhibit a strong patrilateral bias in both postmarital residence and land inheritance.[4] They are slash-and-burn horticulturalists, and to some extent their social organization must be seen as an adaptation to a situation where they are squeezed onto small government land cooperatives (*ejidos*) and engaged in intense conflicts over land rights and sometimes bloody confrontations with local owners of large cattle ranches. In bilateral inheritance, all offspring should in principle have the right to inherit land to farm. A severe land shortage, however, has created a situation of de facto primogeniture where the oldest brother is the only one who actually inherits sufficient land to support a family. Younger brothers are forced to wait until land becomes available in the village, search for land elsewhere, or unite and, at great risk, attempt to expropriate land from a local *mestizo* rancher. Northern Veracruz and the surrounding region has a reputation of being marginal to Mexico as a whole and a lawless and dangerous place because of the almost constant violent struggles over land (Lomnitz-Adler 1992:51–55; Schryer 1990). Daughters expect to get married and move away with their husbands and are often dispossessed of the family patrimony. However, conflict among siblings, including sisters, may arise over the disposition of family property.

I define household as a group of kinsmen who live together, prepare and consume food in common, share a common domestic budget, and store the staple corn in a common facility or section of the house (for a thoroughgoing treatment of households from an ecological and economic perspective see Wilk, ed. 1989, 1991; Wilk and Ashmore, eds. 1988:2–6). Nahuas call the people who constitute such a functioning household *nocalpixcahuaj*, and they describe the household arrangement as *se kosa tekiti* ("working for a common thing") (Taggart 1975b:348; see also Nutini 1968:206–7). Because of bilateral descent, individual villagers are usually able to trace kinship relations to a number of other people both in and outside the community. They call this larger kindred-like grouping of active kinsmen *noteixmaticahuaj.*[5] In sum, the household is not equivalent to the Nahua family. Marriage is prohibited between first or second cousins among the Nahuas. There is no rule of exogamy or endogamy, although because the village is small (fewer than six hundred people), many young men and women must look outside the community to find a partner. Contrary to Lévi-Strauss's discussion of house societies, I was unable to detect any ranking of kin groups, and there are no clear lines of wife-givers or wife-takers to constitute the basis of such a ranking. In fact, the Nahuas have a very strong ideology of intra-village egalitarianism and generally suppress expressions of wealth or status difference (Chamoux 1981:255–59; Sandstrom 1991:199–200).

I have detailed information on 81 households in the community over a fourteen-year period, and it was only by documenting changes in these households through time that I was able to clarify the domestic cycle and shed light on the workings of the kinship system as a whole. The domestic cycle of the Nahua family—that is, systematic changes that occur in family structure and composition as members pass through stages of their lives—is guided partly by cultural rules and partly by economic and political realities of village life (see Robichaux 1997a, b). For the Nahuas, post-marital residence is ideally patrineolocal. It is the stated goal of every married couple to establish their own household in their own separate dwelling. I will begin describing this cycle at the point when a man and woman decide to get married. At this stage, the man is normally living in his father's household. Following the rule of patrilocality, the wife moves in with her new husband and begins to share domestic tasks with her mother-in-law and husband's sisters.

Pressures on the new wife during this period are strong as she works under the critical eye of her mother-in-law, and she may be treated almost like a servant by other household members (Taggart 1975a:179–82). A small proportion of marriages end after only a few days if the new wife finds her situation unbearable. The groom is often caught between the demands of his family and the desires of his wife, particularly if relations deteriorate. His best option is to busy himself gaining access to sufficient farmland to support his own separate household. There are a number of strategies for accomplishing this, but the most common is to wait patiently, sometimes for years, as the father doles out parcels of land to his sons. In this way, at least the oldest will eventually have enough to maintain his household.

After perhaps a year or more, and often at the urging of his wife, the husband begins to build a house in the same clearing as that of his father. If there is no room in the clearing, he will try to build nearby. All the while, he continues to work the patrimonial land in common with his father and brothers while accumulating small parcels for his private use. He relies on the help of other adult males in his group as well as friends and workmates in tending his fields and constructing the dwelling. James Taggart calls this phase of the division of the house "segmentation" (Taggart 1975b:348). After the couple move into the newly finished house, they begin to separate their domestic budget and corn supply to create a new household in a process Taggart calls "fission" (1975b:348). By building in the vicinity of the groom's family, the newly married couple form what Hugo Nutini calls a "non-residential patrilocal extended family" (Nutini 1967:385, 1968:241–43) and David Robichaux calls a "localized limited patriline" (Robichaux 1996:16). The arrival of children cements the marriage and begins the domestic cycle anew. As the years go by, the groom's father often dies first, leaving his widow with their youngest son. It is a responsibility of the youngest son to care for his aged mother, and in return he inherits the house (see Robichaux 1997a, b). During the processes of segmentation and fissioning and afterward, the male relatives of the groom continue to cooperate in a number of ways, particularly in the cycle of work associated with cultivation and other efforts, such as house repair or construction. This mutual aid is a key component of house organization, as discussed below.

The cycle of creating a household that then divides itself into nearby dwellings as sons marry gives Nahua villages a disorganized appearance to outsiders. The community is composed of a group of widely scattered clearings in the dense tropical forest with from two to eight houses built in each clearing. The clearings are often quite isolated and are connected to each other by a network of trails. I call a clearing with its attendant buildings a "compound"; the equivalent Nahuatl word is *caltinej*, meaning "houses." As mentioned above, the ideal is for each nuclear family ultimately to occupy its own individual dwelling. In a survey of the community in 1985–86, I found that 50 households (about 62% of the total sample) contained either complete or fragmented nuclear families. Another 27 households (about 33%) were occupied by patrilocal-extended families. These households included one or both parents, immature children, and one or more married sons with their wives and children. Four remaining households (about 5%) contained matrilocal-extended families. These included one or both parents, immature children, and daughters with their husbands and their children. These figures have artificially frozen the domestic cycle, but the ratio of about twice as many nuclear-family households to extended-family households seems to hold constant at any given time.

In mapping a Nahua village, the results are much messier than one would be led to expect, given the relatively simple domestic cycle described above (see Sandstrom 1991:169). Compounds usually do contain houses of members of a patrilocal extended family, but in almost all cases during the survey period houses of non-kinsmen were also present. When asked about these seeming exceptions, people responded that the anomalous dwelling was the house of a friend who had quarreled with his family, or that the house was occupied by a very distant relative, usually labeled a "cousin." Interestingly, a few compounds contained houses that were not linked by kinship at all. Added to this apparent confusion were the four compounds in which the people occupying the houses were linked through female ties. In fact, contrary to expectations, maps of the village made at this time revealed that in many cases females were able to live in houses closely associated geographically with the compound of their parents and brothers. Villagers informed me, and I confirmed their statements with observations, that these apparent exceptions were very common and well within the range of acceptable behavior.

Closer examination of the village map revealed something else unexpected. It will be recalled that the non-residential, patrilocal-extended family is the ideal family according to the testimony and behavior of villagers. This type of family has a vertical structure encompassing two, three, or in some cases, four generations. The basis of loyalty to the group is descent from the parental pair. It will also be recalled that groups of brothers form core cooperative groups and that ideally they should be living in the same compound. The Nahuatl term for such a group of cooperating siblings is *noicnihuaj* (literally, "my siblings"). Villagers are clear that brothers who stay together will reap advantages such as reliable work partners and allies in the event of political trouble. These sibling sets may be diminished by migration or death, but they are continually being recreated as children grow to adulthood. During my research in 1985–86, after a period of relatively high out-migration from the village and the two recent incidents of village fissioning, I found that the community was actually dominated by sets of siblings. Of the 81 households in the sample, only 8 were not connected to other households through a sibling tie. I recorded 44 sibling sets, 41 of which included at least one brother. There were 21 sets that included two or more brothers, and these brothers headed 51 of the village households (63%). The village, in short, was largely composed of groups of brothers who, despite heavy odds against their doing so (due mainly to land shortages), had managed to stay together.

Even more surprising was the number of sisters living in the village. Three of the sibling sets were sisters with no brothers (although two of these sets were old women who had outlived their brothers). Within the 21 sibling sets that included two or more brothers were found 16 of their sisters. These women had married local men and had managed to stay close to their other siblings. Of the 44 sibling sets found in the village, 20 were composed of a single brother and one or more sisters. It is clear that sisters are more likely to remain in the village if they have at least one brother there. In a surprising number of cases, as mentioned above, the sisters had even managed to live in houses built relatively close to their brother(s). Brothers have a responsibility to protect their sisters and look out for their welfare. Therefore it is in the interest of the sisters to stay close to their brother(s). However, patrilocal-residence patterns and the way that property—especially land—is inherited are strong forces dividing siblings against each other.

Taggart (1975a:16, 180–91), in a carefully documented study of Nahua domestic groups in the Sierra Norte de Puebla region, has shown the marginal place occupied by sisters in their kin groups. He found that widowed sisters who, following the patrilocal residence rule, had moved away to become part of their husband's compound, had lost all rights to their father's patrimony. Should a brother living in his father's compound die, however, his widow (the surviving brothers' sister-in-law) inherits his land, particularly if she has children. Thus, a widowed sister usually relinquishes the rights to family land to her widowed sister-in-law. The dispossessed widowed sister may try, however, to make a case that she retains rights in the family estate, leading to further erosion of sibling solidarity. This practice serves to alienate sisters from their brothers. And yet Nahua sisters and brothers work very hard to stay together. As seen above, younger brothers are usually forced to leave the village in search of land to farm and, if they are successful, their other siblings, including in some cases sisters, tend to follow them. The fact that so many sibling sets have managed to stay together despite all odds is testimony to the strength and benefits of sibling ties.

Emphasis on the sibling tie in Nahua villages produces fundamental structural contradictions in the kinship system. As mentioned above, the postmarital residence rule creates a vertical, lineage-like extended family at the center of residence groupings. This extended family is composed for the most part of parents, their sons, and the sons' wives and children. The vertical lineal structure is itself a contradiction of the bilateral nature of Nahua kinship. Bilaterality in turn is subverted and contradicted by the land shortage. Scarcity of arable land causes younger sons and daughters to be dispossessed, creating rivalry and jealousy among siblings and hard feelings between the generations.[6] Sibling sets are by definition collateral and constitute a horizontal contradiction to the verticality of the extended family. Brothers loyal to each other and to their sisters subvert the lineage-like nature of compound organization. A related dimension is that Nahua communities are strongly stratified by age and generation. I observed that people tended to be very aware of others in their own stratum but remarkably ignorant of people in the generations above or below them (Sandstrom 1991:181). This age stratification reinforces the horizontal nature of Nahua social organization created by strong ties among siblings. It would appear that at the heart of the Nahua kinship system are fundamental contradictions, some external and others internal to the system, that threaten the viability of village life.

It is my contention that many of these problems can be resolved or at least clarified if we view the compound not as a descent group, following traditional anthropological usage, but instead as a house in Lévi-Strauss's use of the term (Robichaux 1996, 1997b comes to a similar conclusion about Mesoamerica in general, based on the work of French ethnologist Georges Augustins). The contradiction between lineage-based and cognatic kinship ideologies and the problematic nature of marriage ties, both characteristic of the Nahua situation as discussed above, are features that Lévi-Strauss specifically links to house societies (Lévi-Strauss 1987:155, 163–64). Lévi-Strauss claims that a common dimension of houses is a "dialectic of filiation and residence," and he notes conflicts that can result from "dual membership in a group with bilateral descent and a residential unit: village, hamlet . . . ward, or neighborhood" (1982: 180; see also 1987:185–86). These features give meaning to Lévi-Strauss's characterization of the house as a confluence of opposites. To fit the Nahua data better, I suggest an expansion of the concept of house to include the people who live in or near a compound regardless of how many buildings may be found there. In place of a dwelling, a Nahua house refers to a well-defined precinct containing kinsmen and non-kinsmen who share a common interest in the property and who interact with each other as if they were kinsmen.[7] It remains to be seen if additional features of the Nahua compound fit Lévi-Strauss's vision of a house.

Nahuas have a complex naming practice that fulfills the requirements of house-based organizational principles. In dealings with government representatives or local authorities, the people use an essentially Spanish naming system. A first-born child is often called after the paternal grandparent, a practice that can characterize house societies (Lévi-Strauss 1982:175). Names of younger siblings are taken from saints' days listed in the *Calendario del más antiguo Galván*, an almanac popular in rural regions. Following Spanish convention, the child's surname is that of the father and the third element is the surname of the mother. These practices match well with a lineage-based society or a bilateral society with a patrilateral bias. However, in a significant number of cases the pattern is violated. People feel free to change their names, and sometimes close siblings will have different surnames. I inquired about this practice, mainly in connection with the difficulties it caused in census-taking and gathering information on Nahua kinship, and was told that people can take whatever name they want. Most people change their given name, but I have documented cases where people have also changed surnames. I should point out that, despite this freewheeling practice, there are very few surnames in use in the village. I estimated that over three-quarters of villagers have Hernández or Martínez as one or both elements of their names. Thus, the names in themselves cannot effectively be used to differentiate kin groups. In order to specify particular individuals in conversation, people employ a system of nicknames that may or may not be connected to a person's Spanish name. To outsiders, Nahua naming practices confirm the fluidity of their social organization.

Operating simultaneously in many Nahua villages is a complex toponymic system in which people are named by association with the location of their compounds. Lévi-Strauss (1982:172) discusses a similar case of toponymic naming in the Yurok house society. These place-name appellations were disappearing in the village where I conducted field research, so it is difficult to obtain a complete picture of the practice. The inhabitants divide the village into about 25 subareas, each named after a geographic feature or other peculiarity that calls attention to that place (see Chamoux 1981:79–94; Montoya Briones 1964:85–86; Reyes García 1961:30–35; Sandstrom 1991:104–7, 1996:167–68; Schryer 1990:63–66). Examples of such toponyms include "below the poplars," "little plaza," "muddy place," and "flat grassy place."

Each named area may incorporate one or more compounds. In a practice called *caltocayotl* ("house name"), villagers label individual houses or, more commonly, the houses in a single compound based on the same set of environmental features or peculiarities used to name subareas (García Salazar 1975). Often the house name will provide the name for the larger village subarea. For example, a house named "broken earth place" may give its name to a subarea that contains other compounds with different names. What is interesting is that house (compound) names may be taken by people as surnames. This is particularly useful when many individuals have similar names following the Spanish tradition, where, for example, there may be more than one man called Juan Hernández Hernández. Individuals may be distinguished by a nickname in certain contexts, but when discussing matters of kinship or estates, people often attach the toponym in place of a surname. In this example, Juan Hernández Hernández might be referred to as Juan Tlajcocali (John Middle House). What is even more interesting in light of the discussion of house societies is that all the people who live in a compound, whether technically kinsmen or not, will be called by the same toponym. In certain cases of identity, therefore, residence takes precedence over strictly kinship ties. This feature is to be expected in a house society.

Three additional characteristics of compounds indicate that they can fruitfully be viewed as houses. The first concerns the key role played by *compadrazgo*, or ritual kinship, in the formation of houses (see Ravicz 1967 and Nutini 1984 for a general treatment of ritual kinship in Mesoamerica). The Nahuas commonly incorporate non-kinsmen or remote kinsmen into the compound by creating ritual or fictive kinship ties to them (see Lévi-Strauss 1982: 177, 1987:152; Sandstrom 1991:188–92). Ritual kinsmen have special mutual rights and obligations analogous to those of real kinsmen, and among the Nahuas ties of ritual kinship are an important part of social life. This ubiquitous custom is an example of using the language of kinship to create groups only partially based on actual kinship.

A second defining characteristic of the compound is that all members are bound to each other through labor exchange. Called *matlanilistli* (literally "exchange hand") in Nahuatl and known throughout Mesoamerica as *mano vuelta*, every man in the village must participate in labor exchange with a group of his peers in order to complete tasks associated with slash-and-burn horticulture and house-building (see Taggart 1976). Brothers (*noicnihuaj*), sometimes with their father, form the core of most labor groups, but they almost always are forced to rely on some non-kinsmen for mutual aid. Ritual kinsmen are likely work-group candidates. An invariable feature of compounds is that all men consistently form such work groups and exchange labor in their fields. Thus, the overlapping ties of ritual kinship and labor exchange are important dynamics in the creation and maintenance of Nahua compounds. The importance of maintaining close ties with other compound members may explain why people spend more time in their clearings, in sight of one another, than inside their respective dwellings.

The third characteristic of compounds is that land—by far the most important item of wealth among the Nahuas—is relinquished piecemeal by the father to his sons. Lévi-Strauss states that in the contradiction between rights bestowed by "voting" and rights bestowed by kinship in house societies, it is important that property be publicly passed to heirs while the father is still living. This practice serves to garner "the collective consent and [to] neutraliz[e] potential rivals publicly" in a context where strict kinship rules are contradicted by other factors such as residence (Lévi-Strauss 1982:184). As we have seen, a Nahua father doles out parcels of land to his male children over many years. As mentioned previously, however, only the eldest son receives a sufficient amount to support a family of his own, due to the shortage of land.

I am not completely certain what Lévi-Strauss means when he writes that the house is a fetishized objectification of an illusory, unstable alliance (Lévi-Strauss 1987:155–56). Among the Nahuas, as among all indigenous groups in Mesoamerica, the physical house is subject to ritual observance and has a spiritual presence that occupies an important place in religious belief and practice. When a house is being constructed, offerings are placed in the holes dug for the major supporting beams. Each house has an altar on which are kept ritual objects such as pictures of Catholic saints (reinterpreted by the Nahuas as house guardians), a clay incense brazier, paper cutouts of witness spirits to watch over the house, beeswax candles, and cups and plates used in offerings. The fire table is home to *tlixihuantsij* (or simply *xihuantsij*), a hearth spirit who receives offerings during each ritual occasion in the house. This fire spirit guards the house and protects its inhabitants. During curing rituals, the shaman lays out offerings and paper cutouts on the house floor to rid both the dwelling and its inhabitants of polluting and disease-causing wind spirits. When patients visit the shaman for their cure, they bring along a small bag of earth collected from the four corners of their house. This observance insures that the house itself, by being sacralized, will benefit from the cleansing.

I have argued elsewhere that the Nahuas hold a pantheistic view of the cosmos in which the universe itself and everything in it are aspects of a single sacred principle (Sandstrom and Sandstrom 1986:275–77; Sandstrom 1991: 238–39; see Hunt 1977:55). If this interpretation is accepted, then the Nahua house would by definition be an important spiritual presence in the world. It is literally home and hearth, simultaneously the largest object created by the Nahuas and an encompassing sacred presence that provides the members of the household with a refuge. People identify with their individual dwellings, pass them on to their children, and, as we have seen, may even assume their names. The dwelling among the Nahuas is a kind of living entity that is far more than simple shelter or a commodity to be bought and sold.

There is another sense in which the compound assumes a key role in the religious life of the Nahuas. In most older and more established compounds, inhabitants have built a shrine or dedicated a corner of one of the houses for ritual purposes. This shrine is in addition to the house altar found in each dwelling. These larger shrines may be dedicated to seed spirits or to an earth-related female deity associated with fertility named *tonantsij* (literally "our honored mother"). *Tonantsij* is represented on the altar by a small plaster statue of the Virgin of Guadalupe. The seed spirits are in the form of paper cutouts that have been dressed in tiny cloth outfits and are kept in a sacred box along with miniature items of furniture. The sealed box is placed on a special altar and is the focus of periodic offerings and ritual attention. The ostensible purpose of the box and altar is to preserve a pleasant place for the seed spirits so that they will choose to stay in the village and confer the blessing of fertility on the fields. It is important that the compound be kept clean and peaceful so that the seed spirits will find it an amenable place to live. Discord will motivate the spirits to return to their cave home at the peak of a sacred mountain, leaving the village without life-giving crops. The shrine, then, is a focus of ritual activity for members of the compound, a point of identity, and a link between the compound and the most sacred aspects of the Nahua cosmos.

In sum, a number of features of Nahua compounds fit very well with the characteristics of house societies outlined by Lévi-Strauss. Perhaps, since Nahua houses are not classified into wife-givers and wife-takers, the Nahuas have "embryonic" houses, a term applied by Lévi-Strauss to describe the social organization of most African societies (Lévi-Strauss 1987:192). Traditional anthropological theories of kinship are based on the concept of descent or shared substance. People are incorporated into structured systems of obligation and expectation based on the premise that others in the system share their vital essence and therefore their vital interests. The theory works well enough for unilineal systems but falters for cognatic systems such as that found among the Nahuas. Cognatic systems are too sweeping in their inclusiveness and make it very difficult to generate coherent descent groups. House societies create groups, to be sure, but in so doing, they must circumvent the shortcomings of cognatic systems. In fact, if Lévi-Strauss (1987:185–86) is correct, houses are to be found in unilineal societies as well as cognatic ones, since these societies present their own problems for the creation of workable and functioning groups in pre-capitalist societies. The house must also overcome a number of potential contradictions that would seem to make group coherence impossible. Examples already discussed include contradictions between lineal and cognatic principles, antagonisms in the marriage tie, de facto primogeniture in a bilateral society, and the incorporation of non-kin in a group based on the ideology of kinship. What is needed is an operational definition of the house society so that anthropologists can identify the type in various field settings, allowing for a more systematic comparison.

HOUSE SOCIETIES AND A CURRENCY OF INTERACTION

It is critically important that the concept of house society not be so broadly defined that it loses all value in explaining cultural similarities and differences. As a first step toward operationalizing the concept and increasing its potential usefulness for anthropologists, I suggest that something other than the currency of descent (shared substance) must be found to exist in house societies that will serve as a substitute for establishing a kinship-like basis for interacting. This other currency of interaction will most likely be closely linked to life-giving productive activities and will be used by people as a substitute or reinforcement for ties of descent in these societies. By identifying the currency of exchange in a particular society, as well as specifying the degree to which it is used as the basis of social organization, researchers will be in a position to develop a measure for identifying house societies. I would like briefly to examine four ethnographic examples (only two of which have previously been identified as house societies) to see if it is possible to identify such a currency that might replace the shared substance of descent as an organizing principle.

David Schneider's research on Yap has been a focus of kinship studies in anthropology for many years (Helmig 1997:1). In 1984, as mentioned previously, Schneider published a critical evaluation that called into question the whole scholarly edifice of kinship analysis in anthropology. He found that residence groupings on Yap could largely be explained without making reference to principles of kinship and descent. Furthermore, he found that the residence group, called a *tabinau* in Yapese, was riddled with contradictory features similar to those discussed by Lévi-Strauss, including the absorption of non-kinsmen. Schneider went so far as to assert that the people on Yap were ignorant of any biological connection (any shared substance) between father and son, thus canceling the whole principle of descent as a basis of social organization.

Schneider's assertions that the people on Yap were ignorant of paternity and that the anthropological concept of kinship is a product of Western science that does not reflect ethnographic reality have recently been challenged based on a reanalysis of Yapese material by Thomas Helmig (1997). As far as I know, Schneider never called Yap a house society, but he portrayed its social organization in such a way that it is compatible with that system (see also Joyce, this volume). Interestingly, for example, one translation he provides for the word *tabinau* is "house," while an alternative definition is "persons who are related to the speaker through ties to the land" (Schneider 1984:21). In his description, he mentions another Yap word, *magar*, meaning "work," "labor," or "creative effort," as a kind of currency or value through which people become attached to the *tabinau* (1984:27). He states, "it is work that makes and maintains a *tabinau* and people exchange their work for their rights in the *tabinau*" (1984:27). Here, it seems to me, we have some evidence that Schneider is describing a house society with *magar* as the substitute currency for the shared substance of descent.

Susan McKinnon (1991) presents a detailed and complex account of the cultural principles of social organization of people on the island of Fordata in the Tanimbar archipelago of Indonesia. She explicitly recognizes that the people in this region are organized into houses in Lévi-Strauss's sense and that traditional categories of kinship are inadequate to the task of capturing the essence of Tanimbarese life and culture (1991:33). McKinnon's complex analysis defies easy summary, but we can conclude that Tanimbarese houses are dynamic, hierarchically ranked groupings whose inhabitants enter into exchanges with each other in order to constitute themselves as well as their exchange partners. A house in Tanimbar can be described as "the explicit and differential articulation of mutually implicating, contrastive social forms and processes" (McKinnon 1991:282). The people in Tanimbar do not conceive of the group associated with a house to be based on principles of descent. In fact, through a process she calls "adrogation," a man from one house can be "lifted" into another house and assume full rights and privileges (1991:100). If McKinnon is correct, "patrilateral affiliation depends upon the completion of bride wealth prestations" (1991:99). In short, it is successful participation in the arena of exchanges among houses that acts as the substitute currency among the Tanimbarese. Failure to secure bride wealth payments could lead a man to lose his house affiliation and force him into slavery or absorption into another house altogether.

John Monaghan describes a complex system of ritual and social exchange for the Mixtecs living in the community of Nuyoo in Oaxaca, Mexico (Monaghan 1995, 1996). He explicitly describes the Mixtecs as a house society, not in the sense of a structure that generates behavior but as "local articulations of how groups form and accomplish goals" (Monaghan 1995:246, 356). Nuyootecos live in individual households, but their activities and exchanges create a larger coherence Monaghan calls a "great house" (1995:15, 245–46, 259). This concept, while not identical to Lévi-Strauss's formulation, shares key features with it. In a statement that could have come straight from Lévi-Strauss, Monaghan writes that "The image of the house thus encompasses a series of processes whereby separate entities are brought into unmediated unity" (1995:253). As in most indigenous communities in Mesoamerica, traditional kinship categories explain little of the composition of houses or of people's interactions with one another. When Nuyootecos describe themselves as a community they say, "we eat from the same tortilla" (1995:13). These people broaden the traditional anthropological definition of kinship in their belief "that substance is transmitted through nurturing acts, as well as through sexual intercourse" (1995:197). Among the Mixtecs, the exchange currency of social interaction is *nakara*, a term that can be translated as "love" but more accurately is "a willingness to take responsibility for another by providing what is needed for a healthy life" (1995:36). *Nakara* is most often expressed by providing food and clothing to another, and Mixtecs "speak of the household as emerging out of acts of *nakara*, which can occur between a variety of people" (1995:42).

Finally, we return to the Nahuas of northern Veracruz, Mexico. As I have tried to show, the Nahua kinship system and residence groupings present problems for analysis that are similar to those encountered among the people of Yap, Tanimbar, and Oaxaca. If the concept of house society applies to the Nahuas, it should be possible to identify a substitute currency that people use in place of the shared substance of descent. The Nahuas have a cosmology in which human beings are linked to the sacred animating sun through the foods they eat, in particular corn. They say "*sintli ne toeso*" or "corn is our blood" to express this linkage. Corn carries heat from the sun, and by consuming this all-important grain people acquire the energy they need to live. This vital life force and power is called *chicahualistli*, and the Nahuas believe that it is carried in the bloodstream (Sandstrom 1991:247). If one's *chicahualistli* should diminish, that person would weaken and die. One of the greatest ways to look out for someone's well-being is to give the gift of life, namely food. Similar to the Mixtec example cited above, the Nahua house emerges out of the shared labor of the field that provides food and the energy of life to members of a compound. The sine qua non of membership in the compound—the house—is not so much descent as a willingness to work in cooperation with other members of the group. By sharing labor, people indirectly provide *chicahualistli* to each other. A close kinsman who refused to share labor would be forced to relinquish membership in the house and would be obliged to move away. At the same time distant kinsmen or even non-kinsmen could participate fully in the Nahua house so long as they took the responsibility, by sharing their labor, to replenish the lives of the others who live there.

CONCLUSION

It is my contention that the Nahuas fit the definition of a house society sufficiently to merit further exploration. Not all of the features stressed by Lévi-Strauss are present (for example, the ranking of different houses), but enough are found to justify viewing the Nahua compound as a house at least in "embryonic" form. There are many questions that remain to be answered. For one, Do the Nahuas consider non-kin house members to be real kinsmen? In some cases they seem to, but there is some doubt because non-kin members of a house never, to my knowledge, inherit land. Another question is, Do the Nahuas have concepts equivalent to lineage, cognatic descent, affinity, or the other terms used by anthropologists in studies of kinship? This question must be answered if anthropologists are to be able to distinguish clearly emic versus etic modes of analysis (James Taggart, personal communication). The fact is that in Nahua compounds the overwhelming majority of inhabitants are actual kinsmen of each other. I anticipate that the same holds for other house societies as well. It is not yet time to reject the more traditional anthropological theories of kinship. Descent, the sharing of substance, may not be the only factor accounting for houses, but it is certainly an important one. The concept of house fits my observations of the Nahuas because it allows for people who act on their own behalf, to plan, and if possible to manipulate their circumstances to achieve their goals. The concept promises to help ethnographers deal with what they find in the field with all the contradictions, subverting of the rules, and playing the game that characterizes real human interaction. The insight will lead nowhere, however, if we insist on linking it to abstract cultural principles and rules that are impossible to demonstrate and that cannot be shown to have measurable effect on people's behavior. The work on house societies has just begun in Mesoamerica.

I would like to thank María Guadalupe Hurtado Escamilla, Robert Jeske, Lawrence Kuznar, Hugo G. Nutini, David Robichaux, James M. Taggart, Jesús Ruvalcaba Mercado, and Pamela E. Sandstrom for commenting on earlier drafts of this paper.

4

Transformations of
Nuu-chah-nulth Houses

Yvonne Marshall

*The long-term perspective of archaeology and history makes it possible to
trace the life history of structures in concert with that of the people associated
with them, by observing how the transformations of physical houses may materially encode the correlative changes to the social groups that occupied them.
Yvonne Marshall demonstrates the important diachronic perspective in the
analysis of house societies with her meticulously researched overview of both
the stasis and the change experienced by Nuu-chah-nulth (Nootka) houses.
Her examination of a Northwest Coast people, one of Lévi-Strauss's original
exemplars of house societies, also fills in missing details from his defining work
by examining the relationship between the material and social reproductive
aspects of houses. She begins with archaeological evidence some 2000 years
old that reveals not only the remarkable longevity of house form and internal
organization as described by much later European observers, but also the
continuity in house location, a "curation of established house placements." In
contrast, the late nineteenth through early twentieth centuries saw rapid demographic and economic changes, accessible from historical and archival records, that transformed Nuu-chah-nulth society. In this short period the physical
house changed from an externally undifferentiated residence, housing people,
to an externally elaborated but essentially vacant building, housing paraphernalia and symbolizing the increased wealth of the social group that maintained
its ritual and representative functions, materializing accentuated hierarchical
differences. In a matter of decades, even this form disappeared as the social
houses gave way to a new sociopolitical configuration based on wage labor
and a cash economy. These changes in the physical house relate directly to
house formation and definition. Its corporate identity derived from the cooper-*

ative labors of its members in subsistence activities on house-owned lands. With the loss of participation in the communal labor that generated house wealth, the house as an economic institution ceased to exist. Marshall, like Sandstrom, concludes that the house has a fundamental economic and prag-matic base and must be continously "performed into existence" by communal investment in its resources.

One of the most widely quoted passages from ethnographies of the Nuu-chah-nulth people of the west coast of Vancouver Island is Philip Drucker's descrip-tion of the local group: "The fundamental Nootkan [Nuu-chah-nulth] political unit was a local group centering in a family of chiefs who owned territorial rights, houses, and various other privileges. Such a group bore a name, usually that of their 'place' (a site at their fishing ground where they 'belonged'), or sometimes that of a chief; and had a tradition firmly believed, of descent from a common ancestor" (Drucker 1951:220). This description identifies four com-ponents to the local group: a group of people, a house or houses in which they lived, an economic base, and a narrative of social connection phrased in the language of names, kinship, and descent. Given the immense importance anthropologists have traditionally attached to kinship and descent, it is hardly surprising that Drucker privileged the final component as the key defining fea-ture, even though the term *local group* directs our attention to place. Similarly, Lévi-Strauss (1982), in his analysis of social organization among the neigh-boring Kwakiutl people, developed the concept of the house to describe the equivalent social institution. Although his choice of term—house—also privi-leges place, and his definition of the house is remarkably similar to Drucker's local group (Lévi-Strauss 182:174), Lévi-Strauss, like Drucker, was more inter-ested in issues of alliance and descent than of residence. He gave little consid-eration to the three material components of the Kwakiutl house—its architec-ture, inhabitants, and economic base (Carsten and Hugh-Jones, eds. 1995, Carsten and Hugh-Jones 1995).

In this paper I show how the privileging of kinship and descent arises from the ahistorical, synchronic nature of ethnographic data and leads to a distorted understanding of the Nuu-chah-nulth local group, and by implication the Kwakiutl house also. Both the Nuu-chah-nulth and the Kwakiutl can usefully be characterized as house societies in the sense that Lévi-Strauss proposed, and I therefore use the term house in reference to the Nuu-chah-nulth instead of Drucker's term local group. However, the core of a house is argued to be a physical dwelling and the people who choose to occupy it, rather than an abstract set of social connections or positions based on descent, because the corporate identity of a house must be performed into existence by a dwelling's inhabitants through their actions as co-residents. Narratives of kinship and descent draw together specific, contingent groups of house occupants by generating traditions of social connectedness rooted in a distant past, but they do not construct or define the house as social group, they follow from it.

Because the Nuu-chah-nulth recognize bilateral descent and have no prescribed marriage rules, groups defined on the basis of descent overlap in complex ways. This overlap gives people social options, and they can choose to be members of several groups. People exercise social options by physically taking up residence. A shift in residence is both a physical and a social statement (Marshall 1989). House groups remain discrete because at any one time a person is understood to reside in a specific dwelling and is therefore a member of a specific house. As a result a house may always be full but its composition will be constantly changing (Marshall 1989). Thus the social group which forms the core of a house is both a permanent entity and a fluid, shifting contingency.

The same pattern of stasis and change is seen in the structure of house dwellings. Nuu-chah-nulth dwellings are large, substantial, and imposing. They have been known to house 50 and more people (Marshall 1993b). The structure itself consists of a permanent framework to which moveable wall planks are lashed. Houses own dwellings at several seasonally occupied sites, and one set of planks is moved between house frames. Thus a constant movement in planks is anchored by the imposing permanence of house frames. The impression of permanence is enhanced by the practice of partial renewal: "over a long period, the entire roof and siding of a house might be renewed, and one by one the posts and beams would be replaced, but it would be the same old house that had stood in that place since the lineage who owned it had been given the right to build their house there" (Drucker 1951:73).

When viewed as a dynamic social and material process the Nuu-chah-nulth house is seen to consist of a constant flow and redistribution of planks and people. This flow is arrested in contingent moments which are afforded precise physical and demographic definition by containment within a house frame. Narratives of descent are integral to the social identity of a house, but they follow from its contingent composition; they do not produce it. Because ahistorical ethnographic descriptions offer snapshot images, they reduce the house as process to the house as contingent moment. It is only when seen in this reduced, synchronic view that narratives of descent appear to construct rather than describe the house.

The aim of this essay is to place the Nuu-chah-nulth house in a historical context so that the interplay among the four components of the house outlined above can be examined over an extended period of time. It begins by drawing together the archaeological evidence for Nuu-chah-nulth houses, and then briefly reviews observations made about houses by late eighteenth-century European newcomers. The main body considers the dramatic changes occurring during the period 1870–1940. The general Nuu-chah-nulth situation is outlined, and then the Mowachaht and Muchalaht tribes of Nootka Sound are examined in greater detail.

In this historical context, it can be seen that during the nineteenth century the combination of social flexibility and physical solidity which characterizes the house proved a source of strength to a people struggling to survive demographic decimation. However, by the late nineteenth century, an economic transition to a cash economy had set in motion social changes which the Nuu-chah-nulth house did not survive. By 1900 the Nuu-chah-nulth house had become transformed from an externally undifferentiated structure which housed people and symbolized wealth in the form of pooled labor, to an externally elaborated structure symbolizing capital wealth. These houses, which became known as potlatch houses, were empty except for ceremonial gatherings and ritual paraphernalia. By 1940, just as the Nuu-chah-nulth turned the demographic tide and began to increase their numbers, the house disappeared as both a social and a physical entity, and Nuu-chah-nulth social organization consolidated into its contemporary two-tier structure of families living in nuclear family dwellings amalgamated on tribal reserves. But gone, it turned out, was not forgotten. During the 1980s the potlatch house slowly re-emerged in a new tribal form. Although a very different kind of institution, these new houses owed much to their ancestor, the house dwelling (Marshall 1999).

THE ARCHAEOLOGY OF NUU-CHAH-NULTH HOUSES

Archaeological information on Nuu-chah-nulth houses, village layout, and changes in settlement size and plan is limited for two reasons. First, excavation areas are usually small compared to house sizes, so houses are difficult to recognize among the bewildering array of dumping events which make up a typical Northwest Coast midden. Second, little attention has been given to the production of detailed site maps, so surface features indicating house locations have gone unrecognized. Even so, two distinctive features emerge from the few exceptions: a remarkable continuity in the placement of houses and the arrangement of their interiors. Excavations extensive enough to recover houses have been carried out at two sites, Yuquot and Ozette. The oldest evidence comes from the village of Yuquot in Nootka Sound (Figure 4-1b). In stratigraphic layers dated to 2300–1900 B.P. (radiocarbon years before present),

18 semi-rectangular, rock-rimmed firepits were identified (Dewhirst 1980:50). Two were isolated examples, but the remainder occurred as two clusters within which firepits were directly superimposed. One explanation for the clustered, superimposed pattern is that the firepits were located inside a dwelling. "These two clusters indicate that the firepits were maintained in two restricted areas for a long period of time, thus suggesting that the firepit locations were relatively permanent. The long-term restricted and intensively used locations reflect containment in relation to a structure . . . both clusters of firepits are contemporaneous stratigraphically, spatially and by radiocarbon determinations. If we can assume that both clusters were contained within a dwelling, this would suggest the several firepits of multifamily dwellings described in the early historic period" (Dewhirst 1980:50). This evidence suggests that from at least 2300 B.P. on, Yuquot was a settlement of large permanent house structures containing established and curated placements for firepits. The highly structured spatial arrangement of the firepits and their associated houses indicates that social relations were materially expressed in the internal organization of the dwellings and in their arrangement within a village.

More detailed evidence of houses was recovered from Ozette, located on the northwest tip of Washington State (Figure 4-1a). Large areal excavations of a village which had been buried and preserved beneath mudslide deposits were carried out, and detailed data recovered on the size, construction, internal organization, and external arrangement of houses within the village. The Ozette site includes both dry midden deposits and wet mudslide deposits. The dry midden excavations revealed four sequential house floors, stratigraphically separated by sandy beach berms. These floors are undated. Firepits, postholes, and floor deposits defining the first three dwellings were superimposed such that each successive house floor, firepit, and posthole was located directly above the earlier one, despite the fact that deep layers of sterile beach sands intervened between floors (McKenzie 1974). Such perfect superimposition cannot be coincidental. Considerable care was exercised to maintain the exact placement, dimensions, and internal floor plan of the initial house structure when refurbishing the floor and rebuilding the superstructure. Precise spatial layout clearly mattered a great deal.

At the Ozette wet site five protohistoric houses were excavated. Again, concern to maintain precise placement and established internal arrangements across successive structures is strikingly evident, even though deep mudslide deposits sometimes intervene between superimposed house floors. The most dramatic example is the direct superimposition of House 2 over the earlier House 5 (Samuels and Daugherty 1991:23).

Further evidence for the practice of curating established house positions is

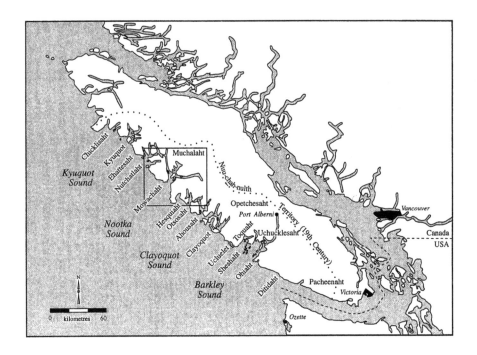

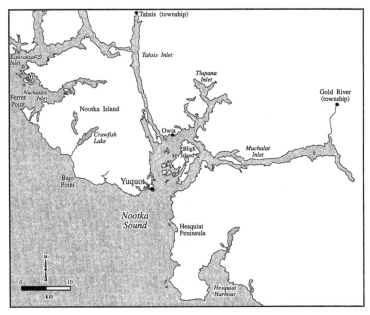

Figure 4-1. a) Tip of the Washington peninsula showing the territorial locations of twentieth-century Nuu-chah-nulth tribes and the Ozette site. b) Enlargement of the Nootka Sound area showing the key site locations.

found in the highly structured arrangement of surface features on settlement sites which have been closely mapped (Haggarty 1982; Inglis and Haggarty 1986; Marshall 1992; McMillan 1996). In Nootka Sound the coherence of the surface features identified on all sites, both large and small, is remarkable. Even on small sites, which have only a few terraces or ridges, these features are well defined and spatially coherent (see site maps in Marshall 1992, 1993b). As sites become larger, surface features increase in number and complexity while clarity of feature definition is maintained. On the largest sites, house depressions are present, and it is apparent that each depression is in part defined by and accommodated to its neighbors. These characteristics of the surface features suggest that the locations of structures, particularly those associated with house depressions, were maintained over long periods, and their placement within settlements was highly curated.

House depressions are argued to define the perimeters of substantial, permanent dwellings. An 1874 photograph taken at Yuquot shows a dwelling with its wall boards removed for temporary use on another house (Figure 4-2). The house frame and skirting boards are therefore exposed. Around the outside edge of the skirting board is a ridge which, if the house frame and skirting boards were removed, would look exactly like a house depression. Such ridges may have been deliberately constructed around the base of dwellings when new; however, this seems unlikely, because the ridges consist almost entirely of rock, even when rock is not immediately available on the site. It is more likely that the ridges were formed around dwellings in the course of their occupation and are composed of discarded boiling stones and hearth rocks. Again, this points to the long-term maintenance of house structures in established positions. As discussed above, house building practices documented by Drucker in the early twentieth century indicate how this continuity may be accomplished.

Taken together, the archaeological evidence from Yuquot, Ozette, and survey maps suggests that the curation of established house placements has been a distinctive feature of Nuu-chah-nulth settlements for at least 2000 years. It was also very characteristic of Nuu-chah-nulth life in the eighteenth century (Huelsbeck 1988; Marshall 1989).

A second feature of Nuu-chah-nulth houses which emerges specifically from the Ozette data concerns the social organization of families within dwellings. Close to complete recovery of house timbers at the Ozette wet site established that at least four of the five excavated houses were shed roof structures with rectangular floor plans measuring 13–17 meters in length and 7–10 meters in width (Mauger 1991). The superstructures of all five houses were very similar, and they would have appeared virtually identical from the outside.

Figure 4-2. A Nuu-chah-nulth house dwelling with the wall boards removed and frame exposed. Note the ridges built up against the outside of the skirting boards. Photographed at Yuquot in 1874. By permission of the Royal British Columbia Museum, PN 10508.

The same cannot be said for the interiors. The houses were internally subdivided into smaller areas by regularly spaced firepits placed just in from and around the walls. House 1 had an additional central firepit (Samuels 1989, 1991). The number and types of artifacts and the proportion of various species in the faunal remains recovered from the vicinity of each firepit suggest that each firepit area was occupied by a different social group, possibly a family (Huelsbeck 1989; Samuels 1989). Croes and Davis (1977) even suggest that, on the basis of the distribution of baskets with slight differences in weaving styles, it is possible to identify the residence areas within houses of individual weavers. In Houses 1 and 5 the greatest density of artifacts was found in two adjacent corner areas. In House 1, one corner contained most of the decorative-symbolic-ceremonial shells recovered at the Ozette site, including a string of more than 400 dentalium shells (Huelsbeck 1989; Wessen 1982). The differential number and quality of artifacts and fauna recovered from around different firepits within a house is interpreted as evidence that the houses were subdivided according to status. Corner areas were occupied by the high status groups who had greater access to goods in general, and to rare or imported goods in particular (Huelsbeck 1989; Samuels 1989). The practice of chiefs occupying the corner areas of houses is widely documented in twentieth-century ethnographies (Drucker 1951:71).

Clear differences were also identified between houses. While all houses contained large amounts of midden from the major faunal species, there were subtle differences in the distribution of minor species. For example, House 1 contained considerably more salmon and halibut bone than Houses 2, 3, and 5, suggesting differential access among households to the restricted areas where these fish could be taken (Huelsbeck 1988). Each house also contained different proportions of various shellfish species, suggesting that households collected their shellfish from different beaches (Wessen 1982, 1988). Huelsbeck (1988:147) concludes "that the occupants of Houses 1, 3 and 5 were members of different resource controlling social groups." A special function is suggested for House 1 because it was the only house with a central hearth. In the vicinity of this hearth, salmon and halibut remains were unusually abundant, and high concentrations of decorative-symbolic-ceremonial artifacts were found in the corners closest to the central hearth. House 1 also contained most of the whaling gear recovered at Ozette (Wessen 1988:195). Huelsbeck concludes that, although Houses 1 and 2 "exploited similar resource territories . . . more of the preferred foods were consumed in House 1 than in House 2. These two households probably were members of the same local group with House 1 ranked higher than House 2" (Huelsbeck 1989:166).

These differences were internal features of the houses. They were not displayed in the houses' exterior appearance except to the extent that house locations carried differential values. Social status and social connection were materially displayed in the placement of each group's residence area within a house and in the kinds of material items and faunal remains recovered from each residence area. High status groups resided in the corner areas. Each household or group of households utilized a distinct resource territory. High status households had greater access to certain foods and materials. A central firepit distinguished the highest status house and special activities were associated with this hearth. Finally, the repeated superimposition of both structures and features indicates that once established, these spatial markers of social relations were tenaciously maintained.

EIGHTEENTH-CENTURY OBSERVATIONS

Observations on houses made by Captain James Cook and his officers when they visited Nootka Sound in 1778 paint a very similar picture (Figure 4-3). Cook noted that "several families live under the same roof" (Beaglehole 1967: 303) and later described the houses at Yuquot as consisting of a "long range of buildings, some of which are one hundred and fifty feet in length" and between 24 and 30 feet in breadth (1967:317). The interiors of these buildings were divided into apartments about 12 feet wide and 18 feet long, using boarded partitions three or four feet high (1967:1407). Each apartment was "the property of one family" (1967:317). Raised platforms covered with mats were constructed around the enclosed sides of the apartments, and these were used for sitting and sleeping. Possessions were stored in large wooden boxes, and a fireplace for cooking was located near the center of each apartment. If the house was wide enough, apartments were placed along both sides and a passage ran along the center, but narrower houses had family apartments on only one side. King adds that the wider dwellings usually housed four families and the smaller ones only two (Beaglehole 1967:1409).

However, the historic records also draw attention to a feature not apparent in the archaeological evidence. Neither Cook nor his officers commented on any observed differences between the apartments of chiefs and those of commoners. Nor was it apparent to them that chiefs occupied the corners of dwellings. Furthermore, all houses appeared alike from the outside. A chief's house could not be distinguished from any other. While Cook does describe carved images placed in a house drawn by Webber, he never suggests they distinguish a chief's residence. For his part, King was perplexed by the presence upon one building of "a tree supported by two posts of an uncommon size, capable of

Figure 4-3. John Webber's 1778 watercolor sketch of Friendly Cove, Yuquot, showing the plain, undecorated exterior appearance of the houses. By permission of the British Library, ADD MS 15514 f7.

making a Mast for a first rate" (Beaglehole 1967:1409). It was not apparent to him at the time that the right to raise such a "tree" was a "privilege," and it marked the residence of a high status family (Drucker 1951:69). In essence then, while status differences certainly existed at Yuquot, and were expressed in both the internal and external arrangement of dwellings, everyday social practice did not draw attention to these markers, so the casual visitor remained unaware of their meaning.

Interestingly, this was not the case ten years later in Clayoquot Sound. When John Meares visited the Clayoquot village of Opitsat in 1788, he found the Clayoquot chief, Wickaninish, living "in a state of magnificence much superior to any of his neighbours" (Meares 1967:230). Wickaninish's house was exceptionally massive, and on the inside was a huge figure whose mouth served as the doorway (1967:136). In May of the following year, Haswell was similarly awed by Wickaninish's huge house and its numerous carved pillars, "so large that the Mouth serves as doorway [sic] into their houses" (Howay

1941:69). This display of material wealth on and in the houses of the Clayoquot, particularly those belonging to Wickaninish, left all visitors, however foreign, in no doubt as to who was in charge.

The differences between Yuquot in 1778 and Opitsat in 1788 may simply reflect the very different personalities and ambitions of their respective chiefs at that time (Marshall 1993a). However, considered in the light of events taking place over the following two centuries, it is also possible they were early indicators of the direction future change would take.

DEMOGRAPHIC AND ECONOMIC CHANGE, 1870–1940

During the nineteenth century the Nuu-chah-nulth people were severely reduced by disease and bitter internecine warfare. Although the wars ended by 1870, population continued to decline. When the first official census was taken in 1881 the Nuu-chah-nulth people numbered 3589. By 1910 population had dropped below 2000, and did not regain that level until the 1950s. By 1990 it was approaching 6000 (Watanabe 1991). The Nuu-chah-nulth were one of the last native groups in British Columbia to make the demographic transition from a rapidly declining to a rapidly increasing population. Overall, the native population of the province had stabilized by 1890, but the population of the west coast of Vancouver Island continued to decline until 1939 (Duff 1964:39). During the same period dramatic changes were seen in Nuuchah-nulth housing. Until 1880, photographs of villages all along the west coast of Vancouver Island show large shed roof style houses similar to those recovered archaeologically at Ozette and recorded by Webber. These houses were built of moveable, split cedar planks lashed horizontally to a permanent house frame. The same villages photographed a decade later still show large houses, but they are constructed from commercially sawn, fixed planking. By 1900 European style frame construction, single family dwellings are widespread (see Sendey 1977 for examples).

Changes taking place in the composition of the households occupying these dwellings are captured in the first official census records, collected by Indian Agent Guillod in 1881 and 1891. In 1881, 3589 people living in 230 households were enumerated (Table 4-1). Households varied in size from 1 to 54 people (Figure 4-4). The extraordinary range in household size is a graphic illustration of this transitional moment. One-third of the households contained fewer than ten people. They would have consisted primarily of nuclear or extended families. Another third included 20 or more people. These were big, multifamily, house-based households composed of several nuclear or ex-

Table 4-1. Nuu-chah-nulth Household Size in 1881

Group	Pop.	Houses	40+	30+	20+	10+	1+	Range	Mean
Chickliseht	148	8	-	-	5	1	2	28–2	19
Kyuquot	655	36	2	4	12	7	11	45–2	18
Ehattesaht	145	6	1	-	3	2	-	42–10	24
Nutchatlaht	146	9	-	-	3	5	1	28–7	16
Mowachaht	254	10	1	3	1	4	1	49–8	25
Muchalaht	92	7	-	-	2	2	3	25–3	13
Hesquiaht	220	14	-	1	2	7	4	38–5	16
Ahousaht	313	21	-	2	4	10	5	31–4	15
Kelesmat	158	7	1	1	2	2	1	40–7	23
Clayoquot	329	20	1	2	2	9	6	54–2	16
Ucluelet	226	15	-	1	3	5	6	36–3	15
Toquaht	32	3	-	-	-	2	1	18–3	11
Sheshaht	174	10	-	1	4	2	3	39–3	17
Opetchesaht	56	5	-	-	1	2	2	20–2	11
Uchucklesaht	56	8	-	-	-	3	5	10–3	7
Ohiaht	232	12	-	3	1	7	1	39–8	19
Nitinaht	270	27	-	1	1	7	18	37–2	10
Pacheenaht	83	12	-	-	-	4	8	17–2	7
Total	3589	230	6	19	46	81	78	54–2	16

Source: Canada (1881).

tended families, related to each other through the household chief. The remaining third of households, which contained between 11 and 20 people, represent households in transition from house-based to nuclear family. Thus, in 1881, about half of Nuu-chah-nulth households were still house-based, and they accounted for considerably more than half the population. However, nuclear family households were growing in popularity.

A decade later this picture was dramatically different. In 1891, only 2863 people were enumerated but they were dispersed among 320 households. The largest household now included only 34 people (Table 4-2; Figure 4-4). Two-thirds of households contained fewer than 10 people, and just under a third contained 10–19 people. Only 8% contained 20 or more people. These figures indicate that by 1891 the vast majority of Nuu-chah-nulth people had moved out of house-based multifamily households into nuclear family households.

This transformation did not occur evenly along the west coast. The general pattern was for the transition from house to nuclear family-based residential units to occur first in the south, and then spread slowly north over a period of

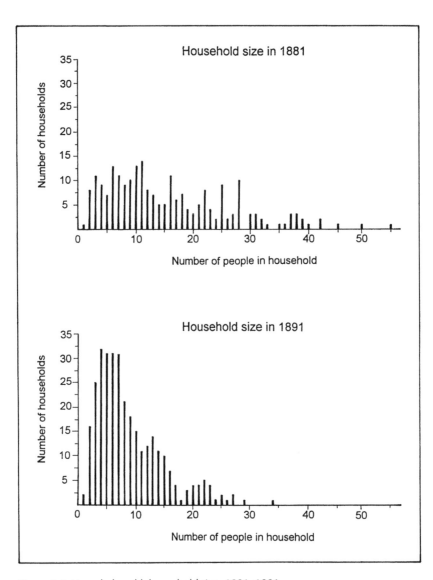

Figure 4-4. Nuu-chah-nulth household size, 1881, 1891.

Table 4-2.   Nuu-chah-nulth Household Size in 1891

Group	Pop.	Houses	40+	30+	20+	10+	1+	Range	Mean
Chickliseht	131	12	-	-	2	4	6	22–4	11
Kyuquot	469	55	-	-	3	17	35	25–2	9
Ehattesaht	115	7	-	1	1	3	2	34–6	16
Nutchatlaht	103	11	-	-	-	3	8	19–3	9
Mowachaht	214	17	-	-	4	6	7	29–4	13
Muchalaht	67	7	-	-	-	3	4	14–6	10
Hesquiaht	209	35	-	-	-	3	32	14–2	6
Ahousaht	279	23	-	-	4	9	10	27–3	12
Kelesmat	86	10	-	-	1	1	8	20–4	9
Clayoquot	253	30	-	-	1	11	18	24–2	8
Ucluelet	181	25	-	-	2	3	20	22–2	7
Toquaht	22	2	-	-	-	1	1	15–7	11
Sheshaht	152	21	-	-	1	3	17	21–2	7
Opetchesaht	65	9	-	-	-	3	6	16–1	7
Uchucklesaht	41	5	-	-	-	1	4	16–3	8
Ohiaht	199	22	-	-	-	10	12	19–2	9
Nitinaht	277	29	-	-	5	6	18	27–2	10
Total	2863	320	-	1	24	87	208	34–1	9

Source: Canada (1891).

several decades. Examination of the census records by tribal group reveals that in 1881 household size was declining more rapidly among the southern groups than among the central and northern groups (Table 4-1; see Figure 4-1 for tribe locations). By 1891 household size among the central Clayoquot Sound groups had declined to a size comparable with their southern neighbors, but the northern groups maintained larger households until around 1900 (Table 4-2). Figures obtained in 1921 by Edward Sapir indicate that throughout the west coast, Nuu-chah-nulth household size had by then declined to an average of 3–4 people (Sapir n.d.).

The slower pace of change in household size among the northern groups can be attributed in part to greater house cohesion. The Barkley Sound tribal groups (in the south), and to a lesser extent the Clayoquot Sound tribal groups, were made up from amalgamated remnants of house groups reduced by war. They often included large numbers of war survivors who had been displaced both socially and geographically. In these cases, displaced people drew on their personal kin ties to locate themselves in a house, and the physical bound-edness of the house dwelling promoted a sense of house identity and definition. But the lineage or descent-based narratives which traditionally underwrote and strengthened house groups became stretched and fragile. When placed under sustained economic pressure, as described below, these amalgamated house groups fragmented easily, and the contemporary two-level social structure consisting of families and tribes emerged quickly. In the north, by contrast, nineteenth-century conflicts had been less disruptive, and houses with strongly integrated social affiliations still formed the sociopolitical core of tribal groups. Although the move to smaller households also occurred in the north, the change was later and multifamily households persisted longer.

Missionary activity sometimes accelerated change, but it was not a driving force. For example, change was unusually rapid among the Kyuquot and Hesquiaht, both of whom had resident priests by 1880. The priests regarded house-based, multifamily households as immoral (Moser 1926), and placed strong pressure on people to abandon them. More important, however, household structure was strategic ground in the clash between the authority of the priests and chiefs. Priests could exert their influence far more effectively once people were divided from one another in small, nuclear family homes (Moser 1926). Chiefly authority remained stronger in large, house-based households, where traditional values could still be lived and practiced in everyday life. The maintenance of house-based households was an active form of resistance to the Catholic church, and the physically imposing structure of house-based dwellings was an important element in that resistance.

If demographic collapse and the incursion of the church had been the only pressures on the Nuu-chah-nulth at this time, the house would almost certainly have survived. Its flexible social structure drew displaced people together and consolidated them within strongly framed, enduring dwellings. These house structures held people together, proffering their resisting walls to the fragmenting pressures of war, disease, and Christianity. But the Nuu-chah-nulth were also under intense economic pressure, ironically, because the period between 1850 and 1920 was a time of exceptional economic affluence. The Nuu-chah-nulth people's remarkable talent for taking advantage of any new economic opportunity that arose led Blenkinsop to remark in 1874 that "without question, these people are the richest in every respect in British Columbia" (quoted in Crockford 1991:39).

Widespread opportunities for employment, particularly as producers of dogfish oil, sealers, hop pickers, and cannery workers, drew Nuu-chah-nulth people ever further into the Canadian commercial cash economy. As more people spent longer periods employed for wage remuneration, cash and purchased products replaced locally produced resources as both basic food stuffs and wealth items. This change affected the corporate structure of the house in two ways. First, a house chief's *ha-hoolthe*, which consisted of major territorial rights (Dewhirst 1990:22; Drucker 1951:247), no longer represented the economic base of a house. Second, people were increasingly at liberty to earn and dispose of cash income independently of the chiefs. The fragmentation of the house-based household into nuclear family dwellings thus occurred in tandem with the fragmentation of the house corporate economy into single family incomes.

During the mid-nineteenth century the primary source of cash income was the production of dogfish oil and sealskins (Jones and Bosustow 1981; Moser 1926). By 1854 a small trading schooner was servicing Nuu-chah-nulth waters (Inglis and Haggarty 1986:51). Chief Charles Jones of the Pacheenaht described dogfish oil production as the work of slaves and commoners carried out as an extension of existing duties as harvesters of the resources located within a chief's *ha-hoolthe*. Although production was generally carried out by individuals or families (Crockford 1991:28), the sale of dogfish oil and its proceeds commonly remained in the hands of the chief (Jones and Bosustow 1981). These proceeds were substantial. In four years, 1854–58, "between five and six thousand gallons [of oil] per year were produced by the Pacheenaht" (Crockford 1991:27).

By 1870 sealing schooners were calling at villages to take on crews to work off the California coast and in the Bering Sea. Sealers usually worked in pairs consisting of a hunter and steerer, who was commonly a son, or during the early years before the schooner captains put a stop to it, a wife or daughter (Crockford 1991; Canada 1913). The Nuu-chah-nulth, especially the southern tribes, were highly receptive to employment as sealers, so much so that Indian Agent Guillod reported in 1889 that the "Nittenahts and Ucluelahts bought schooners for sealing purposes" (Inglis and Haggarty 1986:77). By 1896 the Nitinaht had extended their investments and owned four sealing schooners. Again, the economic rewards were considerable. The West Coast Indian agent noted that "each Indian could make almost twice as much in one sealing season as the average white man would make in a year" (quoted in Crockford 1991:47). Not surprisingly, in 1891 40 percent of Nuu-chah-nulth men identified themselves as sealers (1991:48).

Towards the end of the nineteenth century people were taking regular summer employment in canneries in Rivers Inlet and on the Fraser River, often moving later to hop fields or clam beds in northern Washington. Men were employed to catch fish for the canneries and paid between $1.75 and $3 per day; women cleaned and canned fish for about $1 a day (Crockford 1991:43).

Local opportunities for cannery work increased substantially in the early twentieth century when canneries and reduction plants were built along the west coast to capitalize on the availability of pilchards (Crockford 1991).

Wage labor drew people away from the tasks of harvesting and preserving local resources for the lean winter months, so European foods were purchased to compensate for a lack of winter provisions. Crockford (1991), however, stresses that between 1840 and 1920 wage labor and cash income were only employment supplements, and the core of the Nuu-chah-nulth economy remained embedded in subsistence fishing and hunting. At first, political leaders "extended their authority into commercial enterprise" and chiefs in some cases acted as "labour contractors" (Crockford 1991:79). But individuals and families increasingly won control over the disposal of their cash income (1991: 43), especially after 1900 when canneries and hop picking supplanted dogfish fishing and sealing as the major sources of cash income. As a result, house members no longer depended on access to a chief's *ha-hoolthe* rights at fishing stations. Nor did they depend on each other for the communal labor necessary to exploit those rights effectively. Economic affluence and independence eventually pulled the Nuu-chah-nulth house apart.

A CLOSER LOOK AT WHAT HAPPENED IN NOOTKA SOUND

The general trends described above are better understood when the specific experiences of particular people are considered. This section therefore focuses on the Mowachaht and Muchalaht tribes of Nootka Sound (Figure 4-1a). An unusually rich and varied archival record remains of the Mowachaht/Muchalaht people during the late nineteenth and early twentieth centuries. By drawing these records together it is possible to follow in surprising detail the changes taking place in all four components of Mowachaht and Muchalaht houses. Thus, the changing role of the physical house structure can be understood in relation to the demographic and economic changes occurring at the time.

Demographic decline among both tribes was staggering. In 1881 the Mowachaht still numbered 254, but showed the "waisted" age distribution so typical of a population struggling to recover from epidemic disease (Figure 4-5). The Muchalaht, devastated by a long war with the Mowachaht, were reduced to 92, and demographic recovery seemed doubtful. The situation deteriorated over the following decades. The 1891 census revealed a straightening, and narrowing, of the Mowachaht demographic profile, suggesting they were losing the battle to replenish their numbers. By 1920 the profile had narrowed even further, the proportion of children under 20 was sinking, and

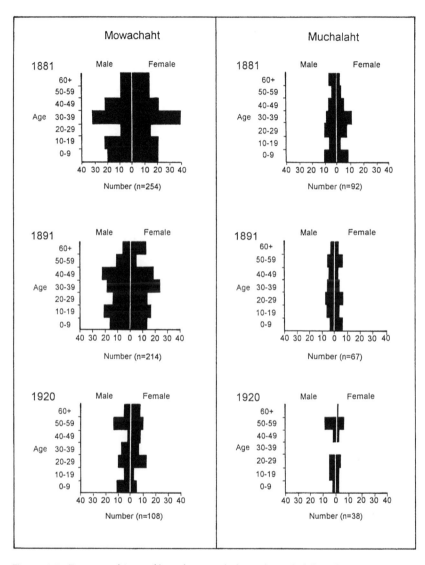

Figure 4-5. Demographic profiles of Mowachaht and Muchalaht tribes, 1881, 1891, 1921 (Canada 1881, 1891; Sapir n.d.).

numbers had dropped to 108. Only 38 Muchalaht now remained, and they moved into houses at the Mowachaht summer village of Yuquot, thus effecting an amalgamation. Despite this appalling situation, in 1939 numbers started to rise. A new generation of only 38 people, who in 1920 were 20 or younger, started a trend toward large family size that eventually led to dramatic demographic recovery.

A clear correspondence can be identified between households enumerated in the 1881 census, ethnographically described houses, and house dwellings shown in archival photographs. Ten Mowachaht households were enumerated in 1881. They can be correlated with ten of the thirteen houses described by Drucker as existing about this time (1951:231). These houses were established at Yuquot in the latter part of nineteenth century when the Tlupana Inlet groups joined with the Tahsis-Yuquot people to form the Mowachaht confederacy. The three groups that in 1881 did not yet have house dwellings at Yuquot emerged slightly later and were given the final three sites at the least desirable northern end of the beach (Figure 4-6a, Houses 227–9).

The photographic record made by Richard Maynard during two visits to Yuquot in 1874 and 1879 is instructive. It shows that in 1874 all houses were of traditional design with movable, split-plank walls (Figure 4-2; Sendey 1977); none stood out. By 1879, the first fixed-plank house had been erected. It was more than twice the height of all other houses, and its location indicates that it belonged to chief Hai'yah, inheritor of the Maquinna title and first ranking chief of the Yaluactakamlath, the first-ranking house (Folan 1972:118–19). The continued use of traditional design dwellings and the close correlation between the number of known houses and the number of enumerated households together document the continuing strength of house-based social groups at Yuquot in 1881. Ten to fifteen years later, the pattern observed in the 1870s was breaking down. A series of photographs taken by the Laing expedition in 1896 show that all Yuquot houses were by then constructed of sawn, vertically fixed planks. A row of large house dwellings lined the beach front, but at the ends of this row, and behind them, single family dwellings had begun to appear (Figure 4-6b).

The beginnings of this new pattern are also discernible in the Yuquot reserve survey conducted in 1893 (Devereux 1893). This was three years before the Laing photographs were taken and two years after the 1891 census was completed. In addition to a new church and related houses which were built in the northern cove in 1889 (Moser 1926:121), Devereux surveyed 25 structures, seven more than are listed in the 1891 census (Figure 4-6a). Despite this discrepancy Devereux's structures can, with reasonable accuracy, be correlated with the houses named by Drucker, and with the households enumerated

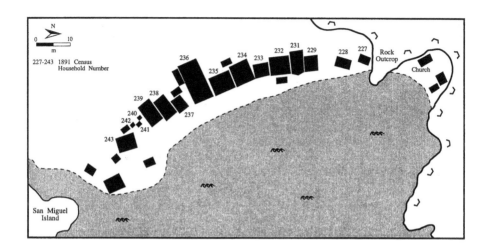

Figure 4-6. a) Yuquot dwellings surveyed by Devereux in 1893. The dwellings are numbered according to the 1891 census. b) Yuquot photographed in 1896 showing houses 236–227. House 236, far left, faces onto the beach and has a painted design encircling the door. House 231 also faces the beach. The ridge pole protruding from the roof front of this house is the carved sea lion pole that in 1874 supported a house oriented parallel to the beach and located at the other end of the village; see Figure 4-2. By permission of the Royal British Columbia Museum, PN 8714.

in the census. Drucker (1951:231) lists the house dwellings at Yuquot in the order in which they stood along the beach front, and Folan (1972:121) was able to correlate these with the dwellings shown in the 1896 photographs. Important names known to be held by particular houses appear in the census lists frequently enough to permit identification of the dwellings of specific houses. They establish that in 1891 the Yuquot households were enumerated in a regular progression from north to south, unlike 1881 when they were probably enumerated in order of rank. This makes it possible to correlate the 1891 census with the 1893 survey and 1896 photograph (Figure 4-6).

What these correlations highlight is that although big house dwellings were still being built, they were beginning to empty of residents. As numbers declined and people moved to single family dwellings, the function of the house dwellings began to change. They were used less and less for everyday living. The internal partitions that had designated the living apartment of each resident family disappeared, leaving a large open space "like a great hall" edged with benches (Folan 1972:154). This change in interior design was already underway by 1894 (1972:154). Eventually, the house dwellings were used exclusively for ceremonial gatherings and other community activities. Interior arrangements continued to accommodate new functions. The "major portion of the house would be set aside for house posts and other display privileges, guests' quarters, feasts, potlatches, Shamans' Dances, an indoor basketball court and, after a floor was put in, roller skating" (Folan 1972:157).

By the turn of the century the house dwellings no longer housed people; they housed ritual paraphernalia, formal ceremonies, and sometimes guests. As their function changed, attention moved from their interior to their exterior appearance. Between 1896 and 1920 almost every house dwelling at Yuquot was rebuilt at least once, sometimes several times, as each house chief strove to "keep up with his neighbours" (Folan 1972:122–29) by constructing ever more elaborate and imposing houses (Figure 4-7). This rapid rebuilding stood in stark contrast to the construction histories of traditional design houses where each post, pole, or board was replaced singly in order to maintain a permanent structure (Drucker 1951:72–73). The older structures powerfully symbolized the eternal, timeless ideology of the house. Superficially, the new style house dwellings with their fixed vertical planks, fancy windows, totem poles, and flagpoles might have seemed more permanent, but in fact, they proved ephemeral. None lasted more than about ten years.

House size and exterior decoration provided dynamic new fields for the assertion of status. By 1891 a very close correlation between lineage rank, household size, and house size had emerged. At the same time exterior displays of house privileges began to proliferate. In the late eighteenth century,

Figure 4-7. Captain Jack's elaborate triple-gabled house at Yuquot, c. 1920. In front stand a totem pole and a flagpole. The house replaced house 232 in Figure 4-6. By permission of the Royal British Columbia Museum, PN 15619.

European visitors to Nootka Sound observed little overt assertion of rank in everyday life. Except for a possible welcome figure marking the house of "the owner of the beach," the person whose task it was to welcome guests, poles and other display privileges were always placed inside houses. In 1893 this was no longer the case. The first-ranking Yaluactakamlath house, whose chief was Hai'yah (Maquinna), was not only twice the size of any other house at Yuquot, it also had a painted sun and *hi'i'Lik* design encircling the doorway (Figure 4-6, House 236). Similarly, the fifth-ranking Tukwittakamlath house (Figure 4-6, House 238) had a ridgepole with a carved sea lion at one end. In 1874 this pole was fully enclosed within the house (Figure 4-2), but in the first decade of the twentieth century the house was rebuilt and reoriented so that the carved sea lion protruded out over the door and faced the beach. At the same time a carved figure of a person holding a copper was moved from the rear interior to adorn the front exterior (Jonaitis 1988:194). Flagpoles became popular. By the opening decade of the twentieth century they stood in front of four houses. The eleventh-ranking Nisaqath house of Captain George sported a totem pole alongside its flagpole, and a few years later the second-ranking Tsisa'ath house of Captain Jack followed suit with a totem pole (Figure 4-7).

As the people moved out of their house dwellings, the house chiefs turned to material culture to assert publicly their rank and status. The frequent rebuilding of house dwellings, the correlation of house size with rank, and the proliferation of exterior privilege displays were strategies for affirming status. Such practices had previously been rare. In 1778 Captain Cook had difficulty identifying chiefs at Yuquot; a century later the casual visitor would have no such problems. In the rapidly changing economic climate of the late nineteenth and early twentieth centuries, the corporate economy of the house came apart. The house chiefs retained their rights to fishing stations, but people were taking their labor elsewhere. A house dwelling no longer housed or symbolized a permanent, enduring social group. Instead it became a stage on which a rapidly changing theater of contested rank was played out. Wealth, and by extension status, was displayed in the size, material contents, and exterior opulence of a house dwelling rather than being implied by the number and corpulence of its occupants. The house structure became a symbol of capital wealth rather than human wealth.

Although people moved out of the house dwellings, the practice of co-residence remained pertinent. People commonly built nuclear family dwellings in clusters behind the house dwellings. In this way the relative residential locations of the people who belonged to the various houses changed little. Even after the large house dwellings had completely disappeared at Yuquot, they remained identifiable in the residential clusters of related families who chose to build close to each other in the general vicinity of the original house dwelling site. This process is well documented among the Kyuquot (Kenyon 1980:97).

Changes in dwelling and household structure were accompanied by a fundamental shift in the relative frequency and socio-political importance of feasts versus potlatches. At feasts only food was given, while at potlatches wealth was also distributed (Drucker 1951:372). When the English sailor John Jewitt lived as a captive in chief Maquinna's house from 1803–1805, he was constantly invited to feasts in other houses (Jewitt 1976 [1807]). As one Nuu-chah-nulth described it to Drucker (1951:370) over a century later, "Every time the chief got a lot of food of any kind, he gave a feast." For Jewitt this meant dining out several times a week. In contrast, Jewitt describes very few pot-latches. Most of the examples he witnessed took place directly after the taking of the *Boston* and involved the distribution of items taken from the ship. To-ward the end of the nineteenth century, feasts began declining in popularity while potlatches became increasingly frequent and elaborate (Drucker 1951: 376). There was also a growing "tendency to give money and gifts at feasts" as well as at potlatches (Drucker 1951:372). Thus the move away from celebrat-ing house and chiefly wealth in displays of labor and local food, in favor of wealth in the form of capital, is evident in house ceremonies as well as house dwellings.

The driving force behind the social changes outlined above was eco-nomic change. In the census of 1881, all 103 Mowachaht and Muchalaht men for whom occupation was given were listed as fishermen. These men probably spent only small amounts of time producing dogfish oil or fish for commercial sale. By 1891, thirteen Mowachaht and nine Muchalaht were listed as sealers, while seven Mowachaht and one Muchalaht were employed making canoes for sealing. Although two households had several sealers, in general, each house dwelling had one sealer and most had one canoe-maker. This pattern indicates that, despite much more widespread participation in wage labor, the house chiefs still retained a significant degree of control over people's access to wage employment. The chiefs had considerable say over who would gain a place on a sealing crew. Native testimonies taken during the Royal Commis-sion on Pelagic Sealing in 1913 explain how it was relatively easy for the chiefs to control sealing employment because the schooners came directly to the village to take on crews (Canada 1913). At the end of the season, the sealers were usually delivered back to their villages (Dawley n.d.).

The mercantile possibilities of this arrangement were apparent, and in 1882 a trading post was established at Yuquot (Folan 1972:25). It allowed the Nootka Sound sealers to sell sealskins and buy goods without making the long trip to Victoria. In 1894, as the prosperity of the sealers increased, a more impressive store, operated by Walter Dawley of the Clayoquot-based merchant firm, Stockham and Dawley, opened at Yuquot (Folan 1972:27). In a good season a sealer could earn more than $60, but in a bad year it might be less than $15. In addition to the local store, business was kept local through the "slop chest." This consisted of goods, purchased by the captain or mate prior to setting out, then sold to the crews while at sea. The value of goods bought from the slop chest was deducted at the end of the season from each sealer's earnings. Returns from the slop chest cut into sales at Dawley's Yuquot store, and he lamented in a letter of 1901 how "the slop chest gets a pretty good share of their earnings" (Dawley n.d.). After a bad season people even returned in debt to the slop chest (Dawley n.d.). Warm clothing accounted for the bulk of sales from the slop chest, but more fanciful items included silver watches at $8.00, ladies' brooches at $1.50, and numerous silk handkerchiefs. The local store and slop chest helped sealers circumvent house chiefs when disposing of their earnings.

Another irregular but potentially significant source of income was sea otter skins. In the 1890s skins were routinely fetching $250 and could even make $400 (Dawley n.d; Murphy 1957:5). On one occasion in 1899, Dawley bought five sea otter skins from a local hunter for the sum of $1260 (Dawley n.d.). August Murphy's account of participating as a boy in a 1896 sea otter hunt is insightful. He describes a communal drive in which 24 canoes were used to sweep the reefs for sea otter. Although the whole affair was organized and directed by a chief who led the hunt, he did not retain all the proceeds. When an otter surfaced, all the hunters would shoot their arrows. Participants were paid according to whose arrows hit the target and in what order. A hunter would commonly receive $10 to $20 for a strike (Murphy 1957:3–5).

The adoption of European ceramics for both everyday and ceremonial use provides another indication of how cash income was at the disposal of increasing numbers of people. Archaeological evidence indicates that it was not until the closing decades of the nineteenth century that ceramic tableware became popular. In this regard, it is noteworthy that women as well as men served on sealing crews and women were often preferred as cannery and hop field workers (Canada 1913; Crockford 1991). Ceramic dishes for everyday use, and to enhance ceremonial feasting and potlatch distributions, were among their preferred purchases (Marshall and Maas 1997).

The persistence into the late nineteenth century of a house-based economy in Nootka Sound is also apparent in settlement patterns. In 1890, 11 Mowachaht and six Muchalaht Reserves were set aside. They included one summer village, three winter villages, and 14 fishing stations, most of which were located at salmon spawning streams. The summer and winter villages were congregation settlements where social and ceremonial events usually took place. Almost all houses had dwelling sites at Yuquot, the only summer village, and at one of the winter villages (Drucker 1951:228–35; Murphy 1957). Fishing stations were owned by individual houses. In earlier times, they were occupied for extended periods, and in Muchalaht Inlet, if not other parts of Nootka Sound, fishing stations were even occupied year round. However, by the late nineteenth century population numbers had declined to the point that most fishing stations were owned and occupied by a single extended family, and occupation was brief. Since the ownership and use of fishing stations was central to the maintenance of a house's corporate economy and identity (Drucker 1951; Murphy 1957), intensity of use is a direct barometer of the relative importance of the subsistence versus cash economies.

Devereux's survey of 1893 established the boundaries of the Indian Reserves. These were now the only places the Mowachaht and Muchalaht people could officially reside, although in practice they continued to use many additional places. Archaeological evidence in the form of glass and ceramic artifacts and structural remains has been recorded at more than thirty non-Reserve sites (Marshall 1993b). However, the Reserves were the main settlement locations, and during his survey Devereux recorded the number and dimensions of all standing structures. With few exceptions all were of European fixed-plank construction. As expected, the summer and winter congregation villages had numerous structures. A further indication of their continued intensive use was the large numbers of ceramic and glass sherds archaeologists later found scattered on their beaches (Marshall and Maas 1997). In contrast, the fishing stations usually had only one large or medium-size house, although seven also had potato gardens. By 1893 all fishing stations were occupied only during the spring or fall (Murphy 1957), but this occupation did remain substantial enough to warrant the construction of house dwellings and the planting of gardens.

A decade later the situation was changing. Sealing was on the decline while fishery employment in Rivers Inlet, the Fraser River, and Washington State was expanding. House chiefs could not control who took up employment at these distant fisheries, and their hold over house economies began to slip. Similarly, the ease with which wages could be spent away from the villages also increased, further eroding chiefly influence over the disposal of house income. Thus the house chiefs gradually lost their monopoly over the ownership and management of a house's corporate wealth and resources. This erosion of chiefly control in turn fueled the construction of nuclear family dwellings. Even common and low-ranked people had cash in their pockets with which to purchase sawn lumber and other construction materials to build nuclear family dwellings and assert their new-found economic independence (Folan 1972:156).

With the growth of wages the number of people moving to the spring and summer fishing stations declined, and the length of time spent at these locations decreased (Crockford 1991). The large and medium-size houses that Devereux recorded in 1893 were replaced by small cabins. When the Royal Commission on Indian Affairs conducted hearings in 1914, the Nootka Sound chiefs Joseph, Napoleon Maquinna, and Captain Jack tried to impress upon the commissioner that "houses" or "cabins" still stood on these fishing Reserves, and these places remained economically crucial to their people (British Columbia 1914). Nevertheless, the substantial structures and extended occupation typical of settlement at fishing stations in the previous century were gone.

The definitive point of transition came in 1917 when Nootka Packing Company purchased W. R. Lord's saltery at A'oqtsis, the site where the *Boston* had been taken in 1803, and built a pilchard cannery and reduction plant (Folan 1972:29; Jones 1991:64). The plant operated until 1952 (White 1972: 82). Nootka Cannery, as it became known, was only three kilometers from Yuquot, and virtually the entire Mowachaht and Muchalaht population, along with numerous people from other tribes, moved there "to take advantage of the opportunities for work" (Folan 1972:29). Not surprisingly, "Dawley's store followed them about a year later" (1972:29). The local men crewed the fishing boats that supplied the plant, unloaded fish, and worked in the reduction plant, while "the women were employed in the cannery, cleaning fish and packing it into cans" (Jones 1991:69). Surviving photographs of the cannery in the 1930s show that these workers were housed in a settlement of small houses located just behind the main plant. Even so, some attention was paid to traditional status markers, as Captain Jack, first chief of the second-ranking Tsisa'ath house, had a separate three-room house for himself and family (1991:69).

With the construction of Nootka Cannery, wage labor in Nootka Sound was no longer irregular and distant. It was local, regular, and virtually universal in its availability. People continued to visit their house fishing stations to harvest and preserve salmon for the winter, but in ever-decreasing numbers, for shorter periods of time (Folan 1972). Archaeological evidence for twentieth-century cabins, such as glass, ceramics, and scars left by bark collecting, is present on at least 47 sites in Nootka Sound, but in no case does the evidence suggest substantial occupation (Marshall 1993b). With the exception of the key ceremonial villages—Yuquot, Kupti, Tahsis, Cheeish, and Ahaminaquus—structural evidence at these sites suggests no more than one or possibly two cabins were present within the last 50 years. In most cases, the glass and ceramics date to no later than around 1940 (1993b). Even the major villages of Kupti, Tahsis, Cheeish, and Ahaminaquus were seldom visited by about 1940, although settlement at Yuquot, Tahsis, and Ahaminaquus was expanding.

In Nootka Sound, a strong house-based economy and settlement pattern remained in place until the late nineteenth century, but by 1900 widening access to wage labor and increasing economic independence from house chiefs were eroding the corporate cohesion of the house. As people broadened their participation in the Canadian cash economy, house dwellings emptied into nuclear family dwellings and fewer people spent less time at their house fishing stations. By 1940, when the Nuu-chah-nulth population hit an all-time low and the combined strength of the Mowachaht and Muchalaht tribes was down to 100 people, virtually everyone lived year-round in single family dwellings located on tribal reserves. The house, it seemed, had disappeared as an economic and social entity.

CONCLUSION

Archaeological evidence indicates the Nuu-chah-nulth house has a long antiquity dating back at least 2000 years. Even before it was tested against the changes wrought by European arrival, the Nuu-chah-nulth house had already proved an enduring and resilient institution.

For the first century of European contact, the house stood firm against the ravages of war and disease. As population declined through the nineteenth century, house dwellings drew displaced people into the shelter of their strong walls and corporate economies, holding them together in the face of social upheaval. When further pressed by missionaries, Canadian Government Indian agents, and new laws, the Nuu-chah-nulth house continued to respond with resistance, not acquiescence. During this period the social flexibility of the house was a critical factor in enabling the Nuu-chah-nulth people both to accommodate rapid change and to take full advantage of new economic opportunities.

However, the incursion of the cash economy proved one pressure too many for the Nuu-chah-nulth house. People's economic interests shifted away from the resource wealth that could be generated from the united labor and territorial holdings of houses to the cash-based wealth generated by individual families. As people of all ranks used their new cash incomes to buy social and economic independence, the house dwellings emptied into nuclear family homes. The house was no longer lived in, in an everyday sense. Furthermore, without annual participation in the communal labor that generated house wealth, the house as an economic institution was literally no longer performed and therefore ceased to exist.

Although by 1900 the house was no longer the primary economic and residential unit, it remained the social and political core of Nuu-chah-nulth community life, and the early twentieth century saw an elaboration of the sociopolitical function of the house. As the performance of socio-political ceremonies expanded, house dwellings were transformed into potlatch houses. In this new role the exterior appearance of the house became all important. Size increasingly mirrored rank, and new potlatch houses acquired windows, gables, carved and painted exterior figures, flagpoles, and totem poles. In short, the material frame of the potlatch house enclosed and inscribed symbolic capital (Bourdieu 1977, 1990), while the house dwelling had housed people and constituted them as a discrete social entity.

This sociopolitical elaboration of the house proved a short-lived phenomenon. The political functions of the house gradually devolved to the tribal group, and the ceremonies which underpinned chiefly positions were performed less and less often. By 1940 the Nuu-chah-nulth potlatch houses had disappeared. However, viewed in a longer perspective the demise of the potlatch house and its ancestor, the house dwelling, appears less complete. Beginning in the 1980s Nuu-chah-nulth tribal groups began building a new style of potlatch house in which to hold community functions and traditional ceremonies. Perhaps, then, 2000 years of history is not so quickly erased.

5

Temples as "Holy Houses"
The Transformation of Ritual Architecture in Traditional Polynesian Societies

Patrick V. Kirch

The life history of houses interrelates the physical changes experienced by the structures with the life cycles of their inhabitants; this is especially the case with the common practice of placing the dead (or objects that represent them) within the house itself. Having become ancestors, representing origins, precedence, and a concentration of spiritual power, the dead sanctify the house, increasing its value and status. Patrick Kirch pursues the material manifestations of the ritual aspects of Polynesian structures as part of a study on the evolution of Austronesian house societies. First, drawing upon Tikopia as a type case for Polynesia, he reviews Raymond Firth's ethnographic work to argue that the Tikopian paito, "house," fits the defining criteria of Lévi-Strauss's house, and as such has significant utility for interpreting the island's archaeological remains, providing a more complete and continuous picture of Tikopian social and architectural forms. Combining historical linguistic and archaeological data, Kirch goes on to demonstrate that the well-known Polynesian temple complex evolved out of an older and more widespread Austronesian pattern whereby ordinary dwellings were sacralized over time by the interment of the dead within their walls. In the process these "holy houses," embodying ancestral origins of the high-ranked groups, diverged as a separate form from residences, and usually included additional features, such as open spaces, raised platforms, and upright posts that are visible archaeologically. Significantly, the transformation from house to holy house in eastern Oceania differed in its architectural configurations from its counterparts in the west. Archaeology thus provides good evidence for the regional transformations of social configurations, just as ethnographers have determined for living house societies.

HOUSES, RITUAL, AND ANCESTORS IN
AUSTRONESIAN SOCIETIES

Lévi-Strauss's brief but provocative discussion of "house societies" or "*sociétés à maisons*"—almost a passing digression in *The Way of the Masks* (1982)—has spawned a fruitful line of ethnographic inquiry, particularly among Austronesian scholars (e.g., Carsten and Hugh-Jones, eds. 1995 and various chapters therein; Fox, ed. 1993; Macdonald, ed. 1987; McKinnon 1991; Waterson 1990). The term *Austronesian* refers, of course, to those ethnographically attested societies geographically distributed between Madagascar and Easter Island, whose members speak languages belonging to the Austronesian family (Bellwood et al. 1995). The greatest number of such Austronesian societies are found in Island Southeast Asia and in Oceania, and include the Polynesians, on whom this paper concentrates. The core definition of "house society" has been reviewed in Chapters 1 and 2, and need not detain us here. Rather, I will begin with a few introductory remarks about some widespread systemic patterns linking houses, ritual, and ancestors in Austronesian-speaking societies, as background to the specific hypothesis I will develop for Polynesia.

Jim Fox (1993:1) has drawn attention to the central presence in most Austronesian houses of what he calls their "ritual attractor." Ranging structurally from beam, platform, to altar—but often most particularly a specific post or upright—this ritual attractor "has a pre-eminence among the other parts of the house." "The rituals of the houses acknowledge this attractor, generally from the moment of construction" (1993:1). Roxana Waterson further develops these linkages, observing that while the Austronesian house is a "key social unit," it often functions "less as dwelling (it may even be unoccupied) than as origin-place, ritual site, holder of ritual offices and storage-place for heirlooms" (1995a:54). The relationship between houses and ancestors is especially critical. "Ancestors may be literally considered to be present in the house," as indeed they are sometimes buried there or their bones kept as heirlooms, "or at least symbolically represented" (Waterson 1995a:54).

Of particular interest to the hypothesis I will develop here is a common temporal process of increased ritual importance as a house ages, as its original builders and occupants themselves grow old and pass away to become ancestors, the venerated objects (often buried in the house itself) of house ritual practiced by their descendants. Various well-attested ethnographic cases document such a temporal progression in Austronesian houses. Maurice Bloch (1995b) describes how the house of a fruitful marriage among the Zafimaniry of Madagascar gradually takes on ritual significance, how it is embellished and built up by the founding couple's offspring. Such houses increasingly come to be referred to as "holy houses," "where one goes for blessing from God and the ancestors" (1995b:80). In Tana Toraja, the founding houses of noble families become over time *tongkonan*, "origin houses," highly elaborated and ornamented, the principal sites of ritual activity (Waterson 1990, 1995a). Among the Ara of Sulawesi (Gibson 1995), houses also have a life cycle with important ritual aspects; houses have spirits which must be ritually fed by placing offerings at the bases of distinctive male and female supporting posts.

Among the Tanimbar islanders of the central Moluccas, as reported by McKinnon (1991, 1995), a fundamental distinction is made between "named" and "unnamed" houses, which stand in relation to each other much as "elderyounger same-sex siblings" (1991:98). A named house, whose members actually reside in nearby, separate residences, is the physical and ritual center of its kin group. At its core, the named house contains a *tavu*, an elaborately carved altar panel, and various heirloom valuables (see McKinnon, this volume).

An ethnographic case from Island Southeast Asia with particular relevance to the Polynesian model I shall develop is that of Lio in Flores (Howell 1995). The Lio have semantically and physically separate categories of "House" (*sa'o*) and "temple" (*kéda*), yet these are intimately related, along with the social categories of "families, clans, and lineages." As Howell explains: "While descent categories regulate inter-group relations of a strictly human kind such as marriages, births, deaths and property, Houses regulate intra-group relations and relations with House ancestors. The temple orchestrates the cosmogonic and cosmological anchoring" (1995:153). What is more, ceremonial houses and temples are "similar in their general layout and construction" (1995:155). Both are elevated off the ground, although the *kéda* is smaller and has no walls, only a roof. Dead priest-leaders are buried in an elevated space at the edge of which stands the temple. The *kéda* provides a cosmogonic link with major deities and with the original ancestors, and only those "that can maintain a claim of direct descent from one of the original people . . . who came from the mountain may build a *kéda*" (1995:158–59). In essence, *kéda* are "holy houses," in which resides the spiritual essence of the cosmogonic primal pair, a brother-sister couple.

Although Howell's account is strictly ethnographic and hence ahistorical, it is not hard to imagine that the Lio *kéda* arose out of an earlier system involving ranked houses, these quite probably with ancestral burials, much as described for other Austronesian societies in Island Southeast Asia. Rather than an actual dwelling house becoming a temple over time, the Lio substituted a permanent category of sacred house as physically distinct from the secular dwelling. It is just such a historical transformation that I will propose for Polynesia, arguing as well that this transformation may be revealed in certain historical linguistic, comparative ethnographic, and archaeological evidence.

POLYNESIAN TEMPLES AS "HOLY HOUSES": THE HYPOTHESIS

The ethnographic cases I have briefly described are all drawn from the *western* subregion of the Austronesian-speaking world, that is, from Island Southeast Asia and Madagascar. Clearly, in the majority of these societies, the house doubles not only as principal residence and key social unit, but also as the main center of ritual action. With rare exceptions such as the Lio, there is no formal distinction between house and temple. As Green (1996) has argued, this was probably the case for the Proto-Oceanic (POC) speakers who migrated into the southwestern Pacific archipelagoes around 1500 B.C., and who are represented archaeologically by the Lapita cultural complex (Kirch 1997). Some Oceanic languages in the Melanesian region still retain reflexes of the old Austronesian term (POC *Rumaq*), and archaeological evidence from Mussau and New Britain indicates that these were stilt-houses elevated on posts.

In the eastern, or Oceanic, region of Austronesia, however, a physical and semantic distinction between houses and temples is relatively common. This is especially so for the Polynesian societies, to which I now turn my attention. Indeed, Polynesia is well known for its elaboration of temple architecture, as exemplified by the *marae* complex of central Eastern Polynesia, the *ahu* of Easter Island, or by the *heiau* of Hawai'i (Emory 1943). *Heiau* and *marae*, while including specialized structures that resemble houses, were not residential complexes, and at first consideration would seem to represent a marked departure from the western Austronesian pattern described above.

The hypothesis I wish to explore here, however, is that the Polynesian elaboration of the temple complex is in essence only a more formalized version of the widespread (and probably very old) Austronesian pattern of transforming ordinary houses into "holy houses." Moreover, I am suggesting that in many Polynesian islands a historical transformation of this sort may actually be *archaeologically* attested in the physical remains of stratified temple sites. This does not mean that I literally expect to find a house site under every Polynesian *marae*. It does mean that I think that the Polynesian pattern is more congruent with that of other Austronesian societies than has perhaps been realized. The full historical linguistic, comparative ethnographic, and archaeological evidence in support of this proposition is too extensive to report in detail here (but see Kirch and Green in press). I therefore will discuss only three specific cases, beginning with ethnographically rich Tikopia, and then moving briefly to archaeological evidence from Hawai'i and Easter Island (Rapanui).

TIKOPIA AS A "TYPE CASE"

Tikopia, a small Polynesian Outlier in the eastern Solomon Islands, achieved anthropological fame through the pioneering ethnographic research and voluminous writings of Sir Raymond Firth (e.g., Firth 1936, 1967, 1970). The island and its people are of special interest in the context of developing a theory of house societies, for it is as clear an example of a *société à maison* within the eastern Austronesian or Oceanic region as one could hope to find. Indeed, Firth's analysis (1936) of the *paito*, or "house," reveals all the core characteristics originally pointed to by Lévi-Strauss (1982:174), such as a corporate body holding an estate of land, the persistence of the house name over time (and its transmission to the principal occupants of the house), varying methods of kinship affiliation to the house, the transmission of titles, valuables, heirlooms, and rituals, and of course, the central role of eponymous founding ancestors.

Tikopia is moreover of special interest to my hypothesis regarding the linkage between Polynesian houses and temples, for it is the only Polynesian society in which the traditional ritual system was ethnographically observed and carefully documented as a functioning system, prior to missionization (Firth 1967). The richly textured detail of Firth's ethnography yields a wealth of information on Tikopia temples and their association with *paito* or houses. In Tikopia the principal temples (*fare*) were thatched structures, in all but a few details identical with ordinary dwelling houses (*paito*). The Tikopia term *fare* is, of course, a reflex of the Proto-Polynesian term **fare/fale*, cognate reflexes of which are the usual term for "dwelling house" throughout Polynesia (e.g., Hawaiian *hale*, Tongan *fale*). Thus the Tikopia have retained the older Polynesian term for "house" as their word for "temple," while innovating a new term, *paito*, for the residential structure. (Actually, the term *paito* has a broader semantic referent than simply "dwelling structure," for it explicitly encompasses the concept of "household, family, lineage," and thus truly represents "the house" in Lévi-Strauss's sense; see Firth 1985:326.)

To understand the role of the *fare* or temple in Tikopia society, let us follow Firth as he describes the temple of the Kafika clan, situated in the sacred district of Uta, along the inner shore of the lake Te Roto:

> An adjournment was then made to a temple standing on the seaward side a few yards nearer to the lake shore. This large building, known by the name Kafika [same

name as the "house" of the chief], is extremely sacred and is the ceremonial heart of the clan, erected by their ancestors in the time when men were as gods and gods were as men. Each clan has its temple of this type, a lofty building bearing the clan name, sheltering the sacred adzes and other ritual objects, and serving as the scene for most esoteric rites. They are called by the name of *fare*, in distinction to the more ordinary *paito* . . . They are in fact edifices now used solely for religious purposes and presided over by the principal deity of the clan, of whom however no image or figured material symbol is preserved therein. The temples are floored with coconut leaf mats, of the same type as used in dwellings, with the qualification that each mat marks the burial place of an ancestor, or is representative of him. (1967:68)

Elsewhere, Firth (1967:198) elaborates that there are actually three sub-types of temple. The first consists of actual dwellings still in use—though only by chiefs or lineage elders and their immediate households—but which have "the grave-mats of noted ancestors therein, with one or more of the house posts dedicated to gods of the kinship group." An example of this type is Motuapi, residence of the Ariki Tafua, situated in Matautu village (and incidentally still standing and occupied during my own fieldwork in 1977–78). The second category consists of those houses, such as Kafika just described above, which are no longer regularly occupied, because, having become the repositories of large numbers of ancestors buried therein, they are "too sacred for ordinary use" (1967:199). This second category is specifically called *fare tapu*, "sacred houses/temples." The third category comprises the oven houses (*fare umu*) attached to the more important temples, where the food destined for rites is prepared. "No ancestors have been buried in them, but they are sacred because of the gods associated with the oven" (1967:199).

As might be surmised from the differences between the first two types—those *fare* still occupied by persons of rank, and those which have become too sacred through generations of interment of ancestors—the Tikopia temple is essentially a "holy house," associated with the origin of the clan, and serving as its ritual center. The transformation of dwellings into temples, as a temporal process, is clearly conceptualized by the Tikopia, and was so described to Firth by the ritual elder Pae Sao in 1929: " 'Sacred buildings are houses of old; people used to live in them constantly but as time went on they went away from them and didn't live in them. As they stood, not lived in and people went there only to make the kava [the core religious rite of offerings to ancestors], they decayed' " (Firth 1970:114).[1]

One other component of the Tikopia ritual landscape must be briefly mentioned: this is the *marae*, a "type of open air temple," consisting of a cleared space delimited on two or three sides by rows of upright volcanic stone slabs (Firth 1970:120ff; Kirch 1996). Typically, *marae* are situated on the seaward (ritual) side of a dwelling house used as a principal temple. *Marae* Matautu (Firth 1970: fig. 2) situated immediately seaward of the *fare* Motuapi in Matautu village, is a typical case. The upright stone slabs, called *noforanga* (literally "seating place"), each represent a spirit (*atua*) or ancestor. In essence, *marae* can be considered as adjunct ritual spaces to the temples. In Eastern Polynesia, it is these *marae* spaces with their stone slab representations of ancestors that were architecturally elaborated.

It seems clear, then, that the Tikopia temple complex fits comfortably within a broader Austronesian cultural pattern of "holy houses" in which the principal dwellings of ancestors—origin houses if you will—gradually become imbued with such sacredness that they are transformed into god houses. Certainly this is both the emic Tikopia viewpoint, as well as the etic model of Firth as ethnographer-observer.

In 1977–78 I was able to spend eight months carrying out the first systematic archaeological investigation of Tikopia (Kirch and Yen 1982). As a part of this study, I excavated at two important temple sites, providing an archaeological window to this model of temples as transformed houses. At Sinapupu and Takaritoa, I mapped and excavated a stone structural complex held by the Tikopia to be the former village site of the Nga Faea, a social group who, according to oral traditions, had been expelled from the island during a war over land, probably in the late sixteenth or early seventeenth century A.D. (Firth 1961). The site includes a *marae* plaza with upright stone *noforanga* slabs, as well as a rectangular stone house foundation (site TK-1, Kirch and Yen 1982:91 ff: fig. 28) with the proper name Tarengu, identified by informants as the "Kafika" or temple (*fare*) of the Nga Faea. Excavations in the Tarengu structure revealed that in its final stage it had served as a sepulcher, with two burials exposed in the 6-meter trench; this would be entirely in keeping with its purported function as a temple house. However, abundant midden materials and domestic artifacts within the Layer II deposit associated with construction of the foundation also revealed that this site had been a domestic habitation. Moreover, the Layer II structure capped a deep deposit of more than 3 meters of stratified occupation deposits. The temple of Tarengu was simply the last phase in a very long sequence of domestic habitation. This seems to me to be excellent archaeological verification of the Tikopia notion that temples are houses which through time have become sacred.

The second site I investigated is Vaisakiri, described by Firth as "the principle temple of the Ariki Fangarere, having come down to him, with the orchard in which it stands, from Fakaarofatia, the ancestor of his clan, by gift from Pu Resiake of Taumako, mother's brother of this ancestor" (1967:222). Seen by Firth, who participated in the rites of Vaisakiri in 1929, the thatched *fare* itself had largely decomposed by 1977, with only a single half-rotted main post still standing (Kirch and Yen 1982:180–82, Fig. 75). At the request of the current Ariki Fangarere, we did not dig in the foundation of the *fare* itself (for the graves of his ancestors would be found there), but two excavation units were completed less than 5 meters to the east of the temple. These demonstrated that underlying the entire temple area is a domestic midden some 50–70 cm deep, evidence again that the area had a long history of residential occupation.

HOUSE AS TEMPLE IN ANCESTRAL POLYNESIAN SOCIETIES

The Tikopia case provides both a paradigmatic ethnographic model for the transformation of house to temple, and some diachronic archaeological evidence in support of actual physical dwellings changing to ritual structures over time. The question may now be posed: Is the Tikopia case as reflected in ethnography and late prehistoric archaeology a local innovation, or a conservative retention of an older Polynesian pattern? If the latter, then it has considerable relevance to understanding Polynesian ritual spaces and their varied transformations among the more than 30 different Polynesian cultures.

Elsewhere (Kirch 1984; Kirch and Green 1987) it has been argued that all the ethnographically attested Polynesian cultures ultimately descended from an Ancestral Polynesian Culture which can be geographically localized to the Western Polynesia region (the area of Tonga, Samoa, and certain smaller islands such as Niuatoputapu, Futuna, and 'Uvea), and dated to the period between about 500 B.C. and A.D. 1, prior to the differentiation of the Proto Polynesian language, and dispersal of Polynesian populations to the eastern and more marginal islands and archipelagoes. Green and I (Kirch and Green in press) have been engaged in a detailed reconstruction of Ancestral Polynesian culture and societies, based on the application of a phylogenetic model and what we call the "triangulation method," using historical linguistics, comparative ethnography, and archaeology. As part of this project, we have reconstructed the Ancestral Polynesian ritual and calendric system, and the ritual spaces in which this was practiced. The detailed evidence will be published elsewhere, but our reconstruction suggests that the Tikopia system has, in fact, been quite conservative and retains many of the key aspects of its Ancestral Polynesian antecedent.

Our reconstruction is based on the presence of certain essential components of Polynesian ritual spaces that are consistently present throughout the three main subregions: Outlier Polynesia (of which Tikopia is an example), Western Polynesia, and central Eastern Polynesia. Such features are unlikely to represent independent innovations in all three subregions, and are thus taken to be shared retentions of an Ancestral system: (1) The fundamental and consistently present element is an open space, sometimes elaborated into a formal courtyard, almost always denoted by some reflex of the term *malae/marae*. (2) Also invariably present is some form of god house (*fale* or *fale*-adj.) attached or adjacent to the court, sometimes associated with ancestral burials. In central Eastern Polynesia this sometimes becomes miniaturized (even to the extreme of a symbolic box, as in the Tuamotus). (3) Also consistent is the use of either posts or upright stones (often under the term *pou*) as symbolic representations and/or manifestations of deities. The position of these ranges from around the perimeter or at one end of the court, to within the god house itself. (4) Seemingly present only in Eastern Polynesia is a raised platform or altar, called *ahu*, situated at one end of the court. However, there is linguistic evidence to suggest that this was simply a transformation of the original *foundation* of the god or cult house, as found in Outlier and Western Polynesia.

These core architectonic components have corresponding Polynesian terms, which can be robustly reconstructed to Proto Polynesian (PPN) language. Most important is PPN **malaqe*, which Biggs (n.d.) glosses as "open, cleared space used as meeting-place or ceremonial place." Second, we have some form of compound term, **fale*-adjective, with the adjective denoting "sacred," "spirit," or "god." We believe that the most likely PPN form of this term for the sacred house attached to a **malaqe* was **fale-qatua*, based on reflexes in both Western and Eastern Polynesian languages. Third, there is PPN **pou*, a general term for 'post,' but arguably also one that was applied to house posts and/or upright stones which were regarded as representations or temporary receptacles for deities.

Finally, there is PPN **qafu*, a term which requires closer examination. The term is represented by reflexes in 21 Polynesian languages, but its meanings vary considerably. In Eastern Polynesia, it frequently refers to the raised platform or altar at the end of the temple court. In other instances it means a mound, or to heap or pile up. In both Fijian and Yasawan, critical extra-Polynesian witnesses to the reconstruction of PPN, it means "foundation mound of a house." And in Vaitupu, the cognate reflex *afu* refers to a "shrine" (Kennedy 1931:314–15). From this evidence, Green and I construct the following semantic history hypothesis: In PPN, **qafu* referred to the foundation of a house, which may at times have been a slightly elevated mound of earth, or possibly a stone platform. In central Eastern Polynesia, as the god house (**fale*-adj.) itself became miniaturized or abandoned within temple architecture, the **qafu* foundation nonetheless remained, and in time became elaborated as an altar, the most sacred part of the temple. We can only speculate on why this PPN *qafu "house foundation," became Central-Eastern Polynesian *ahu, "temple altar," but it may well have had to do with the practice of interring deceased ancestors under the floor of the *fale-adj. god house.

In short, comparative ethnographic, archaeological, and lexical evidence yields the following reconstruction of Ancestral Polynesian ritual spaces: Architecturally, these were probably simple affairs, consisting of an open, cleared space (*malaqe) to the seaward side of a sacred house (*fale-{qatua}), constructed upon a base foundation (*qafu). The sacred house may or may not have been an actual dwelling of the priest-chief (*qariki), and may or may not have contained the burials of ancestors (*tupuga or *tupuna) although we believe this to be likely. But we are reasonably confident that one or more posts (*pou) within the sacred house were regarded as ritually significant. Such a ritual emphasis on posts was probably a continuance of an older Austronesian practice of designating posts or other key architectural elements of a house as "ritual attractors," as Fox (1993) and others have recently argued.

EASTERN POLYNESIAN TRANSFORMATIONS: SOME ARCHAEOLOGICAL EVIDENCE

That the Tikopia have largely retained the Ancestral Polynesian ritual architectural system seems particularly convincing, given the congruence of ethnographic, oral traditional, and archaeological sources. But what of other Polynesian societies, especially those of Eastern Polynesia noted for their structural elaborations of ritual architecture? I will briefly mention two Eastern Polynesian cases, adducing some archaeological evidence for the transformation of houses to temples. Of course, the argument will need to be refined and elaborated in future studies; my aim here is merely to demonstrate the likely power of this hypothesis.

The temple architecture of Hawai'i is among the most differentiated and complex in Polynesia (Kirch 1985, 1990). Could the varied Hawaiian heiau possibly be interpreted within the broad Austronesian pattern of "holy houses"? One demonstrated archaeological case suggests that this may be a fruitful avenue to pursue. In 1989, Michael Kolb (1994) excavated at the temple of Molohai, in the uplands of Kula District, Maui. In its final construction phase, Molohai was a typical stone enclosure of "notched" plan, with an area of 625 square meters, fairly typical of a mid-sized community temple (it was most probably a heiau ho'oulu'ai). Kolb's excavations revealed a four-phase sequence for the site, spanning about five centuries. Notably, the earliest phase (radiocarbon dated to 770 ± 70 radiocarbon years B.P.) consists of a domestic midden. This was superseded by the construction of a stone pavement, also associated with domestic midden deposits, which may or may not represent the first use of the site for ritual purposes. Only in the third and fourth phases (dated to 420 ± 60 and 260 ± 60 B.P. respectively) did the temple become enclosed, and take on the architectural manifestations of a classic Hawaiian *heiau*. Here, it seems to me, is remarkable evidence that at least some Hawaiian temples were constructed atop former dwellings, in keeping with the general Austronesian pattern, and with what we have reconstructed for Ancestral Polynesia.[2]

For my concluding example, I turn to the remote southeastern corner of the Polynesian triangle, where the unique statuary temple complex of Easter Island (Rapanui) has long intrigued ethnographers and archaeologists alike (Métraux 1940; Routledge 1919). The Rapanui temples with their imposing stone *moai* appear as anything but transformed dwellings. Can they possibly represent an endpoint in the transformation of "holy houses"? I cannot here explore this issue in depth, but I believe that there is considerable archaeological evidence to support just such an interpretation. One of the most sacred of all Rapanui temples, the famous Ahu Naunau at Anakena, rises above the beach held in tradition to be the landing place of the island's founding ancestor, Hotu Matua. The temple itself has been archaeologically shown to have been constructed in a lengthy series of phases spanning at least seven centuries. Most notably, based on the excavations by David Steadman and colleagues (1994), it is underlain by a domestic midden deposit dated to approximately A.D. 900.

In a recent reconnaissance of several *ahu moai* temples on Rapanui, I observed that in many instances where the seaward construction faces are exposed by erosion, midden deposits can be seen underlying the later, complex stone constructions. In particular, the site of Hanga Mahiku, along the southeast coast, revealed a wonderful example of two superimposed, low single-stone course platforms (associated with midden and presumably habitation sites) stratigraphically underlying the later temple platform. Certainly such evidence deserves careful investigation and will, I suspect, strengthen the case for interpreting Rapanui ritual architecture—despite its elaborations—within a broader Austronesian framework.

No lengthy conclusion or summation is required. My aim has been to explore one aspect of the concept of "house society" as recently developed by Austronesian scholars, specifically the hypothesis that there is a pervasive and presumably ancient cultural pattern among these societies in which the houses of the living become transformed into houses of the ancestors. Specifically, I have argued that Polynesia—in spite of the apparent architectural elaboration of its ritual spaces that makes it appear to stand apart—can indeed be understood as fitting well within this Austronesian pattern.

Portions of this chapter have been adapted from Chapter 9 of Kirch and Green (in press).

6

The Continuous House

A View from the Deep Past

Ruth Tringham

That the continuity of house location over time was socially meaningful is further demonstrated in Ruth Tringham's diachronic analyses of domestic architecture of the Neolithic era in Southeast Europe. Most of the houses in that time-place were made of clay, and they were frequently burned as part of the life cycle of individual dwellings. Far from being a simple act of destruction, the firing of clay houses transformed them into enduring phenomena. It also facilitated their incorporation into a new structure that replaced the old at the same location, even after the passage of many years, creating a social memory of place in the purposeful action of materially incorporating what had been there before into a new incarnation. Understanding the importance of the endurance of the house, as the most salient material manifestation of the social group associated with it and with the land upon which it was built, is greatly facilitated by the concept of house societies, even in the deep past for which specific information on kinship or marriage alliances is lacking. From a larger perspective, Tringham's comparison of Neolithic house continuity patterns in Southwest Asia and Southeast Europe—the basic dichotomy of "tells" and "not-tells" or "open" sites—reveals an unwarranted bias in understanding the social motivations of house replacement practices, which feeds into the common assumption that Southwest Asia was more precocious in its advancement towards urbanism. She suggests that instead of experiencing differences in a linear evolutionary sense, the peoples of these two regions developed different trajectories in siting their houses—manipulating the built environment—to maintain a continuity of place.

In Europe there are times and places in prehistory when the archaeological record seems to be full of houses—dominated by remains of domestic action. The

Neolithic of Southeast Europe—a time and place where I do my research—is one of these. And there are times and places when houses cannot be found and the record is full of burials, death, and enclosed empty spaces. The subsequent third millennium B.C. over much of Europe is one of these. Why is this? People surely continued to dwell, to be. Is it just a question of preservation? To a certain extent, yes. Yet the question of what gets preserved and what does not is more complicated than the variable effects of the laws of physics and chemistry.

One of the explanations for the variation that perhaps resonates with the "house society" concept is Ian Hodder's contrasting structures: "Domus-focused" (house/home/household social action) versus "Agrios-focused" (field/public arenas/the outside), as seen in his volume, *The Domestication of Europe* (Hodder 1991b). This is the one archaeological work about Europe referred to in *About the House* (Carsten and Hugh-Jones, eds. 1995). In Hodder's volume, the Neolithic of Southeast Europe is thought of as a "Domus-based" society and the third millennium B.C. of Europe is thought of as "Agrios-based."

THE AGE OF CLAY AND ITS ARCHITECTURE

The 8th–5th millennia B.C. in Southeast Europe and the Near East comprise an enormous increase in material elaboration of one material in particular—clay. Clay is made into ceramics, furniture, figurines, weights, balls. In this essay, I am focusing on the use of clay in architecture—in the construction of house walls and floors, immovable furniture, fire installations (ovens, kilns), and the construction of roofs. My colleague Mirjana Stevanović has even gone so far as to call this the Age of Clay (Stevanović 1996, 1997).

The Neolithic[1] architecture of Southeast Europe is characterized by rows or concentric circles or random distributions of detached buildings. These are gabled-roofed rectangular dwellings 6 meters wide and 6–12 meters long, often divided into two or more rooms, that were traditionally built on a framework of upright wooden posts dug into the ground with walls of planks, logs, or wattling covered on one or both surfaces by a thick layer of clay daub (Stevanović and Tringham 1998; Tringham 1991c; Tringham et al. n.d.). Universal firing of the houses at the end of their use-lives has led to this period also being dubbed the Burned House Horizon (Stevanović and Tringham 1998; Tringham 1990).

On the archaeological site the structures appear as a bright orange or red mass of burned collapsed clay rubble in which are impressed the shadows of the wooden framework. The mess made from this event certainly contributes to the good preservation of houses and domestic materials in general. But I think we have to ask *why* in this period were they constructed of clay, and why were they all burned. By contrast, the buildings of Neolithic Anatolia are constructed of walls of unfired mud bricks glued together with thick mortar and plastered over by fine white clay. In some cases they have been burned. They do not seem to form detached buildings, but rather contiguous accretions of flat-roofed rooms around a courtyard.

TELLS AND NOT-TELLS

It is said that in the Southeast European Neolithic there are two kinds of settlements: settlement mounds—closed settlements—known from their Arabic term as "tells," and open settlements, villages that may have a history of several centuries with houses stratified one above the other, but that do not form mounds (Chapman 1989; Tringham 1990; Whittle 1985, 1996). Tells are also characteristic of much of Near Eastern prehistory from the Early Neolithic, for example, at Çatalhöyük, Turkey, to the present day (Lloyd 1980; Mellaart 1975). The apparent absence of non-tell sites in Near Eastern prehistory may not be as universal as we are led to believe by current research.

The physical elements that contribute to the formation of a tell are quite familiar and unambiguous: intensive, not necessarily continuous occupation of a restricted area in combination with vertical—or near-vertical—superimposition of later houses, with settlement debris piling up as each house is placed on top of another and a new house uses the old for its foundations (Rosen 1986). Architecture that uses a large amount of clay is an essential component, as this is a material that is added to the natural landscape and helps mound formation. If the clay is burned, the accumulation is dramatically increased, as is shown in the Southeast European tells.

In Europe, many of us have recognized significant differences between the "tells" of the north and west Balkans (Serbia, Macedonia; e.g., Gomolava, Vinca) and those of the east Balkans (East Bulgaria, Southeast Rumania; e.g., Karanovo). Those of the east Balkans have a greater degree of vertical superimposition of buildings and apparent continuous occupation than those further north and west (Chapman 1989; Tringham 1990) (Figure 6-1). In South Bulgaria, tells started to form from the earliest Neolithic settlements, in contrast to those of West Bulgaria and Serbia. In these latter areas, tells were only rarely formed, and then only once agriculture was well established in the later Neolithic.

At the same time, in some "open" settlements, such as Opovo, there is partial vertical superimposition (the same as partial horizontal displacement) of

| | Tells with vertical superimposition of buildings | | Tells with near horizontal displacement of buildings |
| | Tells with partial vertical superimposition of buildings | | "Open" sites with complete horizontal displacement of buildings |

Figure 6-1. Spatial distribution of Neolithic tells and open settlements in Southeast Europe and Anatolia.

buildings. In Central Europe there is almost no record of "tell" formation at any period; the settlements are all "open" settlements displaying complete horizontal displacement of subsequent houses. On the other hand, in many areas of the Near East, tell settlements were established from the early preceramic Neolithic period, with a much greater degree of vertical superimposition than is ever observed on European prehistoric settlements, with new houses being built within the foundations of old houses (Banning and Byrd 1989).

Thus, an essential variable in understanding the formation (or not) of tell settlements lies in the pattern of replacement of houses. How do we explain this variability in patterns of house replacement? Why does it lead to tells sometimes and at other times not? Is a tell intentionally formed? How, moreover, do we explain the lack of stratified sites, let alone tells, through most of European history? Are European settlements therefore less long-term, less continuous, and concomitantly "less complex"? These are the correlations that are frequently assumed, but that need to be questioned by reference to the empirical data.

The Social Formation of Tells

The formation of tells has traditionally been explained as an adaptive response to particular topographic restrictions on settlement, such as a river or marshland, or even the need for defense. Other possible explanations include unequal social access to land through inheritance and ownership. Douglass Bailey (1990) traced the continuity of specific houses through the twelve "building horizons" recorded in the stratigraphy of a tell (Todorova et al. 1983). He envisaged a world in which there was increasing competition for claims to locus of residence on the mound (tell) and a need to legitimize such claims because of an increasing population. Thus families with an older history would have a stronger claim to residence on the mound itself. Such a need was especially acute in light of Bailey's and Todorova's suggestion that the tells of Southeast Europe were periodically abandoned because of flooding (Bailey 1997). Bailey has an interesting idea that small clay house models that occur in the archaeological record of the "tells" are symbolic aids to the legitimization of these claims during the re-occupation process.

His and some other more recent models draw on the idea of long-term (if punctuated) continuity of occupation and institutionalized attachment to a place as being something that characterizes tell settlements. I would agree with the importance of continuity as a significant variable in the life of a tell. In this essay, however, I shall argue that "open" settlements are not necessarily without such a feeling of continuity and attachment, and that an important variable is how continuity is expressed and achieved through manipulation of the built environment, especially through the aspect of house modification during the latter days of its history and its eventual replacement.

Sedentism or Continuity

The concept of continuity is heavily bound up in archaeological practice with the concept of sedentism. Sedentism dominates (albeit implicitly) all the models of the "Neolithic Revolution" in which it is argued that sedentism is a precondition of complex social organization (Harris 1978; Kaiser and Voytek 1983; Price and Brown 1985; Tringham 1990, 2000; Voytek and Tringham 1988; Wilson 1988; Zvelebil 1989). In order to establish whether a society is "sedentary," archaeologists have defined degrees of sedentism along a continuum, depending on how long the spaces are occupied and to what extent the duration of occupation is the result of intentional planning or of serendipity (Kent, ed. 1989; Kent and Vierich 1989; Rafferty 1985). In social evolutionary terms, the more "permanent" settlements are given more value as probable locations of more complex societies. One of the criteria for defining where along this continuum a space-occupation lies is its apparent continuity of settlement, demonstrated by habitations stratified one above the other in a long sequence.

It has been assumed that the establishment of tell settlements represents a definite increase in sedentism and commitment to a particular location through many generations of time. Tell settlements in Europe and the Near East have been privileged as indicators of early continuous occupation of spaces, that is, sedentism, indicating furthermore that their occupiers were well on their way to social complexity. However, "apparent continuous stratified deposits" can be interpreted in different ways. My aim here is to suggest that, if open sites can be demonstrated to be no less "continuous" in terms of the construction of continuous places, then the absence of tell settlements in most of European prehistory must indicate not so much a lack of social complexity among their inhabitants, but a very different intention in the production of continuity and a very different use of architecture in the construction of remembered places.

HOUSE SOCIETIES

It seems to me that the concept of house societies has a valuable role at this point in enriching our models of how the "continuity of house" itself can have variable meanings and how this can be variably expressed in architecture. As Carsten and Hugh-Jones (1995) observe in their introduction to *About the House*, Lévi-Strauss barely mentioned architecture in his writings on house societies. He was, however, interested in continuity and social memory: "Lévi-Strauss stresses that the house as a grouping endures through time, continuity being assured not only through succession and replacement of its human resources but also through holding onto fixed or movable property and through the transmission of the names, titles and prerogatives which are integral to its existence and identity" (Carsten and Hugh-Jones 1995:7).

Always in the back of the archaeologist's mind in considering "houses" and "households" is the fact that archaeological architecture can be interpreted with more or less equal plausibility in many ways (Tringham 1991a, 1995; Wylie 1992). This means that we can rarely be certain (at least in "prehistory") that a building was a "house," or that a "house" was a "House" in the house society sense, or that a "house" was the place of residence of a "household." Fortunately, this has not prevented archaeologists from using the ideas and data from "household anthropology" to inspire their interpretations and models (Ashmore and Wilk 1988; Tringham 1990; Wilk and Rathje 1982). For example, I have found a valuable source in Eugene Hammel's study of the *zadruga* in Serbia (Hammel and Laslett 1974) for my interpretation of the settlement data of Neolithic Southeast Europe in terms of households as the units of analysis and of social reproduction (Tringham 1990).

There are some elements of the concept that Roxana Waterson (1995a) and a number of others in *About the House* have extracted from Lévi-Strauss's concept of house societies which offer significant contributions to understanding the Neolithic of Southeast Europe and do go beyond "household anthropology" and its economics of land ownership, division of labor, and patterns of inheritance. These include: 1) the meaning of "house" beyond the house building (Ingold 1995); 2) the inclusion and absorption of the culturally constructed landscape, such as trees, in the "house"; 3) the identification of "house" with individuals who dwell in it; and 4) the ability of houses to render invisible and inaudible individual members within the house and within different parts of its segments.

Ensuring Continuity of "Houses" in Neolithic Southeast Europe

Many of the elements I mentioned at the beginning of this paper as being specific to the "house-based" Neolithic Southeast Europe—intense use of clay, burning of houses, tell-formation—can be interpreted as leading towards en-

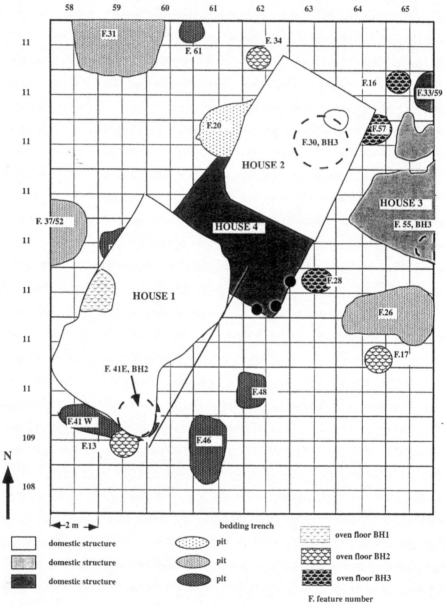

Figure 6-2. Plan of the excavated area of Opovo and the four overlapping house remains.

suring the continuity of houses in the house society sense. In excavating the late Neolithic village of Opovo, Yugoslavia[2] (Figure 6-1), we tried to construct the life history of the 200 years (perhaps eight generations) of the village's occupation in a way which transcends the limitations of the traditional building horizon excavation strategy by investigating each house as though it had a unique life history (Tringham 1994a, 1995). In the area we excavated, we observed four houses with overlapping histories, that is, partial vertical superimposition (Figure 6-2). The builders of the later structures at Opovo (Houses 1 and 2) were probably well aware of the remains of earlier buildings (Houses 3 and 4). The vitrified central part of the remains of House 4 would have been easily visible to the builders of House 1 and 2. But it seems that the exact location of the previous house may not have been known. This impression is made more plausible when we see that the corner of House 2 was placed directly over a former well that had been filled in immediately after the firing of the old house 4. This led to the subsequent partial collapse of the floor in House 2 (Tringham 1994a). Thus we can see at Opovo evidence of direct observation, partial knowledge, and hazy memory of old houses on the place where a new house was built.

Old ovens were frequently incorporated into the foundations of new houses (Figure 6-2). We could interpret these efforts in a rational economic architect-designer mode by suggesting that the builders of the new houses used these old remains to their advantage in the construction of their dwellings, allowing old ovens and clay floors to provide a stable foundation layer and avoiding places of obvious weakness, such as filled-in pits. This may be so, but the intentional treatment of old house material, especially ovens, in this way also ensured a continuity of place. Clay ovens have the triple significance— ugly as they may appear to be to us—of containing fire, being made of clay, and being usable in their indestructible (burned) form (Stevanovič and Tringham 1998; Tringham 1991c).

Clay is a resource that is found close to all the settlements of this time and place. It is full of meaning that can be "read" in many different ways by those willing to try. Its meaning can be read as digging into the bowels of Mother Earth, the Great Goddess, as a material that is feminine because it can be made into anything except a sharp edge, or as the ultimate domestic material. It is heavy, awkward, and hard to carry long distances, and requires water in its use. Yet it is infinitely malleable and boundless in quantity. It can be made into an infinite number of portable and nonportable artifacts. When clay is burned, it is transformed chemically into an indestructible material. Thus clay containers can be used wonderfully for holding, carrying, and storing. It is difficult to burn clay walls, but when they are burned they are preserved forever.

The "Burned House Horizon" has traditionally been taken for granted in European prehistory (e.g., Gimbutas 1991). It has been assumed that no explanation was needed beyond an intuitive common-sense reasoning that the fires were accidental, resulting from the increased use of fire within houses or the denser crowding of houses within villages; or that they were deliberately set due to intersettlement competition, unrest, raiding, and even invasion. Once one starts to question such an assumption, however, and to suggest that the coincidence of the apparently universal occurrence of house fires with socio-economic changes, such as the intensification of production, permanence of settlement, and organizational importance of autonomous households, may be very significant, then the way is opened for a very different research strategy to investigate the burned houses.

This was, in fact, the basis of our systematic investigation of the causes of the house fires at Opovo in Yugoslavia (Stevanović 1997; Stevanović and Tringham 1998; Tringham 1990; Tringham et al. 1985, 1992). On the basis of empirical data from a number of sources at Opovo, we have interpreted the universal burning of houses in the Southeast European Neolithic-Eneolithic as separate house fires, rather than village-wide fires, probably deliberately set (Stevanović 1997; Stevanović and Tringham 1998; Tringham et al., eds. n.d.). This conclusion may be interpreted in a number of ways. It may be explained, for example, as a measure to eradicate pests, insects, or disease. In keeping with examples of house societies, however, I have suggested that a house was set on fire intentionally to signify the death of the household head as a symbolic end of the household cycle, in effect to "kill" the house. Thus the identification of the house with its members has certainly been at the basis of my constructions of these prehistoric places (Tringham 1991a, 1994b).

Efforts were made, sometimes immediately after the burning events, to flatten the burned rubble of the houses and deposit it in pits, in one case filling a probable well. In many other cases the rubble was not used until long after it had lain on the surface and had weathered, to top off garbage pits just before new building was started. The deposition of their rubble in garbage pits and even in a well at Opovo is perhaps part of the "burial rites" of the dead houses to ensure continuity of place. As an alternative interpretation, Mirjana Stevanović (1996, 1997) has recently suggested that burning the wattle-and-daub houses at high temperatures vitrified the clay, thus ensuring that the physical house and its place would be identifiable and remembered for ever—modern farmers can attest to that!

Thus, some of the material remains of the previous houses at Opovo were still observable; others were only memories. To help envisage how continuity of the place we call Opovo-Ugar Bajbuk might have been established through

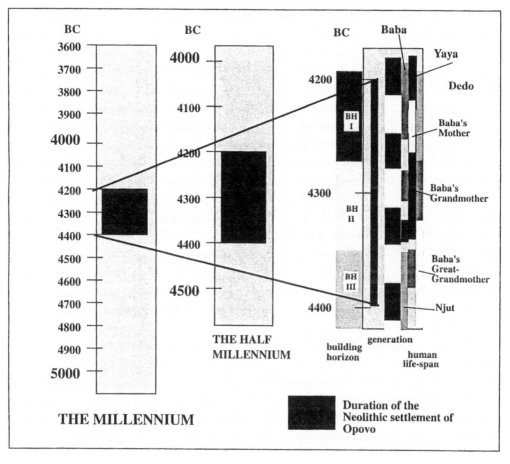

Figure 6-3. Chronological context of the 200 years of occupation at Opovo, from multiple scales of view (Ruth Tringham, the Chimera Web, CD-rom in preparation).

oral memories of the discontinuous cyclical kind that both Paul Connerton (Connerton 1991) and John Berger (Berger 1972) refer to, and through material physical reminders, I have used a narrative format (Tringham 1991a, c, 1994b). I have also tried to express this visually. For example, in the multiscalar chronological chart of the 200 years of occupation of Opovo (Figure 6-3), an evolutionary "bird's-eye" scale can be seen on the two left-hand columns, which are linked along the right-hand side to the microscale "hearth-side" perspective of some imagined social actors living in different houses at Opovo.

This chart is taken from a hypermedia interpretive web of the Opovo

Archaeological Project called the Chimera Web, which has many more such narratives linked to the data. The actors each have a biography, as well as many stories that are like memories of their own experience or that they have heard from others or half-dreamed about. For example, Yaya, who has helped to burn House 1 in the latest building horizon at Opovo, has heard that there was a well (Feature 30) of an old house (House 4) under the one where she dwells now (House 2), since in Divostin (Figure 6-1) she had heard a story about it from Baba's (her co-wife's) mother, who had heard it from her grandmother . . . who used to have to draw water from the well. . . .

Such a narrative format does not produce any "true" facts or picture of prehistoric social action. It has enabled me to follow through an interpretation of the significance of stratified sites, continuity, and memory. It is a means to imagine moments of social action that are linked closely to what we call "moments of archaeological deposition," that is, actual observation of the archaeological record. This is actually the scale at which archaeological excavation is conducted.

When historians, geographers, and ethnographers consider social action and places, they have a wealth of information on individual life histories to which archaeologists just have no access. Archaeologists, however, need not throw up their hands in despair of being able to theorize at a microscale and contribute a prehistory of engendered social action and places. This kind of interpretive dialectical interplay among material remains, comparative historical or ethnographic observation, and imagined actors, acts, and places is designed to encourage and enable us to put into practice a self-critical celebration of the ambiguity of archaeological data.

ENSURING CONTINUITY IN ANATOLIA:
THE ÇATALHÖYÜK EXPERIENCE

I offer, as a contrast to the expression of continuity in an "open" site, my recent experience of the study of the formation of the large East Mound at Çatalhöyük, Turkey[3] (Figure 6-1). This large tell settlement was excavated in the 1960s by James Mellaart (Mellaart 1967), and, since 1993, by a team, under the direction of Ian Hodder, from Cambridge University (Hodder 1997). Since 1997 I have been directing a team (BACH) in close collaboration with this latter group. In this project our aim is to understand the details of the life histories of the different buildings and rooms that led to the formation of the tell in order to investigate the expression of continuity through the built environment.

From the excavation of Building 1 in the northern area of the East Mound have emerged the details of a complex house history (Figure 6-4). The house dates to Mellaart's Occupation Horizon V or VI, but this terminology really does little justice to the complex life history of this building of six phases of modification, including a phase of burning and partial abandonment. Moreover, its meaning clearly did not remain constant through time; part of it was deliberately fired and, through a sequence of more than 50 burials under its floor, at the end it may have been more of an ancestor place.

Çatalhöyük has been popularly claimed as the world's "first city." On the basis of the new excavations, however, it is already clear that the formation of Çatalhöyük is more complex in terms of which parts of which houses were occupied at any one time, and which parts had other meanings and uses at other times, such as garbage dumps, "dead" ancestor places, storage places, and so on. The two neighboring buildings (Buildings 1 and 3), currently being excavated at the northern end of the mound, seem to have been occupied at the same time, but careful microstratigraphic excavation reveals that they were not. Elsewhere on the site, detailed excavation shows that what look under superficial scrutiny to be party (shared) walls are not, and that access from one space to another changes during the history of a house. In other words, its formation is not like a layer cake, but more like an anthill.

Our preliminary research on this topic suggests that continuity of settlement at the tell of Çatalhöyük is explicitly expressed in the life histories of the houses themselves, from the location of new rooms in close proximity and relation to formerly active rooms, through the constant and regular renewal of living surfaces, to the final abandonment of rooms by everyone except the ghosts of the many skeletons buried beneath their floors.

TELLS AND NOT-TELLS AGAIN

These details of house positioning and life histories, the re-use of old features, the memory about the house as place, are all part of the variable pattern of house replacement that holds the key to understanding the distinction between tells and not-tells. In order to develop this idea, I have to make a short excursion to the macroscale of social evolution and cultural variability between continents. In addition to the marked contrasts in prehistoric architecture between Europe and the Near East that I described at the beginning of this paper, a contrast in historical trajectory between the two land masses has long been an accepted part of "common knowledge": Europe north of the Mediterranean

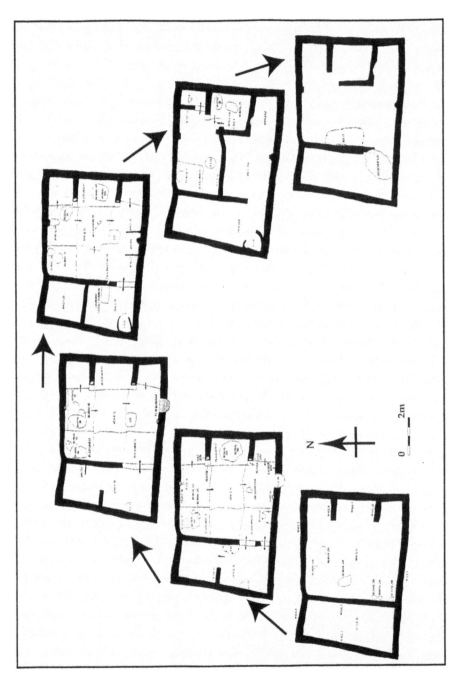

Figure 6-4. Schematic drawing of phases in the life history of Building 1 at Çatalhöyük.

littoral characterized by a lack of urban settlements and centralized authority until the end of the first millennium B.C., in contrast to the Near Eastern pattern of cumulative growth of population density and centralized organization toward fully urban settlements by 3000 B.C. or even earlier. This contrast may have been noticed, but it has rarely been thought of as needing an explanation beyond "the challenge of the European environment," the "distance of interior Europe from the early centers of agriculture," lack of "creative incentive," and so on. Many complex explanations, however, have been devised for the development of urban states in the Near East, starting with V. Gordon Childe (1951). The creativity of archaeologists for devising explanations for their absence in Europe has been remarkably impoverished (Tringham 1996).

One traditional viewpoint suggests that the Neolithic settlements of Southeast Europe (or Old Europe) would have progressed toward an urban state by the third millennium B.C., had not the Indo-Europeans from the east invaded and brought this process to a swift halt (Gimbutas 1991). An alternative explanation is that, in Europe, the social structure based on the organizing functions of the household as the unit of social and economic cooperation, including the control of labor and land that had been established in the late Neolithic period, remained the dominant social unit of economic and social action throughout the prehistory of Europe, until the Romanization of Europe (Bogucki 1988; Chapman 1990a; Tringham 1991a; Tringham et al. 1992). I can even expand this idea to suggest that throughout European prehistory there was a resistance to centralizing trends by decentralizing and fissioning of settlement along household lines.

John Chapman (1989, 1990b) has suggested, however, that this model of the household as a unit of social reproduction may not be applicable to the tell sites of the east Balkans in Bulgaria. He has suggested that the close-knit and clearly conforming plan of houses on the Bulgarian tells indicates a centrally organized authority at the village level who maintained control of land tenure and inheritance, of labor in production and reproduction, and of the intentionality of house construction, destruction, and replacement as well as the use of land for cultivation, for pasture, for the disposal of garbage, and for the burial of the dead. He contrasts this situation on tells, such as Karanovo and Polyanitsa, with the hypothesized situation in "open" settlements, such as Selevac and Opovo, where, it has been suggested, each household could and did act independently in these regards. If I extend John Chapman's idea to the tells of Anatolia, such as Çatalhöyük, I could suggest that from the very beginning of Çatalhöyük's existence the household was never an independent unit of social reproduction but always part of a centralized village-wide organization. The question would still have to be posed *why* that particular social formation was

	EUROPE "open" sites (e.g., Opovo, Selevac)		ANATOLIA tells (e.g., Çatalhöyük)
Method of house replacement	"Open" sites with complete horizontal displacement of buildings	↕	Tells: of vertically superimposed buildings
Passage between and within houses	Detached houses in independent space	↕	"Houses" are contiguous rooms, accretions around a courtyard
Burials	Burials distant from residence	↕	Frequent burial within houses under floors and platforms
The end of the life history of a house	"Killed" by burning	↕	Changed into "ancestor place"
Symbolic expression	Anthropomorphic figurines deposited broken in pits	↕	Murals and relief sculpture decoration on walls
Patterns of dominance	Aggregate of independent households	↕	Village of centrally organized households
Means of resistance	Ability for single household to fission	↕	Fixed attachment to place makes it difficult to fission.
Social memory of place established by	Informal gossip and storytelling	↕	Formal ritualized performance

Figure 6-5. Continuum of house replacement patterns and other material correlates, from Europe to the Near East.

adopted. But is it possible that this was one of the crucial variables that set the settlements of the Near East on their path to urbanism, thus reifying the contrast between the Near East as "cradle of civilization" and Europe as its "periphery"?

In an effort to resist a simplified seductive dichotomy, I have attempted to construct a continuum of material correlates with the open sites of Serbia (and much of the rest of Europe) at one end, and the Near Eastern tell settlements such as Çatalhöyük at the other (Figure 6-5). By extension I think we can even propose a difference (after Connerton) in how social memory of place is established by formal ritualized performance (the right side of the chart) versus by informal gossip and story-telling (the left side).

In looking at the absence of tells and vertical superimposition and ancestors in the houses of Europe as resistance to, rather than a lack of a direction *toward* complexity, we can view the "open sites" of much of European prehistory as following an alternative trajectory in which the creation, maintaining, and memory-making of places is of a *different* kind. Neither the open site nor the tell site is more nor less continuous. In these different trajectories, an essential difference has been the use of the built environment to create the continuity of place. Tells become explicit symbols of continuity as soon as vertical superimposition of houses starts. Open sites are always invisible or rather more subtle places. I believe, however, that this more subtle use of building materials was an equally powerful means.

Archaeology Contributes to the "House Society" Concept

I don't think that we yet understand all the variable ways that continuity of place can be expressed by house replacement, either archaeologically in the ground or in ethnographic settlements. That is, the idea of continuity of place has yet to be explored in detail. The concept of house societies is designed to enable this exploration. Much of the house society literature seems to describe a static situation of what *is* at a particular place and time, whereas archaeology is necessarily focused on transformational contexts—evolutionary change and historical trajectories and life histories. For now, therefore, the significance of the Burned House Horizon and Tells and not-Tells distinction, and the time-and-place with houses and without houses is nowhere near resolution. On the other hand, not to seem inappropriately ambitious, I would like to hope that by its focus on time, history, continuity, and memory of the "house-place," archaeology can make a contribution to coaxing the house society into dynamic historical explorations.

CONTINUITY AND SOCIAL MEMORY OF PREHISTORIC PLACES

The distinction between tells and not-tells as I have described it thus far can seem to have far-reaching consequences for our understanding of the different historical trajectories of Europe and the Near East. But for the many inhabitants of Turkey, Bulgaria, Yugoslavia, and Greece, whose lives my archaeology has touched, it remains essentially an academic intellectual problem that could have ramifications in some mysterious echelons of power in the European Union. Tells are huge mounds that emerge from the surrounding plain or river valley. Like the megalithic monuments of Atlantic Europe, they make a difference to the skyline, and are obvious relics of the cultural heritage (Bender 1998). They have always been the focus of archaeologists' research, wherever they occur. Like the megalithic monuments of Britain, they direct the archaeologists' construction of the past. In Britain, where local viewers of megaliths are as likely to have gone to Eton or Cambridge University as the archaeologists, there is a strong commonality of intent between archaeologist and non-archaeologist in the preservation of what is seen as the cultural heritage of Britain.

Archaeologists are surprised, however, when these tells are not viewed with the same reverence by villagers in Southeast Europe and Anatolia. The mound of Çatalhöyük, for example, is one of the very few prehistoric sites that have been classed as a World Heritage site to be protected by international law. A condition of Ian Hodder's permit set by the Turkish government is quite rightly the conservation of the prehistoric buildings. Their desire is the preservation of what they see as a national treasure, one that should be visited and appreciated by people from all over the world for many generations to come. A vast educational interpretive center is being planned. In the National Antiquities Museum in Ankara, Çatalhöyük warrants a whole gallery to itself, and it is constantly packed with visitors. However, David Shankland, a social anthropologist from Lampeter, has been able to glean very little interest in the site and its history on the part of the local villagers who live and work around Çatalhöyük. This mound is simply not interesting to them as a place, apart from the gossip that somebody recently was buried on it.

In Bulgaria, the tell of Podgoritsa, which I excavated as part of an ill-fated project in 1995, had been partially plowed over until it became registered as a national historic monument in the early 1950s. Strict laws from Sofia protected monuments from agriculture and looting. With the de-communization of Bulgaria in 1990, the laws were not changed, but they were more loosely enforced, and the lure of private enterprise encouraged a huge increase in the looting of prehistoric sites. Tells and burial mounds were obvious targets for a metal object, or a clay figurine, or even a pot, all of which would bring wealth on the free market. At present, looting is a huge underground industry there, definitely with organized crime connections (Bailey 1993). The site of Podgoritsa had a large looter's trench that had been dug with a bulldozer sometime between 1990 and 1993. That's one side of the story.

The other side of the story is that a condition was added to our permit to excavate, namely, that our research should not stop until we had excavated to the base of the tell with a profile that stretched across it. This caveat is attached to many sites in Southeast Europe—to excavate in your chosen area down to the sterile subsoil—and is intended, I think, to prevent research that is stopped halfway through lack of interest or funds, so that at least a chronological picture is retrieved of when a site was created. In the case of Podgoritsa, it meant that we had a mandate to excavate half of the whole mound, and possibly more. Not only was this an elephantine task in itself, but in the way we would be excavating, it would take certainly the whole of the rest of my lifetime, and I doubted it could be funded.

Another element also crept into the equation. I became increasingly uncomfortable with the idea of destroying a place that had been part of the landscape of rural Northeast Bulgaria for 6000 years. But my construction of this place was clearly different from that of my Bulgarian colleagues, who felt no such discomfort, and it was clearly different from that of the local Bulgarian villagers, who viewed our activities as a source of work and money and as the construction of future good agricultural land. In the end, I terminated the project, and the tree on top of the mound survived. My feeling toward the preservation of Bulgarian cultural heritage was definitely a factor, but there were other reasons that I will be happy to discuss. I am ambivalent about excavating tells, of destroying these places in the name of science. I could discuss this in relation to the poetic geographer Douglas Porteous's concept of topocide and domicide (Porteous 1995), and see whether I can resolve what I am doing at the much larger tell of Çatalhöyük, but I believe this would take me into realms of another paper.

It is a very different experience to excavate in an "open" non-tell site. The sites of Opovo and Selevac in Yugoslavia both started off as cultivated fields and ended as nicely turned more fertile fields after we had removed the debris of burned clay rubble. Even though there was no obvious sign on the landscape, however, the farmers who plowed the field were just as aware of these sites as prehistoric places, if not more so. In coming into contact every day with burned rubble, ceramic sherds, stone tools, in the regular daily and seasonal cycle of cultivation in their fields, it seemed that the villagers had incorporated these places into their village's social memory (Connerton 1991). They talked about them, they were interested in them, they would come for hours to watch us excavate them, they would take an active interest in excavating with us. These places were not something "other" to them like a mound, they were not their link to "the past," they were just part of their enduring memories that had been gossiped about through many generations and made part of their village's experience (Berger 1979:9).

Similarly, in Kipling's *Puck of Pook's Hill*, his history of England emerges out of visits that his time-traveling heroes make, not to explicit monuments of the past—megalithic tombs or burial mounds or standing stones—but to subtle places that had been constructed in the past by social action—a path, a spring, a tree, or a field (Kipling 1951 [1906]). It is the subtlety of these prehistoric places, which I have shown may have had as much continuity (or more) as places as the more explicit obvious symbols of the past, that I find heartening.

I'll end with a story, told to me first by Ilia Radulovic (later I heard it from others)—for her it was part of the social memory of her village, on the opposite hill—of the site of Staro Selo near the village of Selevac. "Once there was a great place there, with houses that were so close together a cat could jump from one roof to another. One day, the whole village was burned and destroyed in a great fire and the people moved away." So much for our idea of separate intentional conflagrations! Remember, this site was occupied for 500 years 6000 years ago; no subsequent remains are known in its fields. The houses are about a yard apart, but we were the first to excavate at Selevac. And—yes—we did find the remains of a cat!

7

Maya "Nested Houses"
The Ritual Construction of Place

Susan D. Gillespie

Lévi-Strauss's minimal discussion of the physical house concerned how, as a central symbol of unity, it was conceived and created as a miniature image of the universe. The representation of the house as microcosm has been well documented for many societies, including the Maya peoples of Mesoamerica, and is related to overlapping notions of the house and the body, a means by which people and houses are co-identified. Susan Gillespie draws on ethnographic and archaeological data encompassing over two millennia of Maya occupation to look beyond the mere form of the Maya house as microcosm and examine the active agency of the social house members who used their dwellings and analogous constructions to orient themselves and the spirits with whom they interacted within a specific locus in space. These spirits include the ancestral dead, who are ritually contacted at domestic altars that are miniature houses at the same time that they are made to resemble beds, resting places associated with immobility, permanence, and potency. Archaeological evidence demonstrates the longevity of this practice, which once involved burying the dead under altars or beds within the house compound and constructing miniature houses as containers for certain spirits that were part of the intangible estate of noble houses. In enclosing and thus unifying diverse elements, the house is a means of creating place and sociocosmic order within the landscape. Building such order into existence requires specific ritual actions to produce and activate all these material houses, actions undertaken by those who thereby define themselves as a group with a common stake in the house.

In choosing the word "house" to name a social category , Claude Lévi-Strauss (1982:172) recognized a very common indigenous practice whereby the term for a social group is the same as that for the physical structure in which house members live or carry out ritual activities, or which otherwise can represent their ties with one another and with other houses. He never developed an analysis of the physical house, concentrating instead on the corporate group and the strategies of kinship and affinity that reproduced it (Carsten and Hugh-Jones 1995:45). Nevertheless, his ideas have led others to pay more attention to the relations constructed and dynamically enacted between houses as buildings and houses as social groupings (Hugh-Jones 1995:251), especially in house societies, where a heavy load of significance is borne by the physical house precisely because of its close identity with its inhabitants (Keane 1995:110). In house societies there is a more immediate co-signification of the physical house as place—a specific location in a spatial network—and the social house as place—a locus within a network of relationships. These two allied concepts of house as place anchor people within society in both practice and ideation (Forth 1991; Waterson 1990:91–92).

Another common means of expressing the joint identity of people and houses is conceiving the house as a living being, that is, personifying the house (Carsten and Hugh-Jones 1995:43). This is discursively expressed by using the same terms to names body parts and house parts, indicating an analogous, even homologous, relationship between the two. Both are containers for the entities that inhabit them—the person within a physical body, the group of such bodies within a house (e.g., Errington 1979:13; Kan 1989:63–64).[1] Houses also have a life cycle like humans (Carsten and Hugh-Jones 1995:42)—they must be brought to life, regularly nurtured, and mourned upon their deaths, and they may experience reincarnation. As living entities, houses are often thought to have a spiritual counterpart or soul. Roxana Waterson's (1990:115) study of the "living house" linked these beliefs in Southeast Asia to the widely shared concept of a vital force that animates the universe, referred to as *semangat* or its cognates. Everything shares in this life force, which is sometimes viewed as a soul, a discrete portion of invisible energy housed, or made manifest, within a material container. The house may acquire its life force from the method of construction, for example, by being built of living trees that are "planted" in a prescribed way as house posts, or it may become animated via a ceremony performed when the house is completed or dedicated (Waterson 1990:121, 1993: 223–24).

The link between the house and the body goes beyond a sharing of form, identity, and life force: "the body and the house are the loci for dense webs of signification and affect and serve as basic cognitive models used to structure, think and experience the world" (Carsten and Hugh-Jones 1995:3). It is with regard to the house as such a model that Lévi-Strauss made his brief remarks on the physical house, commenting on how the dwelling could function as a fetish in house societies, such as the Karo Batak of Sumatra and the Atoni of Timor, among whom "the wealth of decoration, the complicated architecture, the symbolism attaching to each element in the total construction, the arrangement of furniture and the distribution of its inhabitants make of the house *a veritable microcosm* reflecting in its smallest details *an image of the universe* and of the whole system of social relations" (Lévi-Strauss 1987:156, emphasis added).

The sociocosmic symbolism of the physical house is especially well documented for Southeast Asian house societies in studies that explicate the analogies between the categories and organizing principles of residential architecture and those of society in general, and ultimately of the cosmos itself as the largest order representation.[2] Some of these studies have been criticized, however, for privileging the house as the most unitary or exemplary cosmic representation. As Roy Ellen (1986:3) and Roxana Waterson (1988:54, 1990:xvii) have observed, the house is one of several such symbolic models, along with the human body and the village, for example, "all of which feed into each other and within which the meanings of symbols or their opposition to each other may shift according to context" (Waterson 1988:54).

In this essay I draw on ethnographic, ethnohistorical, and archaeological information to examine the physical house as a microcosmic model for Maya peoples that both anchors people in place and orients their proper movements in space. "Maya" refers to a large cultural-linguistic subarea of Mesoamerica whose geographic boundaries extend from the Yucatan peninsula south to the Pacific coast, encompassing southern Mexico and parts of adjacent Central America (Figure 7-1). This region was populated by persons speaking related (Macro-Mayan) languages throughout most of the known prehispanic period (ending c. 1525 A.D.). Large, complex polities developed here in the Classic period (c. 250–1000 A.D.), especially in the tropical forest lowlands of the central region. The famous hieroglyphic texts inscribed on stone monuments and portable objects date to this period. The last centuries of the Classic into the subsequent Postclassic period (A.D. 1000–Spanish conquest) saw a decline in population in the southern lowlands, but important political developments occurred in the northern lowlands of the Yucatan peninsula and in the southern highlands bordering the Pacific Ocean. Ethnohistoric evidence recorded in the early Spanish Colonial period referring to Postclassic practices and beliefs is especially rich for these two widely separated regions, and it is here that most descendants of the ancient peoples, several million Maya speakers, live today.

The Maya construct artificial images of their universe in multiple manifes-

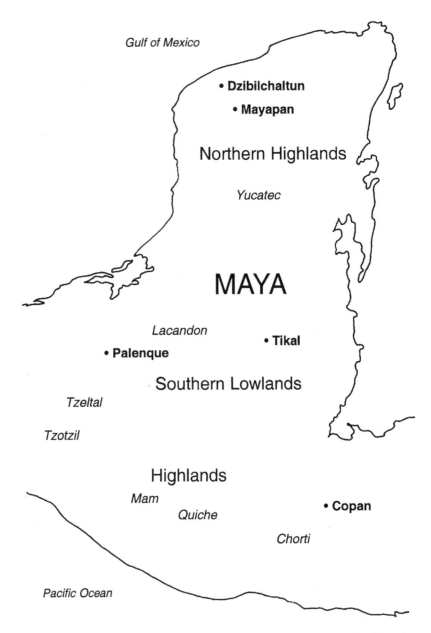

Figure 7-1. Maya area showing its division into subareas, with major archaeological sites and modern language groups mentioned in the text.

tions within the landscape, notably their farm fields, houses, and the altars they use in domestic rituals. In addition, small nonfunctional houses have been recovered archaeologically and may be interpreted as having a meaning similar to that of the altars, sheltering the spirits of gods and ancestors. In practical discourse these various phenomena are linked because they share a common form—a square or rectangle with marked corners—referencing the four-quartered universe. However, this iconic analogy is inadequate, first because it is static, based only on the form of things and not their creation or use, and second because it is incomplete, since some nonrectilinear objects are also referred to as houses. Furthermore, these phenomena are all spatially interrelated according to a dominant concentric orientation to space, such that multiple microcosmic models are nested one within another and therefore evoke one another within a proxemic structure or "semiospace"—space as a system of signs (Drummond 1996).

Creating and activating these cosmic models requires both utilitarian and ritual actions, and it is this agency, not the resulting form, that is highlighted here. The ritual actions in particular manifest another major structuring principle that underlies the system of social relations within space—the complementary opposition of passivity and movement associated with centers and peripheries, which is also common, and better described, in Southeast Asian societies (e.g., Cunningham 1965:372; Errington 1989; Waterson 1990:192–93). Among the Maya, passive behaviors—sitting, resting, and sleeping—are intimately connected to houses; one who is seated in his house is in his place, representing a microcenter. Spirits and ancestors are also petitioned once they have been immobilized, usually by sitting in their own houses. But creating a house as a still and stable center requires the actions of people around its periphery, often enacted as a counterclockwise movement in a ritual that simultaneously identifies the persons who engage in it, or on whose behalf it is undertaken, as a specific social group localized to that space.

The "house" is thus an exemplary symbolic structure represented in multiple material constructs, including actual dwellings. It represents the conjunction of the concrete/visible and the immaterial/invisible components of life. It is a product of the enabling actions of specific impermanent, mortal persons to foster empowering contractual relationships with the generalized unchanging, energetic force, manifested as ancestors and gods. This force originates on the periphery of the world (the space-time of the primordium), a place of dangerous potency, but portions of it can be invoked and even monopolized by social groups if properly contained and located within the boundaries of a house. When materialized and ritually activated, real houses and related microcosmic models—each individually bounded in its spatial extent but simultaneously interpenetrating, one inside another—can potentially provide every-one and everything a proper place.

MAYA HOUSES AND HOUSE SOCIETIES

Although Maya house builders today are rapidly converting to modern mate-rials, earlier in this century many houses were still being constructed in ways little changed over the last 2000 years or more (Wauchope 1934:123–24). Despite some variation in overall form (rectilinear or oval), shape of the roof, and building materials, houses today and of the past conform to very similar techniques (Wauchope 1938).[3] The buildings are generally framed with tree trunks at the four corners and along the sides, their bases placed in deep holes excavated into the earth. The tops of the trunks are cut off where the branches emerge, leaving a notch to hold the transverse beams that run along the top of the walls. The roof frame is built separately and erected on top of the wall structure, often with an attic of slender poles laid out across the transverse beams, and the roof itself is thatched. The walls are composed of split sticks or canes (sometimes covered with mud, leaves, or plaster), of earth mixed with plant materials, or of sun-dried mud bricks (Wauchope 1934:125–26). Fur-nishings are sparse, usually consisting of beds or hammocks, a table altar, and low stools or tiny chairs for the men to sit on. Close by the main house are other buildings (kitchens, sweat houses, storehouses, a shrine building, animal pens, raised seed beds, and subsidiary dwellings), together with cleared spaces used for many activities, forming a residential compound with surrounding fruit trees and nearby agricultural fields.

The houses sheltered the dead as well as the living. Ethnohistoric evi-dence from Yucatan in the early colonial period indicates that most of the dead were buried under or immediately around their houses (Landa 1982[1566]: 59), although high-ranking persons were interred (as inhumations or crema-tions) in special shrine buildings (1982:59), or, in the Guatemala highlands, on mountain-tops (Las Casas 1967[1555–59]:2:526). Burial under house floors was also known as late as the turn of the last century in some remote settle-ments (e.g., Blom and La Farge 1926–27:2:361–62; Thompson 1930:82), and the Chorti Maya maintained family burial plots within the individual house compounds (Wisdom 1940:119). One explicit reason for this practice was that it would allow the soul of the deceased to re-enter the corporeal world in the body of the next child born in that house or an adjacent one (Thompson 1930:82). This practice reflects a common Maya belief that the souls (and names) of ancestors are passed down to succeeding generations (Carlsen and

Prechtel 1991:26; Vogt 1969:372–73; Watanabe 1990:139). Today the dead are usually buried in community cemeteries.

In the prehispanic era, commoner houses were not much different from those described ethnographically. However, archaeological evidence provides many examples of how the Maya nobility expressed their differences from commoners in the elaboration of their houses and their associated graves. Noble or upper-class houses may have been made of similar materials but were larger and raised up on earthen or stone platforms. Some buildings were elaborate stone and masonry constructions with vaulted roofs and multiple rooms, erected on huge rubble-filled platforms faced with cut stone. They were ornamented with decorations in stucco, paint, and carved stone. In the Classic period stone slabs with engraved portraits and accompanying hieroglyphic texts were erected within the royal house compounds of the paramounts who headed the major Maya polities.

Archaeologically identified house compounds, built around common patio areas, are presumed to have been inhabited by social groups who maintained an identity and association with a single place over many generations, for many of them were constantly modified and enlarged (Hendon 1991). The compounds often include recognizable shrine structures for the veneration of family ancestors (e.g., Haviland 1968:109, 1981, 1988; McAnany 1995:66, 104; Tourtellot 1988), an interpretation based on information provided by ethnohistoric sources and contemporary Maya peoples (e.g., McAnany 1995; Nash 1970; Watanabe 1990). Associated with some of these shrines were the actual physical remains of deceased persons. The rarer cases of shrines of the royal dead include impressive temples built atop tall pyramidal platforms erected over subsurface tombs (Welsh 1988:190).

The Maya today view their ancestors as a generic, generally anonymous group that includes both males and females, whose ties to their living descendants are not delineated beyond four to six generations at the most (Gillespie 1995). Ancestors are frequently referred to as "mother-fathers," a term that recognizes relationships through both the paternal and maternal lines (Watanabe 1990:139). Nevertheless, despite the absence of a uniline of named forebears, among the Maya as among peoples of Southeast Asia (e.g., Fox 1993:16–17) the continuity of houses and their claims to land and other property was and still is grounded in ties to their ancestral origins. "As keepers of the land and givers of life . . . [Maya] ancestors fuse local affinities and generational continuity to the very landscape itself" (Watanabe 1990:139).

While the long-lived multifamily groupings that occupied the prehispanic residential compounds are usually interpreted as patrilineages (e.g., Haviland 1992; Hopkins 1988; McAnany 1995), multiple lines of evidence indicate that the ancient Maya, like the central Mexican Aztecs,[4] were organized into houses in the Lévi-Straussian sense, although our best information pertains only to the upper stratum of society (Gillespie 1995, 1999; Gillespie and Joyce 1997).[5] Following Lévi-Strauss's example, it seems wise to consider Maya concepts and terminology to understand their social groups. The most frequently encountered word for the multifamily group with its own identity and estate is "house" (e.g., Vogt 1969:140; Wisdom 1940:248). A common lowland Maya term for house is *na*; a highland Maya cognate is *ha*. Documents from sixteenth-century Guatemala relate epic legends of the origins of the four intermarrying noble houses, the *nimha* (literally "great house" in Quiche Maya), each of which had attached vassal groups and was further objectified by a temple-shrine in the capital city for commemorative rituals to its ancestral origins (*Popol Vuh* 1996; *Título de Totonicapán* 1983:38, 204 pictures the four house shrines).

In the lowland Cholan and Yucatec languages, a distinction is made between a house in general (*na*) and one that belongs to someone, a possessed house (*otot* in Cholan, *otoch* in Yucatec). Both categories of houses appear in the prehispanic hieroglyphic inscriptions in which houses are individually named, especially in the context of dedication and termination rituals (Freidel and Schele 1989; Stuart 1998). For example, the Late Classic site of Palenque, Mexico has long texts that relate the local version of the cosmogony, part of a marvelously detailed life history of the ruling house at the turn of the seventh century. In this account a primordial creator deity metaphysically established a named house, *otot*, in the sky as the first significant act of the creation. The text continues with the activities of legendary predecessors followed by a historical event—the dedication of a real named building (*na*) as an *otot*—by the paramount who commissioned the inscription (Schele and Freidel 1990:246–51).

Because of the great geographic extent and vast time span of societies encompassed by the term "Maya," Maya houses and house societies are likely to represent the same degree of diversity found in other world regions, such as Indonesia (e.g., Macdonald, ed. 1987). Nevertheless, across the Maya area past and present, the definitional critieria for the house established by Lévi-Strauss can be found, and it is possible to speak generically of the Maya house. Moreover, even if the Maya were not all organized as house societies, it remains the case that ethnographic and archaeological evidence reveal how the Maya conception of the house as an exemplary model emerges from their experiences of inhabiting and operating within and around their house compounds, and of organizing productive relations as social houses. The physical house is more than an objectified text reflecting social and cosmic relations; it is a locus and frame for daily activities out of which meanings are constituted (e.g., Earle 1986; see also Bourdieu 1973; Errington 1979; Lok 1987; Ruan 1996).

THE MAYA HOUSE AS MICROCOSM

Many Maya ethnographers have commented on the overlapping symbolic structures represented by the house and the cosmos. For example, the highland Quiche Maya construct their houses to mimic the vertical dimensions of their mountainous terrain. The walls are of mud brick made from earth taken nearby, but the attic and roof are all of wood, brought from the forests on the mountain slopes. Thus, the vertical dichotomy of mountain and valley is repeated in the vertical orientation of trees and earth as construction materials (Earle 1986:166).

More frequently, the horizontal segmentation of the cosmos into four cardinal directions or quadrants is signified by the form and structure of houses and certain analogous phenomena, especially the table altar and the maize field (*milpa*). Evon Vogt (1976:11) cited a Tzotzil Maya informant's statement that the universe is "like a house, like a table" and concluded that "all preeminent cultural symbols are square." Charles Wisdom (1940:43) made the same observation for the Chorti Maya: "The square is the only sacred plane, since it has the form of the milpa and the altar and has four corners. *The milpa and altar represent the universe in miniature.* The Indian sometimes refers to his altar as his little milpa, and to the world, as a great milpa. It is said that houses must be rectangular or square in order to be like milpas. The candles set up at the four corners of the altar are said to be both its corner posts (as if it were a house) and its boundary markers (as if it were a milpa [marked at each corner by a coral tree])" (emphasis added).

The house, the table altar, and the milpa are all four-sided; hence they mimic the cosmic form. Though not actually square, villages are also thought of as having four sides, each with an entryway guarded by a shrine composed of one or more crosses atop a stone or masonry altar (e.g., Nash 1970:292–93 for Tzeltal Maya; Sosa 1989 for Yucatec; Vogt 1976:11 for Tzotzil). The cited examples indicate that the square form is explicitly marked on its four corners or its four sides in some way—the corner posts of a house, the trees that mark the corners of a maizefield, the candles set on the four corners of the altar, and the cross shrines at the four entrances to the village.

Maya houses, like those elsewhere, are also considered analogous to another microcosmic model, the human body. The overlapping of names of house and body parts is not uncommon. However, in this respect, it is more often the body that is presumed to take primacy for orienting spatial relationships; the house derives its organization of fixed parts from the body (Earle 1986:163). For example, the door is the "mouth" of the Quiche house, and the porch posts are its "legs." Additional terms from Tzotzil Maya include the house wall as a "stomach," the foundation rock as a "foot," the corner as an "ear," and the roof as a "head" (Vogt 1969:71). The Tzotzil also place their own bodily detritus—the hair that is combed from their heads—into the cracks of the house walls each day to further materially mark their co-identification with their houses (1969:465). The same body part names are also given to other phenomena, including mountains, maize fields, and tables. In more general terms, a mountain, a field, a house, a table, and a human body are oriented to a single spatial model (1969:580).

The Tzeltal Maya give an additional rationale for equating humans, houses, and the cosmos based on their shared origins. In their cosmogonic accounts, the earth was created from the sea, the first humans were made out of this earth, and the houses they build likewise have earthen walls. From this homology of creation comes the idea that houses, like humans, must be fed or nourished, and a ceremonial "meal for the house" is provided when the structure is first completed (Nash 1970:13; see Vogt 1969:462 for the Tzotzil Maya). It is also at this house dedication ritual that the house acquires a soul or spirit inhabitant—ch'ulel in Tzeltal and Tzotzil (Nash 1970:16; Vogt 1969:71). Among the Quiche of Chinique, the house spirit is personalized and believed to be the soul of the original owner of the house who must regularly be offered "rent" in the form of candles and incense; otherwise, the house will "die." When a new Quiche house is to be built, the house altar is the first thing constructed at the site, and it is here that the spirit, the original house owner, has its place (Earle 1986:164–65). For the Yucatec (Redfield and Villa Rojas 1962 [1934]:147) and Tzotzil Maya (Vogt 1969:71), however, the house spirit guardian is more impersonalized, consisting of a portion of the diffuse vital force that, like its Indonesian counterpart, animates the Mesoamerican cosmos.[6]

Ancestors, as spirit beings, are sometimes believed to live in their own houses, which may or may not be the houses they occupied while living. Among the Quiche of Chichicastenango, the spirits of the dead have definite places of residence, especially within their former houses. Here they are "invoked as private persons, as family men and women maintaining order in their homes" (Bunzel 1952:270). Among other groups, the ancestors reside in natural features that are within the visible landscape, but usually beyond the settled areas. The Tzeltal Maya of Tzo'ontahal believe that the ancestors dwell in a specific cave (Nash 1970:22). Their Tzotzil neighbors say that certain mountains contain the houses of the ancestors (Vogt 1969:298–300). The ancestors are the metaphysical link connecting the members of the house to their origins, and they continue to intervene in the daily experiences of the living. They protect their collective descendants from evil, but will also punish them for breaching social and ritual mores, especially those codified as *costumbres,* "customs" (Bunzel 1952:268; Vogt 1969:300; Watanabe 1990).

The focus for venerating ancestors and similar guardian spirits is an altar or shrine, often located within the house or immediately outside, although some groups also erect ancestral altars on their farmland or other property they claim which is guarded by their ancestors. Altars consist of a raised flat surface provided by a table or platform upon which objects are placed, including crosses (which can be very large), images of saints, food, liquor, candles, incense, flowers, and other offerings. The altar can thereby function as the "ritual attractor" of the house, some object which "has a pre-eminence among the other parts of the house and, as such, represents, in a concentrated form, the house as a whole" (Fox 1993:1). As already noted, the altar is constructed according to the same spatial referents as the house and is considered a small-scale model of the cosmos (Earle 1986:165; Sosa 1989:139; Vogt 1969:403; Wisdom 1940:283).

Although the altar appears to be a Christian introduction—the table form was introduced by the Spaniards and the altar is topped with Christian symbols—it has prehispanic roots (Deal 1987). It is a place for performing rituals to ancestors and indigenous earth deities as well as Christian saints. Even the cross has prehispanic origins and non-Christian signification. The Yucatec Maya refer to the cross as the *ya'axche',* "green tree" (Sosa 1989:137). This same word names the silk-cotton tree (*Ceiba pentandra*), whose branches take on a cross-like shape when the tree is young. The ceiba tree, which grows to be very tall with a large canopy of leaves, is the premier *axis mundi* in Maya cosmology. Ceibas are frequently planted in town centers and used in rituals (e.g. Redfield 1936), and some Maya peoples posited that their ancestors emerged out of the earth via the roots of the ceiba tree (León-Portilla 1988:139). The souls of the virtuous dead were believed by the colonial Yucatec Maya to rest in the shade of a great ceiba (Landa 1982[1566]:60), and their later Christianized counterparts stated that this same tree was a ladder used by souls to climb to heaven (Tozzer 1907:154).

The green color of the *ya'axche'* cross indicates that is is alive (Sosa 1989: 137). Cross-trees are not simply living things; they contain within them the potent force that animates the universe. For example, the four Yucatec town crosses specifically shelter the spirit guardians of the town (Sosa 1989:138). The living aspect of a tree is also the salient factor in choosing materials to make Tzotzil crosses. The wooden cross of the Tzotzil Maya is really a framework for draping fresh green pine boughs, and if no cross is available, arranging boughs on the ground or against a house wall to form a cross shape will serve just as well (Vogt 1969:586). The Tzotzil cross shrines are likewise points of contact with the spirit world, places where ancestors will sit and wait for offerings (Vogt 1964:499–500).

The analogy between the house as a container for the living and the dead, and the altar with its crosses as the place for the souls of the dead or other animating spirits, can be carried further in that the altar is often made or viewed as a miniature house. The Yucatec Maya of Chan Kom build an altar, loosely referred to as a table (using the Spanish word *mesa*) but constructed in the same way as the house. The parts of the wooden altar (the four forked corner posts and the transverse rods that rest in these forks) bear the same names as the corresponding parts of the house (Redfield and Villa Rojas 1962:131). The Chorti Maya altar is also built in a way similar to that of a house, and is sometimes referred to as a house (Wisdom 1940:382).

In a similar vein, the Tzotzil Maya of Zinacantan represent in metonymic abbreviation the physical aspects of the house of the living to contain their dead. Now the dead are buried in cemeteries rather than under house floors, but their graves are often topped with roof thatch (or pine needles to represent thatch) in order to make the grave a replica of a house for the dead (Vogt 1969: 220). In northern Yucatan the dead are often disinterred from their graves, and their bones are placed in small concrete mausolea made to resemble miniature houses or churches. Thus, the structures built to enclose the dead and the ancestors are also houses, as is the case in many societies of Southeast Asia (Waterson 1990:217). In this respect, the house does seem to be privileged as an exemplary architectural model, a manmade container for both the living and the deceased, and the altar as a miniature house is a material point of contact between the living and their revered dead, denizens of the spirit world.

MAYA ALTARS AS SLEEPING HOUSES

In addition to mimicking a house in its form and method of construction, the altar is built in the form of a bench or bed (Gillespie 1999). Beds and altars were traditionally constructed in the same manner, raised up on wooden posts that were topped by slats or latticework to form the upper surface; to be used as a bed, it was covered by a woven sleeping mat (Landa 1982[1566]:34). Both beds and altars were still being made in this way in recent times, and as in the past, were often built into the house wall (Sosa 1989:139; Vogt 1969:87–88; Wisdom 1940:132, 382). This homology of form signifies another important referent for the altar that provides clues to a complex of beliefs concerning the ancestors and their behavioral connections to their descendants. Beds and benches have a specific function—they are loci for sitting, resting, and sleeping. The guardian spirits of Yucatec towns, who are housed within the crosses at the four town entrances, are believed to rest on their benches (k'anche'), the stone altars that support the crosses (Sosa 1989:138), just as men today sit upon wooden benches (k'anche') in their houses (Hanks 1990:112); and as noted above, Tzotzil ancestral spirits sit at the cross shrines (Vogt 1964:499–500).

The Quiche Maya ancestral shrine, a small stone rectangular box, is explicitly referred to as the warabalha, the "sleeping house" of the ancestors (Tedlock 1982:17). This term is related to ideas of where the house spirit, the "bed and foundation" of the house, rests (Earle 1986:166; see above). This complex of beliefs is thought to have its origin in earlier practices described for sixteenth-century Guatemala (Las Casas 1967[1555–59]:2:527) in which altars were erected over the graves of important persons to serve as shrines for rituals and offerings (Cook 1986:148; Welsh 1988:194). Thus, beyond the metaphysical function of altars as resting places for spirits, there once was a more literal juxtaposition of altars with the quiescent dead. As late as the early twentieth century in some areas, the dead were still being buried under their own beds within their houses (Blom and La Farge 1926–27,2:362).

Additional evidence linking beds, altars, and the dead comes from the prehispanic period, during which altars and bench-beds were virtually identical forms, and both were frequently erected over graves. In high-ranking households, benches and altars were masonry constructions built into the wall. Those identified as "altars" are shorter in length than beds and are usually located just opposite the doorway of the main dwelling or a separate shrine building. Identically built larger benches, or those located against the other walls, are interpreted as beds used for sitting and sleeping (Adams 1970:492–93; Thompson and Thompson 1955; Webster 1989:31), although the distinction between altars and benches is difficult to maintain archaeologically (Andrews and Andrews 1980:307; Webster 1989:31) and benches probably doubled as altars for some rituals (Welsh 1988:192). Burials and cremations were commonly placed under or adjacent to existing benches and altars, or new benches were erected over graves. This long-standing practice extends from at least the Classic through the Postclassic periods in the Maya lowlands (e.g., Andrews and Andrews 1980:307; Rathje 1970:370; Smith 1962:221; Thompson 1954; Welsh 1988:192).

While these bench-altars served as actual sitting and sleeping places for the living, and marked those same places for the dead below, the dead, too, were often laid out on their own beds, as can be seen in the upper-class tombs. Within the subsurface tomb of Temple I, Tikal, Guatemala, the body of a Late Classic paramount was laid on a woven mat that topped a large masonry bench

Figure 7-2. Miniature house carved in stone (16"l x 13"w x 25"h), from the periphery of an elite household south of the main center of Copan, Honduras. An anthropomorphic deity seated on a bench can be seen from the doorway. A hieroglyphic text is on the reverse side of the roof. Peabody Museum, catalog 92-49-20/C20,C21. Photo by Steve Burger, Peabody Museum Photographic Archive, negative 32904, © President and Fellows of Harvard College. By permission of the Peabody Museum, Harvard University.

(Sharer 1994:163). Sometimes a wooden bed was used for the deceased, e.g., at Classic period La Milpa, Belize (Hammond et al. 1996:89). In a Calakmul, Mexico tomb, pottery vessels laid out below the body were described as serving as a kind of bed, on which a woven mat was laid (Folan et al. 1995:321).

There is some evidence from ethnohistoric sources that immobility was a valued quality associated with centrality and ruling power in Mesoamerica (Gillespie and Joyce 1998), although it is not as well documented here as it is in Southeast Asia. In the latter area, "Immobility and fertility seem frequently associated with the centre; the idea of rulers or ritual specialists 'staying put', often actually in a house, recurs with noticeable regularity. . . . Immobility thus is utilized as a way of representing a concentration of creative, supernatural or political power" (Waterson 1993:230). The Maya references to sleeping, resting, or sitting in the use of altars and benches do connote a condition of fixity. They also relate to the notion of being in one's proper place (e.g., Forth 1991: 60). Among the modern Maya of Yucatan, there is a "cultural premise" that everything alive, including spirits, occupies a stable place from which it will occasionally move, but to which it will eventually return (Hanks 1990:344, 389). As for people, being in their own particular place also involves an activity, namely, to sit within their houses (1990:344; see Monaghan 1995:99 for similar Mixtec beliefs). One's link to the ancestors is thus achieved in part via a replication of their behaviors, which complements the notion that the living are the replacements (k'ex) for the dead and thus share in their identities, including their recycled souls (Carlsen and Prechtel 1991). The living house members sit and sleep on their beds, and in the prehispanic period the dead "slept" within or under similar bench forms; today their spirits (as ancestors) use the analogous altars (bed-houses) as a place to sit and rest.

Archaeological information dating to the Classic period has also revealed the use of miniature houses for ancestor veneration rituals of the noble class. These small house replicas served some of the same functions as the ancestral altars, further materializing the conceptual overlap between the altar and the house form. At Copan, Honduras, in the eastern Maya lowlands, several small stone sculptures carved in the shape of houses were found in association with a Late Classic noble residential compound, in an area that suggested their use in commemorative rituals to the revered dead (Andrews and Fash 1992:63). There are hieroglyphic inscriptions on one or both sides of these sculptures (Figure 7-2). The text includes the phrase u waybil ch'ul, "the sleeping place of a spirit/divinity" and a personal name (Grube and Schele 1990:3; Freidel, Schele, and Parker 1993:188–89; Stuart 1998:400). The front side shows the doorway in bas-relief, within which a seated anthropomorphic divinity (ch'u(l), Yucatec k'u(l)) can be observed, and in the illustrated example it is sitting on a bench. The naming of a miniature house as the sleeping place of a spirit reveals the same quality as that ascribed today to the Quiche Maya ancestral altar, the *warabalha* (Freidel, Schele, and Parker 1993:188–90), which means "sleeping house" (see above). The personal name carved on these house models may refer to the ancestor of a particular noble house, or to its claim to having divine origins or being under divine protection, since the associated name is in some cases known to be that of a deity (Grube and Schele 1990:3; Stuart 1998:400–401).

Also in the Late Classic period, the ruling house at Palenque went to great effort to record its history, especially its origins and connections to particular divinities active at the creation of the world. This epic story is preserved in inscriptions on tablets within the Temple of the Inscriptions and three adjacent temple pyramids arranged around a plaza; these three are referred to collectively as the Cross Group. Each Cross Group temple has a front and back room, and in the back room was built a complete small masonry house as a shrine, about 3 meters high and 3 meters wide (Houston 1996; Proskouriakoff 1963: 12; Robertson 1991).[7] Inside these smaller houses hieroglyphic texts were inscribed on panels erected against the back wall, opposite the door. The small structures nestled inside the larger ones are referred to metaphorically in the inscriptions as "sweat houses," *pibna*, and each is associated with a specific named primordial divinity said to be under the guardianship of the ruling paramount. As sweat houses, structures to which women have traditionally repaired following childbirth, or in order to give birth, they are linked directly to the notion of origins (Houston 1996).[8]

Like the Copan miniature house models, these small shrines are considered the place of a specific divinity linked to the ruling house, whose claims to legitimacy and identity necessitated the objectification of the houses of these spirits as a medium for localizing and possibly immobilizing them. The named primordial divinities (the "Palenque Triad") housed in the three Cross Group shrines apparently endowed the royal house with its most treasured sacra (certain costume elements), according to the inscriptions. Conceivably these specific divinities were the "house spirits" that were ritually coaxed (using the metaphor of birth) into their own special houses in the Cross Group compound, which is adjacent to the royal residences, in dedication ceremonies that were the main subject of the inscriptions. The Copan house miniatures probably served a similar function, albeit on a smaller and less expensive scale.

Furthermore, if what sets high-ranked houses apart from low-ranked houses, or from groups that do not belong to named houses, is the strategic and economic means to concentrate value (e.g., McKinnon 1991, this volume), then such immaterial property as specific gods and ancestors can be considered part of the value or resources claimed by a house. The paramount of Palenque who commissioned these three buildings on behalf of his royal house, at enormous expense, did so in an effort to concentrate his house's spiritual property by concretizing it. Other valuable material objects were also cached within the buildings, thereby taking them out of normal circulation and rendering them non-transactable (Joyce 1992; see Joyce, this volume).

Palenque also has a most unusual ancestral altar as a sleeping place, constructed literally to contain the remains of one of its paramounts in a tomb beneath the Temple of the Inscriptions (Ruz Lhuillier 1992); this tomb itself is apparently referred to as a named house (na) in the inscriptions (Stuart 1998:382–83). Rather than simply being laid out atop a masonry bench-bed, this man—named Pakal in the inscriptions—was actually encapsulated within his bench. His body was placed within the hollowed-out interior of a great rectilinear limestone block, which was raised up on legs as a bench (Figure 7-3). Similar legged stone benches served as thrones for the rulers at Palenque and other Maya sites (Robertson 1985, Figs. 418–35; Gillespie 1999:240). The bas-relief design on the upper surface of his stone coffin depicts Pakal himself with a great cross-shaped ceiba tree, like the tree-crosses that Maya peoples today still place on their ancestral altars. On the four sides of the box are ten depictions of Pakal's named predecessors, both male and female. Only the upper halves of their bodies are shown, and they seem to erupt out of the surface of the earth (Robertson 1983:65).

Besides representing an ancestral altar as a bench, within which an ancestor was literally immobilized, the sarcophagus within the tomb-house itself resembles a house. It is a four-sided enclosure for a human body (and its spirit), and the icons engraved upon it represent the vertical dimensions of the cosmos in their proper orientation. On the lower portion of its four sides is the earth band, from which the ancestors emerge, each juxtaposed against a fruit tree, while the cover design is framed by a "sky-band" border. One scholar has thus described Pakal's sarcophagus as "a small cosmic house inside a large cosmic model" (the temple-pyramid itself) (Benson 1985:185).[9]

MICROCOSM OR MACROCOSM?

Contemporary and ancient Maya houses and house altars exemplify a concept that Evon Vogt (1976:11), speaking of the Tzotzil Maya of Zinacantan, referred to as "scaling"—conceiving small or large-scale models of cultural categories. But he noted that the scale can run both ways; just as the Tzotzil house is a miniature cosmos, so the great mountain in which the ancestral gods live is

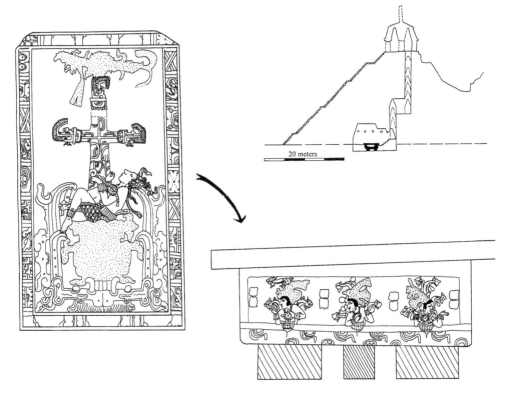

Figure 7-3. Temple of the Inscriptions, Palenque. Upper right, schematic cross section showing the vaulted interior stairway leading to the semi-subterranean tomb chamber. The chamber holds the hollowed-out coffin or sarcophagus, with four large legs at the corners and two smaller supports in the center. Lower right, east side of the sarcophagus, displaying three of the ten persons who emerge out of an "earth band," each with a fruit tree. The person on the right is female. Left, main sarcophagus cover with the portrait of Pakal falling into the earth, represented by the double-profile maws of skeletal serpents. Behind him is a ceiba tree with serpent heads on the tips of its branches. The scene is framed by a "sky-band" composed of celestial symbols. Some motifs have been simplified and others, along with the hieroglyphic inscriptions, have been deleted in this composite drawing (based on Ruz Lhuillier 1968).

considered to be a larger version of a Zinacanteco house. As Ellen (1986:3) demonstrated in his study of the Nuaulu (Indonesia) house, microcosm and macrocosm are relative to a specific point of view. If the house is a microcosm of the universe, can it also be that the universe is a house? The Postclassic Aztecs of central Mexico stated the latter point of view explicitly. According to the sixteenth-century Aztec ethnographer Fr. Bernardino de Sahagún (1963[1575–77]:Ch. 12, 247), the sky was believed to be the roof of a great house whose walls reached down to join the sea which encircled the earth, forming the floor. J. Eric Thompson (1970:214–16) suggested from iconographic evidence that the prehispanic Maya may have shared a similar notion that the world was contained within a great house known as *Itzam Na*, "iguana house." Itzam Na appears in colonial Yucatec Maya dictionaries as a deity name representing the totality of the incorporeal primordial power that existed before the creation, also referred to as Hunab K'u, "the one (unique) god" (1970:210).

On what basis are Maya scaled replicas, macrocosm or microcosm, identified? As noted above, ethnographers have recorded many statements comparing houses, altars, maize fields, and the cosmos because they share a four-sided form (replicated in the benches and sarcophagi of the prehispanic Maya). However, some Maya miniature houses are not square. The Lacandon Maya of the ethnographic present make ceramic incense burners, which they call "god pots" (*läk-il k'uh*; McGee 1990:45) because each is used in rituals to invoke specific deities. They are essentially bowls with a modeled anthropomorphic face on the outer rim; the mouth of the face is "fed" offerings. They are kept in the "god house," a special structure built to replicate the metaphysical houses that these powerful invisible spirits are believed to inhabit. Within the god house is the shelf where the pots are kept, which is the god pots' "bed" (Tozzer 1907:186), while palm leaves are spread out on the ground to form "stools" for the gods to sit on (McGee 1990:76), all means of immobilizing these portable objects. Set to one side of the god house is a dugout canoe in which *balché* beer is brewed to feed the gods, and it, too, is conceived as a house, although it is not square. It is painted with the same red circular designs as those that decorate the beams in the god house, and when not in use it is covered with thatch, just like the thatch-roofed houses (McGee 1990:55).

Because it is an intermediary between humans and the spirit world, the god pot of the Lacandon Maya is equivalent in its function to the cross shrines and similar altars elsewhere in the Maya area (McGee 1990:51), although in keeping with the co-identity of peoples and houses, it said to have a human form. The pots are not made to resemble any specific god; on the contrary, they represent a generalized human body, and their parts are named according to the parts of the body. In addition to the modelled face attached to the rim (the sole iconic representation of a human), the front of the bowl is called the "chest," the base is the "feet," and five cacao beans placed inside the bowl represent the major internal organs (1990:52). Since the god pot has a function fulfilled elsewhere by an altar and is likened to the human body, it is referred to, not surprisingly, as a house (*na*) for the god. It is so addressed during the ritual when a new ceramic vessel is being dedicated, so that the invisible god will willingly reside within it. This is the same motivation as that for house dedication ceremonies described elsewhere among the Maya—to invoke a house spirit or soul to come dwell within (described below). It even is provided with furniture: inside the god pot is a little stone that serves as the stool for the god to sit upon when it consents to occupy the god pot. The ash from burned incense that covers the stone is likened to the thatch that roofs a house (McGee 1990:52; Tozzer 1907:186).

The Lacandon god pot and beer-brewing canoe as miniature houses indicate that something more than a four-sided icon is the prerequisite for this analogy. These objects emphasize how the house is a container for the contained, and how the contained involves some aspect of the invisible animating force, as has been argued for house symbolism elsewhere (e.g., Carsten and Hugh-Jones 1995:42; Hugh-Jones 1995:233; Rivière 1995:195). Significantly, it is the process of creation or activation, both utilitarian and ritual, of such containers that frequently involves tracing its circumference, its outer boundary. Ordered space is created out of special types of movement involving ritual circuits in prescribed (usually counterclockwise) directions. These circuits often trace boundary markers, especially at corners, which mark out a path that returns to its initial point (Hanks 1989:100).

This ritual process began with cosmic creation itself, as characterized in a colonial Quiche Maya text (*Popol Vuh* 1996:63–64) as an act involving

the fourfold siding, fourfold cornering,
measuring, fourfold staking,
halving the cord, stretching the cord
in the sky, on the earth,
the four sides, the four corners, as it is said,
[the work of] the Maker, Modeler,
mother-father of life, of humankind.

Their Yucatec Maya counterparts explained the creation of world order by the progressive erection of trees to hold the sky up above the earth. They arose in order in the east, north, west, and south, and finally in the center appeared the green tree, *ya'axche'* (Roys 1967:100), the ceiba tree that was actually planted in the centers of towns and, as a cross, tops many domestic and community altars.

Although cosmic creation was the work of gods, people must continually construct, maintain, and ritually activate their own microcosmic models. Entire communities are annually sanctified by the ritual processions of shamans following a path marked by cross shrines or sacred mountains around the community's perimeter (e.g., Sosa 1989:135); the Quiche Maya call this procession the "sowing and planting" of the town (Tedlock 1982:82). Members of each Tzotzil *sna* (literally "possessed house," the local group) in Zinacantan regularly make a counterclockwise ritual circuit to the cross shrines within the lands that form its own domain, a legacy from the ancestors, thereby marking off that territory from unused areas and from those that belong to other houses (Vogt 1969:141–44). Vogt (1969:144) observed that this biannual ceremony is what "links together the descendants as common worshipers and members of the same sna . . . [and thus] symbolizes the unity of the sna as a structurally significant unit in Zinacanteco society."

Similar paths are traced on a smaller scale to dedicate a house and endow it with a soul. Among the Tzotzil, this ceremony, *ch'ul kantela* ("holy candle"), is performed when a new house is completed and is given its house cross shrine (Vogt 1969:462–65).[10] This single ritual succinctly demonstrates the complex aspects of house symbolism. It requires an interior counterclockwise circuit stopping at each of the four house corners, where offerings of candles and chicken broth are made and pine boughs are planted. The roof is also "fed" a meal of liquor and chicken broth. In the center of the floor, a rooster is buried, the earth tamped down in the same way as for a human burial in a cemetery. After the house has been fed, its occupants eat a ritual meal (also chicken). Then the husband and wife who will occupy the new house make a ritual circuit to shrines in the four holy mountains, giving offerings and prayers to the ancestral deities who reside there. Thus the encircling movement to feed the house and emplace its the soul is repeated on a larger scale within the sacred universe of Zinacantan, calling on the generic ancestors who are the keepers and disbursers of the souls (*ch'ulel*) that are distributed to humans and other animate phenomena.

On an even smaller scale, the circuit of the four corners is repeated when a Yucatec Maya shaman "activates" his altar, converting a table into a sacred locus. He does so by invoking specific animate spirits in turn and metaphysically tying each one down, in sequence, to a corner of his altar, thereby immobilizing them and allowing him to interact with them (Hanks 1990:336–38). William Hanks has shown that such ritual circuits are often represented as encompassing four corners, linked to the four directions, and that a center is actually defined by the circuit of the four corners, creating a five-point cardinal frame exemplified by altars, maizefields, the earth and sky: "The path connecting the five points defines the perimeter of the space and hence distinguishes inside from outside. Without its perimeter, a place has no unity and is potentially dangerous" (Hanks 1990:349).

Going back in time to the prehispanic Maya, a common verb in the inscriptions for the ritual dedications of houses and other objects, *hoy*, means "to circumambulate" in Cholan languages (Freidel, Schele, and Parker 1993:418) and "to encircle, enclose" in colonial Tzotzil (Laughlin 1988:214), a likely reference to a circuit-completing movement through the four directions. This verb appears in the Palenque cosmogonic text in reference to the raising of the metaphysical house in the sky by the creator deity (see above). While such ritual actions are often unrecoverable archaeologically, texts and images provide clues to their importance.[11] For example, the ten ancestors with their fruit trees whose images surround Pakal's sarcophagus may reference the peripheral encirclement that centered Pakal's "house" and his accompanying ceiba tree. A more explicit case of counterclockwise movement through a circuit comes from the three buildings that form Palenque's Cross Group (each with its interior smaller house). They are oriented to the cardinal directions and contain inscriptions that reveal a sequence in their ritual activation (Robertson 1991:12–13). By the chronology of the birthdates of the gods who were sheltered in each shrine, the reading order for the buildings is north, west, and east, referencing a counterclockwise circuit that was probably enacted by the ruler and other notables when the buildings were dedicated and used.

The Cross Group is believed to have been ritually terminated, following the death of the paramount who commissioned it, by the construction of a small structure (Temple XIV) between the main temples of the north and west. Temple XIV blocks the main access to the central patio and hence to the stairways that lead to the temples (Robertson 1991:55). This building also has an interior house shrine, whose tablet shows the deceased paramount himself in a sidestepping posture moving from north to south, as if from the north building towards the west building. He is making the same encircling procession that was begun, according to the inscriptions, in primordial times, but is now frozen by the imagery in perpetual motion.

The spatial division of center and periphery in this recurring model, associated with the ranked complementarity of stability-mobility, reflects the dichotomous character of the social house as described by Shelly Errington (1989:239), in which the timeless and unmoving center is represented by ancestors or house origins, while the periphery, the people who serve the house estate, are mobile both in their actions focused on the center and in the transient quality of their mortality (see Chapter 1). For the Maya, as Hanks (above) observed, orderly movement around the periphery is what creates and animates the stable center. There is a necessary and reciprocal, even contractual, relationship between people and the divine forces that they have stabilized in the center, each defining the other (Watanabe 1990). Those who participate in these circuits express their common interest in defining or preserving the estate that they thereby enclose (on multiple spatial scales), and their actions link them to the ancestors and creator divinities who initiated this manner of ritually constructing one's place.

Understanding the intentional actions that produce spatial order is one basis for viewing the house as a microcosm. Houses, and the spaces and other buildings associated with them, are places where order has been created by building according to specific plans and materials, and dedicating these spaces by ritual processions. This movement creates a sanctified "inside" and opposes it to an "outside." This spatial categorization must be ritually renewed, and the perimeters of the container so enacted are not impenetrable. Villages, houses, and bodies are susceptible to invasion by dangerous, potent forces. By the same token, their animating spirits or souls can escape their bodily (or other) confines, and the protection provided by ancestors and guardian spirits can be withdrawn, resulting in illness and general misfortune (see Errington 1979 for similar concepts in Southeast Asia).

It is important to note that the house as an ordered place may extend beyond the building itself. Among the Tzotzil Maya of Zinacantan, the term for house (na) refers to the extended family that occupies a residential compound (sna, possessed house), but it also signifies the space that encompasses the dwellings, granaries, sweat houses, maize fields, fruit trees, and surrounding fence. This entire unit is included in the house dedication ceremonies described above, when the house acquires its soul, ch'ulel (Vogt 1969:71).[12] Significantly, the Tzotzil Maya place their altars, which are platforms with three tall crosses upon them, outside the dwelling of the senior family member rather than inside. The house cross shrine is the pre-eminent material symbol identifying the existence of the house as a social unit (Vogt 1969:128–29; see La Farge 1947:114–15 for similar Kanhobal Maya practices). The shrine is called the krus ta ti' na, the "cross at the edge of the house" (Vogt 1969:127). This phrase may indicate that the cross is placed at an invisible boundary of the na as encompassing all of the ordered space used by the members of the social house, rather than the house as a single dwelling. The cross shrine is also referred to as a "doorway" to the soul of the house, connoting the same idea of a threshold or boundary to this non-corporeal dimension of the house. When people come to visit the residential compound, they must ritually enter this doorway by making the proper gestures to the cross shrine (1969:128). Thus, instead of the house enclosing the altar, the cross shrine metaphysically encompasses the individual dwellings of the extended family as well as their yard, small fields, and outbuildings.

On a larger scale, the Tzotzil divide the local world into two parts. Areas used by human beings and under human control are all referred to as naetik—

"houses"—in contrast with the forest, representing the wilderness; this area is called *te'tik*—"trees." As Vogt (1969:374) noted, this dichotomy is ritually produced: all of the areas designated as *naetik* are annually reaffirmed by ceremonial circuits or processions to enclose them. Among the Yucatec Maya, areas similar to the Tzotzil *naetik*—the house compounds, farm fields, etc.— are under the protection of guardian spirits who watch over these spaces from positions at the four corners or four sides of those spatial units, and to whom ritual offerings are regularly made (e.g., Hanks 1990:341; Redfield and Villa Rojas 1962[1934]:113).

Thus, in addition to the formal similarities and ritual actions that link Maya houses and altars as miniature houses, their spatial juxtaposition references another logical principle of their interrelationship, one which conforms to the Mesoamerican concentric world view. The sarcophagus of Pakal as a bench/ altar/house/womb was placed within a vaulted tomb chamber, nestled within the Temple of the Inscriptions within the royal residential area. The adjacent house shrines of the Cross Group, conceived as sweat houses/wombs, were built inside other structures that were also within the ruling house's immediate domain. The miniature house sculptures from Copan were probably originally kept within a shrine structure in a noble residential compound. Both ancient and modern ancestral altars are built within houses or erected in maize fields, which are their analogue.

Vogt (1969:571ff.) saw in the ritual circuits of Zinacantan, carried out at various levels from the *sna* to the entire municipality, the manifestation of a principle he called "structural replication." The nestedness of houses and the agency to produce them can also be understood as a generative and transposable schema, following William Sewell's (1992:8) notion of structure as "generalizable procedures applied in the enactment/reproduction of social life." The spatial association of nestedness or encompassing concentricity is what links humans to these levels of space and these forms to one another, creating of the house an entity that is both contained and container, but on multiple levels.[13] Nested imagery has been used to describe houses elsewhere (e.g., Carsten and Hugh-Jones 1995:42; Hugh-Jones 1993:105, 1995:233; Gibson 1995:146) as a means to represent self-containment and unity, as Lévi-Strauss (1987:155–57) himself suggested the house as fetish should signify.

CONCLUSION

The Maya conceive the universe as a series of concentric containers and materialize this functional imagery for themselves at the local level as a series of nested houses, reflecting the concentric principle of Mesoamerican socio-cosmology that organizes all space (Sandstrom 1996). These houses, great and small, are analogous not simply because their material form is based on a single rectilinear pattern, but because all are ritually created via a circumambulating motion that defines their perimeter (and hence encloses their center)—walking around a village, cornfield, or house, or calling upon spirits to move around an altar. They are interconnected by their mutual encompassment on a graduated scale as the container in turn becomes the contained, and movement between these boundaries requires certain ritual prescriptions; hence, each evokes the others.

These interpretations help to explain why the material models or images of houses as bench-altars and shrines in the prehispanic period refer to more than just an architectural form. As a micro-center, the house is associated with passivity; it is the most appropriate locale for sitting and sleeping behaviors that relate to the notion of properly being in one's place. The ancestors are believed to engage in similar behaviors in the places where they can be contacted by their descendants. These places are materialized in specific forms, most often the altar within the house, which is conceived as and built to resemble a miniature house, but whose shape and method of construction are that of the bench-bed. The altar is usually enclosed within the house, but these relations are reversed when the symbolic referents of the altar—house origins, links to ancestral authority, the animating power of invisible guardian spirits—conceptually encompass the social house and its estate. Beyond the individual house, a larger container is formed by the circumscription of the entire community. Guardian spirits reside at the four entrances to town, or ancestral spirits have their own houses in the surrounding mountains, on the periphery of the familiar landscape. Finally, from the most extensive and abstract point of view, the universe itself is a macrocosmic house.

Considering Maya social organization from the vantage point provided by the house society model yields a meaningful and dynamic integration of architectural and other material remains with the social groups who made and used them. It also has allowed a productive union of ethnographic and archaeological information, but with major caveats. Ethnographic information on house societies demonstrates why archaeologists need to be cognizant that the house as a ritually recognized socio-spatial unit extends beyond the physical building into what may appear to be unmarked space (see also Sandstrom, this volume), it has both immaterial and material qualities, and it need not reference a strictly defined descent group. Moreover, the significant evidence for historical discontinuities is a warning against the facile application of ethnographic "up-streaming" to explain social organization in the prehispanic period. In the past, noble houses were able to retain their estates, which is a principal mechanism of house identity and membership, as the same residential clusters were continually occupied, modified, and expanded over many generations. Ancestors and gods unique to specific houses were venerated, and huge investments of labor, material, and valuable heirlooms were made to properly house the revered dead and localize their spirits. Such is not the case today. Although rudimentary principles for the development of house societies have been maintained in some contemporary Maya villages, where the house remains the most important social unit whose identity is ritually acknowledged via links to the ancestors, the sixteenth-century European invasion eventually terminated the long-lived estates of the Maya elites, as the Spaniards brought to the New World their own version of noble houses.

8

The Tanimbarese *Tavu*

The Ideology of Growth and the Material Configurations of Houses and Hierarchy in an Indonesian Society

Susan McKinnon

The social hierarchy that characterizes house societies is materially manifested in various ways, often most obviously by the elaboration of the house itself, but it can take other forms. Susan McKinnon's elegant analysis of the wooden ancestral altars (tavu) that once graced the interiors of noble houses in Indonesian Tanimbar reveals the intricate means by which they objectified high status and quintessentially symbolized the unity of contradictions that Lévi-Strauss originally suggested the house should represent. Links to ancestral origins are embedded in the physical form of the altar and are enacted in the practical behaviors associated with it. The ancestors are the "root" (tavun) of the house as a social unit, and are represented by the tavu, the image of a standing human figure with upraised arms that seemingly supported the frame of the house itself. The head of the house sat upon the bench at its base, representing thereby the "tip" that developed out of its ancestral "root." The living house head, physically juxtaposed with the image (and also the physical and spiritual essences) of his ancestors, forms a human icon for fundamental concepts of growth and continuity (the future) since the house's ancestral founding (the past), a time depth that is prerequisite for noble status. A hard, enduring object that abstracts the human form, the tavu further indicates the ability of the noble houses to generalize and objectify their relations with allied houses that ensure their noble standing, something that commoners are unable to accomplish. As an image of growth, the tavu represents the tension within any house between the obligation to concentrate value and the strategic desire to invest value in the form of marriage alliances to ensure the social reproduction of the house.

In its evocative abstraction and its splendid spiraling tendrils, the Tanimbarese ancestor statue (*tavu*) condensed into an aesthetic form a world of understandings about the relation between houses and people. It commented upon the relation between ancestors and descendants, between the source of life in the past and its issue as it unfolds into the future, between the anchoring stability of roots and the effervescence of growth, and between the objectification and concentration of value in hard, immovable objects and the extension of value in the softness and fluidity of living beings. To talk about houses in Tanimbar, an eastern Indonesian archipelago, or to talk about Tanimbar as a "house society," is always to talk about the dynamic tension of this double movement, which was so exquisitely represented in the ancestor statues that graced noble houses in Tanimbar through the turn of the century.

There is something of a paradox in the discourse about houses and house societies. On the one hand, Lévi-Strauss and others have oriented us to the ways in which houses represent the "objectification of relations" (Lévi-Strauss 1982, 1987; see Carsten and Hugh-Jones 1995; Macdonald 1987; McKinnon 1991, 1995). This objectification is often expressed in the qualities of permanence, hardness, and immobility that characterize the wooden, metal, stone, and bone objects that constitute the material elaborations of the house. On the other hand, the house is often seen as a living, moving, growing body. Not only is it sometimes structured as a body and thought to breathe or possess a soul (Barnes 1974; Carsten 1997; Carsten and Hugh-Jones 1995; Errington 1983a; Fox 1993; Waterson 1993), but, of course, it also encompasses and contains a proliferation of living occupants. In the Austronesian world, this seeming paradox is resolved by the unifying metaphor of plant growth—which requires both a stable, unmovable root or trunk and an extension of growth in mobile branching tips.[1] This image of plant growth contains the double movement that is so central to the idea of the house in Tanimbar—the objectification, generalization, and concentration of value (in that which constitutes the trunk or root) and the particularization and dispersal of value (in that which constitutes the branching tips).

If one is to understand the hierarchy that structures Tanimbarese society as a particular representation of a house society, it is crucial not to lose sight of this double movement (McKinnon 1991, 1995). Indeed, in Tanimbar the hierarchical order is organized by the differential ability of houses not only to generalize relations and concentrate value in permanent forms (land, enduring marital alliances, heirlooms, ancestor statues) but also to proliferate new lines of growth in less permanent forms (trees, newly initiated marriage pathways, descendants). Both the generalization and particularization of relations (their objectification and personification) and the concentration and dispersal of value are necessary to the generation of life. While named, noble houses are uniquely able to accomplish both, unnamed, commoner houses are unable to transcend the particularity of individual relations or the dispersal of value over time.

The *tavu*—as one of the vehicles through which noble houses objectified their value, power, and rank—captured this double movement in an especially compelling form. By unraveling the multiple strands of meanings embodied in the *tavu*, therefore, it is possible to understand the shape of Tanimbarese hierarchy as well as its underlying ideology.

THE VILLAGE AND THE HOUSE AS RITUAL CENTERS

At the turn of the century, all the villages on the seven main inhabited islands of the eastern Indonesian archipelago of Tanimbar were situated on cliff tops, encircled by thick walls of protective cactus and accessible only by steep flights of wooden or stone stairs, sometimes embellished with carvings of human or animal figures. Among the rows of raised bamboo and thatch houses, the larger and more imposing houses of the nobles reached skyward with their horn-shaped ridgepole decorations (*kora*) (Figure 8-1). The center of the village was marked by a circle of stones (*didalan*) which, in some villages, took the form of a boat with prow and stern boards (*kora ulu* and *kora muri*) of intricately carved stone. Seen as a boat with a captain, crew, and passengers, the village was unified as a ritual community in its worship of the supreme deity, *Ubila'a*, whose main altar found its place on the boat-shaped *didalan*. It was here that the ritual officials of the village had their stone seats (*vatu*); and it was here that offerings were made to *Ubila'a* in connection with any event that unified the village in relation to the outside world—most notably, headhunting raids, warfare, intervillage alliances, and epidemics.

Just as each village placed the altar to the supreme deity at its center, so too did each house place an altar to the ancestors at its center. This was most evident in the noble houses: upon climbing the set of stairs that led up through a trap door in the floor of the house and standing up inside, one would have immediately encountered the striking image of the *tavu*, the magnificently carved wooden panel that stretched from its base on the floor up to the roof beam of the house (Figures 8-2, 8-3, and 8-4).[2] The "standing portion of the altar" (the *tav dardirin*) took the shape of a human figure—abstractly represented in a dance of filigreed designs—with arms spiraling gracefully upward. The upturned arms of the statue appeared to support one of the main roof beams that also constituted the shelf (*kalulun tavu*) upon which were placed

Figure 8-1. Distinguished house with ridgepole decorations (*kora*). Photo by H. Geurt-jens (in Drabbe 1940, Pl. V). By permission of Missiehuis Tilburg.

Figure 8-2. The *tavu* in the Ditilebit house of Awear, Fordata, c. 1920. This *tavu* is currently in the collection of the Koninklijt Instituut voor de Tropen, Amsterdam. Photo in Geurtjens (1941:opp. p. 80). By permission of Missiehuis Tilburg.

the skulls and cervical vertebrae of the ancestors, a plate for offerings to the ancestors, and perhaps also a few small wooden statues of the ancestors (Geurtjens 1917:67, 1941:19–20; Drabbe 1940:36).[3] The heirloom valuables would also have been kept in a small chest (*dolan*) stored on the roof beam above the altar panel. At the base of the altar, there was a bench (the *tav dakdokun*) upon which only the head of the house was allowed to sit during ritual occasions and when marriage exchanges and other matters were negotiated (Figure 8-4).

On the "land side" of the house was the hearth, while on the "sea side" was the "head" or "front platform" (*dedan ulu*) upon which the guests of the house sat during rituals or exchanges. Above this platform, on the sea-side loft,

Figure 8-3. A *tavu* in the collection of the Musée Barbier-Mueller, Geneva. This *tavu* of unknown origin was collected by H. J. Raedt van Oldenbarnevelt around 1900. Height, 130 cm. Photo by P.-A. Ferrazzini, Musée Barbier-Mueller, Geneva. By permission of Musée Barbier-Mueller.

Figure 8-4. The head of a house sitting in front of his *tavu*. This *tavu* is currently in the collection of the Rijksmuseum voor Volkenkunde, Leiden. Photo in Geurtjens (1941:opp. p. 80). By permission of Missiehuis Tilburg.

there was a plate for offerings to the "spirits of the above" (*nit ratan*), while the offering place to *Ubila'a* was on a shelf located on the roof beam opposite the *tavu*—on the sea side of the entrance (Drabbe 1940:36–37). The platform directly behind the *tavu* was reserved as the sleeping place for the unmarried girls of the house, while the other sleeping platforms around the perimeter of the house were occupied by the various brothers of the house together with their wives and children (see McKinnon 1991:86–90).

The *tavu* panel and the altar it supported—complete with the bones of the ancestors, the heirlooms of the house, and the offering plates—provided the ritual center of the house (Fox 1993) and made evident that the house was far more than a domestic space (Waterson 1993). The house was, first and foremost, a temple to the ancestors and a space in which contemporary occupants of a house maintained a vibrant connection with the founding ancestors of the house.

In visiting the Tanimbar Islands today, one will see but very few traces of what has been described above. Most villages no longer occupy their cliff-top sites; with a few exceptions, they are all now situated on beach-front locations, and the old sites, with their beautiful stone boats, have long been abandoned by the descendants of the ancestors whose spirits nevertheless still linger about the land. By order of the Dutch, most of the grand old houses—with their ridgepole decorations, their carved support pillars, and their *tavus*—came down in the decades between 1920 and 1940, and those few that still remained during the war were dismantled for firewood by the Japanese. Now people live in bamboo and thatch houses placed directly on the ground or, increasingly, in cement houses with tin roofs—structures that bear little resemblance to their more stately predecessors. With regard to the *tavu* more specifically, there is not a single one left in Tanimbar today. Dutch Catholic priests and government officials exchanged tokens of European status (priestly robes, heavy woolen coats, and cabinets) for the Tanimbarese *tavus*, which they brought back with them to Europe and placed in the collection rooms of museums. Ambonese Protestant missionaries were apparently more direct, and are said to have simply burned the images of the ancestors.

RELATING SOURCE AND ISSUE IN A FIGURE OF GROWTH

The Fordatan word[4] for ancestor statue—*tavu*—immediately connects the statue to a set of ideas that were central to its meaning as a ritual center (Drabbe 1932a:96). The noun form, *tavun*, refers to the "beginning, starting point, base, or root of something" and is often paired semantically with the words *ni tutul*, "its end or tip." The word *tavu*, then, especially when considered in relation to *tutul*, suggests not only an entity that has a beginning and an end but also a process that connects a source to that which issues from it. More specifically, it suggests a figure of growth, as in plants that have a base or root (*tavun*) and a tip (*tutul*), which is only a provisional ending point, one which has the potential for extending beyond itself. If we assume that the word *tavu*—as it refers to the house altar—is the same root word,[5] then we may well ask, what was the beginning, base, or root represented here, and what, then, would its end or tip be?

There is some confusion in the sources as to what the *tavu* did or did not represent. Forbes (1885:317–18), for instance, claimed that the *tavu* was a representation of the supreme deity, *Ubila'a* or *Duadila'a*. Riedel (1885:722, 1886:280–82) took Forbes to task for his error when he noted that there were no images of *Ubila'a* in the house, only statues of the ancestors, although he did not mention the *tavu* as such. Drabbe, a Dutch Catholic missionary who lived in Tanimbar from 1915 to 1935, claimed that the *tavu* statues no longer had any religious significance and had nothing to do with the worship of either the ancestors or *Ubila'a* (Drabbe 1940:36). However, from the writings of both Drabbe and his contemporary, Geurtjens (1941:19–21), the association of the *tavu* altar as a whole with the ancestors (*ubu-nusi*) is clear: it was the place where offerings were made to them and, indeed, the place where their skulls, neck bones, and images were kept.

The ancestors are, quite literally, the beginning, base, root, and source of the "house" (*rahan*); they are its *tavun*. When one remembers that the place reserved solely for the head of the house was the seat in front of the *tavu*, it is clear that if the ancestors were the beginning, base, and root of the house, their descendants—and, most particularly, the head of the house—constituted the end or tip that had issued forth from them.

A PATHWAY BETWEEN ANCESTORS AND DESCENDANTS

Indeed, the *tavu* was a kind of bridge or pathway between the past and the present,[6] the ancestors and their descendants, the root and the tip. The spirits (*nitu*) of the ancestors were not embodied in, and did not necessarily permanently live in, either the *tavu* or the objects placed above the *tavu*. The spirits of the ancestors cannot be said to be in or of any one particular object or place. But these objects—the *tavu*, the skulls and neck bones, the small statues, as well as the offering plates—were the points of contact between the living and the dead. When, for instance, during a ritual or an exchange negotiation, the head of the house sat in his place directly in front of the *tavu*, it was said that his ancestor descended along the *tavu* and sat beside him.[7] Whereas both the past and the ancestors are necessarily distinct and separate, they remain, at the same time, a vital ever-potential presence in the house and in their descendants. The power of the *tavu* was that it formed a pathway of time and identity—a pathway that related the actions of the past and the ancestors with the actions of the present and their descendants.[8]

If the *tavu* was a pathway, a place of active relation between ancestors and their descendants, that relation was (and still is) about something—about the potentiality for life and death. It is in the power of the ancestors, and ultimately

Ubila'a, to foster the fertility, growth, and health of humans and crops, as well as to ensure efficacy and success in hunting and fishing expeditions and in warfare. It is also in their power to cause infertility and disease, failure and disaster.

The fine line between the two forms of potentiality is constantly negotiated through prayers and offerings. Offerings—of a betel quid, tobacco, food, or some drops of palm wine—were (and still are) made in connection with almost every event, from birth through the life cycle to death; during illness and upon recovery; from the beginning stages of a new garden to harvest; from the initiation of a hunting or fishing expedition to its conclusion; from the first to the last steps in the construction of a house or boat; from the commencement of a war to its final resolution (see Drabbe 1940; McKinnon 1991, 1996). Both *Ubila'a* and the spirits of the ancestors were thought to eat the "soul" (*ngraan*) or the "image" (*walun*) of the offerings, just as *Ubila'a* was said to "eat the person" should the deity allow the person to die (Drabbe 1940:429). Indeed, when people died, they were laid out for the wake with their heads at the base of the *tavu* and their feet pointing toward the door (Drabbe 1925:34–35, 1940:252–53, 379). One might almost say that people formed their own last offering to their ancestors in the process of becoming ancestors themselves (cf. Cunningham 1973:232; Metcalf 1982:107–9).

The *tavu*, as the place where prayers and offerings were made and received, was the meeting place of intentionalities: those of the ancestors and those of their descendants. The course of life, and ultimately of death, revolved around the mediation of these two intentionalities. The house, with the *tavu* at its focal point, was a ritual center—its occupants dedicated to shaping the form of life through their relation to the potentialities inherent in the powers of the ancestors.

HOUSES AND RANK:
DIFFERENTIATED PATHWAYS TO THE ANCESTORS

Yet the relation of every house to these powers was (and still is) not the same. The hierarchical relation between named, noble houses and unnamed, commoner houses within a house complex (*rahan ralan*) is also conceptualized as a relationship between "elder and younger brothers" (*ya'an-iwarin*).[9] Younger brother houses "fall to one side," while at the center and origin there remains the house of the elder. Indeed, the difference between named, noble houses and unnamed, commoner houses can be characterized by their differential ability to maintain enduring pathways that link contemporary occupants of a house to its origins in the founding ancestors. The *tavu* was but one of several such pathways; the others included the "forest estates" (*abat nangan*) and "village estates" (*abat ahu*) of the house and the heirloom valuables of the house.

The estates of named, noble houses encompass two kinds of objects and relations: those that connect them to distant and founding ancestors (the origin, source, and root of the house) and that concentrate and generalize value and power along established pathways; and those that extend and disperse the ancestral life out from the center along new lines of growth that are fragile and impermanent. By contrast, the estates of unnamed, commoner houses encompass the latter kind of objects and relations only.

Hence, the forest estates of named houses comprise both tracts of land and plantations of trees, while those of unnamed houses consist of trees only. Named houses thus maintain a permanent relation to estates of land and their generalized potential for fertility, which were bequeathed by the founding ancestors of the house. Unnamed houses, by contrast, maintain a more tenuous relation to the land through trees alone—trees that were planted by recent forebears and will endure, at best, only a few generations.

Similarly, the village estates of named houses comprise not only the long-established "rows" (*lolat*) of wife-taking houses, which link *houses* through repeated marriage alliances, but also the more recently established pathways of "sisters and aunts" (*ura-ava*), which link specific *people* through newly initiated marriage relations. The village estates of unnamed houses, by contrast, consist of "sisters and aunts" pathways only. The *lolat* rows of allied houses were formed by the marriage alliances of the founding ancestors and by the repetition of marriages along the same pathways over the generations until these have become objectified as alliances between houses rather than marriages between persons. Thus the *lolat* rows that comprise part of the village estates of named houses constitute permanent pathways that link the actions of descendants and ancestors and, in the process, represent a concentration and generalization of value that is not possible in marriages that establish new relations of exchange.[10] Whereas the *lolat* rows of named houses reach back to the founding alliances of the ancestors, the sisters and aunts pathways open new pathways of growth through marriages between men and women of previously unrelated houses. While *lolat* rows are named, extend back through ten to twenty generations, and link houses (as opposed to particular people), sisters and aunts pathways are unnamed, have been in existence for no longer than three generations, and link particular people along particular female blood lines. Again, unnamed houses possess only these more impermanent pathways of exchange—ones that neither extend back into the deep past of the founding ancestors nor have the power to concentrate or generalize relations through the repetition of marriage alliances.

Not only do named houses possess land in addition to trees, and named rows of allied houses in addition to sisters and aunts pathways, they also possess named heirloom valuables—usually a pair of gold earrings (*loran*) and/or a gold breast pendant (*masa*). The history of the origin of such named valuables is not always known. But where the origin is known, it usually involves an exploit on the part of an ancestor who journeyed to the heavens, the underworld, or foreign lands and obtained the valuable from beings who inhabited a world invested with supernatural powers. Heirloom valuables are not only connected with the actions of the founding ancestors and therefore associated with the origins of the house; they are also linked to the sources of otherworldly power (see McKinnon 1991).

In the Fordatan language, heirloom valuables are called the "masters of the house" (*rahan duan*),[11] while in the Yamdenan language they are known as "the riggings of the house" (*das ni mbaretar*) (Drabbe 1940:202). Every important, named house strives to retain at least one heirloom valuable as a sign of its history, stature, and weight. With its heirloom valuables, a house is considered to be "heavy" (*aleman*), while an "empty" house—one which has lost its heirloom valuables (usually in the payment of a debt) or one which never had heirloom valuables—is considered to be "light" (*maraan*) and inconsequential. Associated with the ancestral beginnings of the house, the heirloom valuables constitute the strength and weight of the house.

Although the heirloom valuables are usually kept hidden in a small chest (*dolan*), they were also occasionally represented on the *tavu* as a sign of their underlying constitutive power (cf. Weiner 1985).[12] Most often these are either images of gold breast pendants (*masa*) or golden "male earrings" (*loran*). The male *tavu* image in Figure 8-4 wears a pair of *loran*.

It was not immediately evident to me what these valuables were meant to represent until I read the accession notes for the *tavu* panels in the collection of the Koninklijk Instituut voor de Tropen in Amsterdam. By chance, the only *tavu* I know of (in any collection) for which there is detailed information about its origin is the one collected by Drabbe in 1927, in the village of Awear, from the Ditilebit house—the same house in which I lived some sixty years later (this is the *tavu* shown in its original setting in Figure 8-2). In the accession notes for the Ditilebit *tavu*, Drabbe wrote that "all the valuables of the house" were represented on the statue. I assume that he was referring to heirloom valuables, which remain within the house, as opposed to valuables that circulate on the extended pathways of exchange and may "rest" in any particular house for anywhere from a few weeks or months to several decades (McKinnon 1991).[13]

While the valuables that circulate enable the transference of value from house to house, an heirloom extracts value from circulation and concentrates it in a particular house, where it also then becomes a pathway that links that house back to ancestral sources of power and life. Although valuables circulate through both named and unnamed houses, only named houses are able to immobilize named valuables as heirlooms.

A word might be said here about names. Houses, marriage pathways, and valuables are all differentiated by reference to whether or not they are named. A name is a sign of permanence—of an enduring structural identity—as opposed to the more impermanent, shifting, and ephemeral identities that bear no names. A name also signifies an entity that has concentrated and immobilized value as opposed to those entities that are more dispersed, mobile, and transient. Finally, a name signals the ability to transcend the personal and individual and to objectify relations in a more abstract and generalized form.

Finally, to come around full circle to the *tavu*, it can be said that just as only named, noble houses possess named heirloom valuables, so too, only they would have been distinguished by their possession of a *tavu*. The hierarchical superiority of named houses was marked by their ability to maintain not only a link to their immediate ancestors (through their skull and neck bones and the small carved images), but also a link (through the *tavu* altar and heirloom valuables) to the founding ancestors of the house complex as a whole, and thus to distant and successive ancestral sources of life and power. Although unnamed houses may have kept the skulls and neck bones and the small carved images of their immediate ancestors on an altar shelf, their hierarchical subordination was evident in their inability to establish or maintain an enduring pathway to the founding ancestors of the entire house complex. The relation of unnamed houses to these founding ancestors existed only to the extent that they remained attached as "younger brothers" to named houses (McKinnon 1991).

The character of named noble houses, then, is expressed in their concentration of value and weight in an immobile center, their generalization and objectification of relations in land, *lolat* rows, heirlooms, and *tavu*—all of which served as enduring pathways to the founding ancestors. At the same time, the character of named, noble houses is also expressed in their ability to extend ancestral sources of life into the more impermanent, uncertain figures of growth—in the form of trees, new pathways of marriage, and a proliferation of descendants. By contrast, the character of unnamed houses is manifest in their dispersal of value, their lightness and mobility at the periphery, their particularization of relations in terms of blood, bodies, people, and trees, and their mediated relation to the founding ancestors.[14]

RELATING PERSONS AND THE MATERIAL STRUCTURES OF HOUSES

In its remarkable abstraction of human form, the *tavu* beautifully expressed this generalization and objectification of relation and value that is the special characteristic of noble houses. Yet the *tavu* articulated not only the transformation of persons into enduring structural and social entities (houses), but also the extension of the structural continuity of the house in the form of living human descendants.

The images on the *tavu* are so playfully abstracted that it is difficult to say whether they might have represented a particular (perhaps the founding) ancestor or even whether they represented a male or female form. While Drabbe considered the small ancestor statues (*walut*) to be "soul images" of immediate ancestors, he asserted that the *tavu* itself was not a "soul image" of any particular ancestor (1940:36, 112). The abstraction of the designs of most *tavu* (especially when compared to the relative realism of the small ancestor statues) could be taken as confirmation of this.

Although the human form of the *tavu* was highly abstracted, it occasionally had either male or female references, or both. The *tavu* in Figure 8-4, for example, is obviously male. In the collection of the Museum voor Land- en Volkenkunde in Rotterdam there is one *tavu* that is carved in an unusually realistic manner and clearly shows a figure of a woman wearing shell armbands. In the same collection there is another *tavu* that is rendered in a highly abstract form but, interestingly enough, has a sun and a moon (male and female symbols) carved on either side where the hands would be (photographs of both *tavus* are shown in van Nouhuys 1923:opposite page 5). Various commentators have noted that the position of the arms on the *tavus* closely resembles that of women when they dance (*rsomar*)—arms extended and turned upward, it is said, like the wings of frigate birds. In connection with this, Drabbe quotes a riddle which asks: "Who is the young maid who dances day and night?" The answer is, of course, the *tavu* (Drabbe 1940:289). Other associations, however, clearly link the *tavu* with males and, more broadly, with the highly valued intergenerational continuity of males within a house.[15] The heirloom valuables most often represented on the *tavu*—*loran* earrings and breast pendants—are considered "male" valuables and would be worn by men. That the *tavu* is associated with the male forebears of the house is indicated by the saying quoted by Drabbe: "if someone's father is dead, he says: my *lamngatabu* [Yamdenan for *tavu*] is gone" (1940:284–85). Drabbe also mentions that *lamngatabu* or *tavu* is an honorific term used for the eldest, first-born son of the house—the son whose seat, one day, would be on the bench at the base of the *tavu* (Drabbe 1940:271).

What is most striking about the *tavu* is that, while it unmistakably takes the form of a human (and occasionally gendered) figure, it is, at the same time, so abstracted and overwhelmed by filigreed designs that it almost intentionally seems to negate reference to any particular human. Neither human individuality nor gendered specificity is foregrounded here.[16] Rather, most *tavu* are dominated by abstract decorative designs—S-shaped double spirals (*kilun ila'a*) and single spirals (*kilun etal*), which are also carved into house posts and continue to appear in the *ikat* designs of Tanimbarese weavings. However, unlike other abstract decorative designs that are explicitly meant to depict fish, flags, or half-moons, these spirals have no referential meaning. This nonreferential abstraction produces a powerfully synthetic representation: generations of individual forebears are condensed and abstracted into a generalized image of ancestral potentiality.

Moreover, in its placement within the house the *tavu* was integrated with the structure of the house itself: it appeared to stand as the support for the roof beam of the house. This play between representation and abstraction, between image and architectural structure, was not simply a stylistic convention, but rather a visual realization of a dynamic relation between an ancestral figure and a house that had become an enduring social entity. While the image of the ancestor was abstracted to the point where it was almost submerged into the structure of the house, at the same time the structure of the house was such that it seemed to emerge out of the image of the ancestor. The *tavu* represented the ancestor as a human figure objectified into the structure of the house itself. That which had issued forth from the founding ancestor had become an enduring social entity—a named house.

The *tavu* also, and simultaneously, represented the house as a structural entity that was rooted in human form and grounded in the actions and exploits of the founding ancestors[17] as well as in the continuing practices of their descendants. Indeed, the potentiality of the *tavu* was fulfilled and completed only when the head of the house leaned against it. In Figure 8-4, it is clear that just as the *tavu* was the objectification and generalization of all human relations of the house, so too the head of the house was the particular realization of the original ancestral potentiality for growth. If the *tavu* was the base, root, source, and origin, the man who sat in front of the *tavu* was the tip of the branch that had issued forth.

The *tavu*, in short, consolidated a number of associations that have to do both with ancestral beginnings and the base or root from which the house derives its power and identity. In this way, one man told me, when the head of the house said he "leaned against the *tavu*" (*nebang tavu*), he meant more than that he literally sat with his back against the *tavu*; he meant that he had, as his backing and support, the spiritual power of all his ancestors and the stable grounding weight of all the pathways—the *tavu*, the rows of allied houses, the land, and the heirlooms—that continued to connect him directly to these ancestral powers.

There was, indeed, a kind of condensation of value in the ancestral altars of noble Tanimbarese houses that was the mark of hierarchical differentiation. Here, around the telling and elegant abstraction of the *tavu*, there was concentration of hard, permanent, immobile objects—bones, metals, and hard woods. These objects generalized and objectified the enduring value of the relations of the house so that the house might serve as a stable source, base, root, and origin for future growth and the proliferation of life. The maintenance of this double movement—reaching back to ancestral sources of life and forward in new tendrils of growth—is the unique achievement of named noble houses and what sets them apart from unnamed commoner houses. It is both the ideology of growth and the material configuration of hierarchy.

Research was carried out in the Tanimbar Islands during the years 1978 through 1980 and was assisted in part by a Grant for Doctoral Dissertation Research for Anthropology from the National Science Foundation. Both doctoral research and postdoctoral research (1983–84) in the Tanimbar Islands were assisted by grants from the Joint Committee on Southeast Asia of the American Council of Learned Societies and the Social Science Research Council with funds provided by the National Endowment for the Humanities and the Ford Foundation. This article considerably develops an argument that was originally published in *Tribal Art* (Bulletin of the Barbier-Mueller Museum, Geneva) (McKinnon 1987). Revised portions of that original article are reprinted here with the permission of the Barbier-Mueller Museum.

9

House, Place, and Memory in Tana Toraja (Indonesia)

Roxana Waterson

Houses, as substantial material constructions, represent permanence and con-tinuity, and hence endow a metaphorical immortality on the social groups who identify with them and who ensure their perpetuity by continually re-building them, or, even when the buildings have vanished, by reverencing the empty places in which they once stood. Roxana Waterson explores this theme in her examination of the interplay between the "living" house and the lives of its inhabitants in Tana Toraja, South Sulawesi, Indonesia. The Sa'dan Toraja identify themselves not just with their own dwellings but with those of their forebears on both sides, and ultimately with the highly elaborated noble "origin houses." The physical and spiritual components of house value—the heirlooms, bones, and spirits of the dead as well as the placentas of the newly born—anchor people to place and to their ancestral origins. People's identities are thus grounded in the landscape, the physical house function-ing as a material sign for the social memories that localize groups to cer-tain places (houses, fields, tombs). Houses create simultaneous spatial and temporal networks for conceptualizing how social groups are linked to one another, because of their references to specific historical memories of descent and affinal relationships that are construed as relationships among houses. Waterson's perspective thus moves from the individual house to the entire settlement, and from the individual social group to the "language of kinship and affinity" that connects social groups to one another in the larger com-munity. Her explicitly diachronic orientation demonstrates how meanings of "place" are dependent on the changes that occur over time, resulting in a "biography of built forms."

CONTEXT AND INTERPRETATION IN
ARCHAEOLOGY AND ANTHROPOLOGY

Anthropology, archaeology, and history are disciplines intimately related to each other by their mutual concern with time's arrow. All our data are historical; they belong just as inevitably to a particular place and social setting. We are all engaged in the business of interpreting particular intersections of time and space. Just as the thousands of disparate observations and experiences of the field worker must be woven into some form of coherent narrative to become ethnography, just as history will never simply speak for itself, so, too, for the archaeologist, inferences have to be made. "Things are equivocal," remarks Ian Hodder. "The objective past will not present itself" (Hodder, ed. 1995:9, 13). Therefore, the question for all of us is always how to make the best inferences, the best interpretations possible. Raymond Firth (1989:48) describes ethnography as "a *crafted* job"; so, too, is the work of the historian or the archaeologist (Hodder, ed. 1995:28). Our crafts have much to contribute to each other; this volume represents a valuable opportunity to advance such cooperation.

Already a large literature exists on the question of the possible continuities between ethnographic observations and the sort of historical inferences that archaeologists wish to make about their data. Whatever the pitfalls of using contemporary examples to illuminate possible patterns of past behavior, the need remains, in the absence of people to speak to, to make the best inferences possible about material evidence. Having the widest possible range of ethnographic examples to draw on helps the archaeologist (just as it does the anthropologist) to avoid applying our own unexamined cultural assumptions to the case in hand. Moreover, many of the contributors to this volume are dealing with contexts where there is a marked continuity between archaeological data, available historical records, and a contemporary ethnographic context.

The question of how best to interpret the meaning of landscapes and architectural spaces is one that is fundamental to archaeological practice, yet anthropology alerts us to how elusive those meanings can be, even when we have informants to question. Recent works by archaeologists have given concentrated attention to this question (Blanton 1994; Hodder, ed. 1989, 1995; Kent 1990; Kroll and Price, eds. 1991; Tilley, ed. 1993). Here I should like to draw attention to just a couple of the potential difficulties which may lie behind our customary assumptions about the meanings of space. In Kent's discussion of this topic, some of these assumptions are clearly set out. The first is that "architecture creates boundaries out of otherwise unbounded space" (Kent

1990:2). This is obviously true—or is it? Ethnographic experience cautions us to be aware that exactly how these boundaries may be perceived is no simple matter. What does the boundary mark? Is it a distinction between "public" and "private"?

Anthropologists have had to confront the fact that these categories are already heavily loaded, in European cultures, with meanings which have developed in a particular way since the industrial revolution (Strathern 1984). No doubt Wilson (1988) is fundamentally right in telling us that the building of walls effected a profound transformation in human relationships; yet walls may be highly permeable. Helliwell (1993) describes the experience of living in a Gerai longhouse in Kalimantan, where connecting walls between apartments are deliberately breached and kept in a state of disrepair in order not to hinder communication—at least orally—between families. "Good walls make bad neighbors" might be taken as the model of Gerai notions of sociability. Thomas (1995), writing of the Temanambondro of Madagascar, reveals that domestic space is not in the least private, in spite of the walls around it, and that in this society if you really wish to have a private conversation you repair to the granary. In fact, whispering is called "granary talking" (Thomas 1995:15). Whereas house doors are always open, granary doors are kept closed.

Is the boundary that between kin and non-kin? Here again, interpretation is not always straightforward. Many people belong to a Toraja origin house without living in it, and any individual may trace ties to many different houses, the birthplaces of ancestors on both the mother's and the father's side. To find the outer limits of these networks is difficult; they become visible partly in a ritual context, or else when quarrels arise over claims to rights in houses (Waterson 1995b).

What about the gendered division of space? Within the house, such divisions, where they exist at all, may be as important symbolically as they are invisible physically. It is questionable how far, for example, an archaeologist would be able to infer the complex web of associations which Bourdieu (1973) recounts as shaping the uses of space by men and women in the Berber house. In some societies of eastern Indonesia, floor space is invisibly divided into a "male" and "female" side, yet the significance of such a division is very different here, I would argue, from that in Berber society (Waterson 1990:189, 196–97). Even the image of the house as womb, which recurs in both areas, cannot be taken as simply a universal symbol but carries significantly different connotations. These appear to be largely negative in the Berber case, where women's sexuality and reproductive powers are symbolically opposed to men's spirituality and "excellence," and regarded by men as defiling; but quite the contrary in the Indonesian context, where there is no such religious devaluation of life processes, and where the special association of women and houses as sources of life and nurturance can only be viewed as positive.

Second, there is the assumption, which again must appear obvious, that architectural data *represent* something. But again, the question of *what* exactly is represented can sometimes take years of intimate study to discover. Bloch (1995a:212–13) describes how Zafimaniry house carvers told him firmly that their carvings on the main house posts were pictures of "nothing," and that there was "no point" to them; in the end, he came to see the apparently bland statement that they "made the wood beautiful" as in fact something very profound. The house is intimately associated with a married couple who found it; only slowly does it grow to be a solid structure, especially after the couple have children. As the marriage matures and is seen to endure, so the house acquires more hardwood timbers, and these timbers are honored and "beautified" with carvings. The house is then said to be acquiring "bones." The carvings, suggest Bloch, do not "mean" anything, in the sense of signifying or referring to something else—they are themselves part of the process of growth of a successful marriage and house. They are "the continuation and magnification (as in *magnificat*) of the growth and success of the couple transcending the impermanence of life" (Bloch 1995a:215), for the house will live on after this original couple have become ancestors.

This example alerts us to the extraordinarily close identification between people and their houses which is so distinctive a feature of many Austronesian-speaking societies. It is remarkable in how many of these societies we find that both placentae and ancestors are incorporated in some way into the physical structure of the house. In Tana Toraja, the father buries the placenta in the ground at the east side of the house, the side associated with life and the rising sun. Ancestors were traditionally believed to visit the house, and food offerings for them would be placed in a special basket above the hearth at mealtimes. Among the Tetum, the umbilicus and placenta of the newborn are placed in a bag which is hung on the ancestral pillar in the center of the main room of the house (Hicks 1976:31). In Tanimbar, the placenta is buried in the house floor (McKinnon 1991:109), while the often exquisitely carved ancestral altar was the centerpiece of the house; among the Makasar of South Sulawesi it was traditionally stored in the attic, along with the ancestral shrine (Gibson 1995: 136–38). In the island of Roti, and also among the Austronesian-speaking Paiwan of Taiwan, the dead have customarily been buried in the house floor, and their spirits, in Roti, are represented in the attic by palm-leaf decorations hung from the rafters (Chiang 1992; Fox 1987). The Ata Tana Ai of Flores say that the ancestors are reborn in the form of lianas which are used to bind the joints of the house (Lewis 1988:153 n.12). All of this conveys to us how vividly the house comes to stand as an embodiment of the continuity of a group of kin in these societies.

Among the Toraja, houses also gain prestige by being rebuilt. A timber pile-built house may leave no trace archaeologically, not even a post-hole where the piles rest upon stones, as is typical for the Toraja; so an archaeologist might discover no trace of these successive rebuildings. As a general point, though, this is worth noting, because in other places, and in other materials, traces of rebuilding, or of successive additions, may well remain. This would appear to be the case, for example, among the Maya, where according to Gillespie (1995, this volume), we find fixed house sites, redeveloped over time, incorporating burials, texts and images referring to ancestors. By these means, descendants become "anchored" to a place and connected through it to their ancestors.

I discuss here some aspects of interpretation in my own field work with the Sa'dan Toraja people of highland South Sulawesi, Indonesia. For me, the process of developing interpretations about Toraja society has been essentially a movement toward categories drawn from concepts important to the Toraja themselves. The attempt to move closer to an understanding of these categories is what led me to see Toraja as a "house society," because houses are what Toraja themselves talk about a lot of the time. Even learning to ask the right questions in Tana Toraja meant phrasing questions in terms of relationships between houses rather than, for example, degrees of relationship in the conventional kinship terms familiar to anthropologists, such as between cousins.[1] This specificity does not, however, mean that no generalizations are possible; on the contrary, I have shown in my comparative research (Waterson 1990, 1993, 1995a) the importance of this house-focus in very many other Indonesian societies, in spite of the apparent variety of their kinship systems. As other ethnographers have been arriving almost simultaneously at similar insights about our field data (Carsten and Hugh-Jones, eds. 1995; Macdonald, ed. 1987; Waterson 1986, 1990; and a number of more recent researchers in both eastern and western Indonesia), we have all found ourselves acknowledging a debt to those sketchy but powerfully suggestive ideas of Lévi-Strauss (1982, 1987) concerning "house societies," which have prompted us to look at our data in a new way. The outcome has been a radical re-evaluation of Indonesian kinship systems and patterns of social organization.

In my recent continuing field work in Tana Toraja, as well as from a comparative perspective, I have tried to push further with certain aspects of this analysis. One of these is the extent to which hierarchy should be seen as a necessary dimension of the house society in Lévi-Strauss's sense (Waterson 1995a); another is the resonances of the idea of the house as a living thing, which is more than just a metaphor for many Southeast Asian peoples. Most recently, I have been concerned with the house as an embodiment of history or memory about the past, and the connections memory creates between houses and landscape, thereby contributing to a particular sense of place (Waterson 1997). These themes are interconnected: if houses are considered to be "alive," that means that they have a "life history," too, a "biography" that is intertwined with those of their human inhabitants.[2] And, just as no biography can be written of a person in isolation, so houses are connected with each other by historical relationships. Finally, it is clear that the "life" of a house can outlast that of any of its human inhabitants, and I therefore argue that for Toraja, as for other house societies, identification with the house offers people a kind of immortality.

TORAJA ORIGIN-HOUSES AND THE "LIFE" OF THE HOUSE

The Sa'dan Toraja number around 370,000 and live in the mountainous northern part of the Province of South Sulawesi. Most are subsistence farmers, growing wet rice in rain-fed hill terraces, and cultivating a variety of vegetables including cassava and maize as secondary staples, and cash crops such as coffee, cloves, and chocolate. Many Toraja have also migrated in search of work or higher education outside their homeland, generally continuing to return home periodically for the celebration of rituals, especially funerals and house ceremonies. The majority of Toraja today are Christian; about 10 percent still adhere to the indigenous religion which is called *Aluk to Dolo*, the "Way of the Ancestors." Some rituals in the rich corpus of Toraja ceremonial life have remained so important in the social, economic, and political life of the Toraja that they are still vigorously carried on, even by Christians; others are rarely performed today.

In Tana Toraja, houses are the major points of reference within the bilateral kinship system. People trace their descent equally from houses on both sides of the family, where their parents, grandparents, or more distant ancestors were born. At the birth of a child, the father buries the afterbirth on the east side of the house, so that over time the house becomes the place where "many placentae are buried," and thus should never be moved. It is also spoken of as the starting point for most human enterprises. The origin houses of the nobility are magnificent structures, richly decorated with carved and colored wall panels. The roof ridge is greatly extended, ending in the improbable upward sweep of the gable ends, which project so far that they must be supported by an extra free-standing post at each end, the *tulak somba*. These named aristocratic houses have genealogies attached to them, generally of between ten and thirty generations, which always go back to a founding married couple, sometimes credited with supernatural origins. Sometimes either the husband or the wife may more often be mentioned as the founder, depending on whether the house was constructed on her or his family's land. Noble houses were inhabited by politically powerful chiefs who controlled a village, or small groups of villages, in precolonial times. Most houses are plainer, less durable structures of bamboo or wood. Only a few high-ranking individuals remember long, elaborate genealogies; most people can name their ancestors only to a depth of two or three generations. Yet the principle of tracing descent through houses and remembering places of origin I found to be common throughout Toraja society.

Houses are linked with other structures. To be complete, a house must have its rice barn (*alang*), built facing it at the north side. The house is to the barn as wife to husband, or mother to child—a complementary, or organically related pair. Important origin houses also have their own family tombs (*liang*) cut out of solid rock and used over generations; the house and the *liang* are described as a pair (*sipasang*). Some origin houses also have rice fields and other resources such as coconut and bamboo groves attached to them as inalienable property (*mana'*). Competent individuals ought to know not only what houses they are descended from, and their genealogies, but also the burial places of their ancestors, and the names of rice fields attached to particular houses. Within the Toraja kinship system, then, a web of strong emotional bonds is woven between people and their houses, tombs, land, and ancestors, all of which combine to create a particular sense of place.

Ritual governs the proper construction of a house, and the timbers must be correctly positioned. Posts must always be aligned in the same way that the wood was growing in the tree, with the "trunk" end down, while another set of rules governs the placement of "trunk" and "tip" ends of beams in relation to each other, with two "trunk" ends meeting in the southwest corner, and two tips in the northeast, the direction most strongly associated with the deities and with life. Mistakes in construction are thought to bring harm to the occupants and are sometimes sought out as an explanation for illness or misfortune. Houses are often rebuilt on the same site even if not yet dilapidated, because such renewals are part of the process by which a house comes to be regarded as an "origin house" (*tongkonan*) by its descendants. The willingness to invest in the rebuilding of houses is still a striking feature of life in Tana Toraja, for it secures prestige and social approval. On the other hand, the fortunes of different family branches can rise and fall rather quickly, and it may happen that disunity or lack of funds prevents rebuilding and causes the eclipse of a house. But even if a house is destroyed, for example by fire, it does not necessarily perish altogether. Its name will be remembered, and it retains the right to any ritual titles connected with it, even if they have to be temporarily moved to another house. Special rites are held for an origin house destroyed by fire, which symbolize its continuity and the intention of its members to rebuild it when they are able. Even houses that have not been standing for centuries can in theory still be rebuilt if the descendants wish it.

HOUSES, LANDSCAPE, AND HISTORICAL MEMORY

When people recount their genealogies, they begin, as mentioned, with a founding couple. They go on to tell who were their children, whom they married, and where they moved in order to found new "branch" houses of their own. Some accounts also provide details of named supernatural heirloom valuables that were taken along by each descendant as his or her inheritance.[3] Founding and branch houses are sometimes characterized as "mother" and "child" (*indo'na/anakna*), sometimes as "trunk" and "branch" (*garonto'/tangke*), or the original founding house may be termed *ongi'na* (*ongi'*: "stem") as in the stem of a fruit; when demonstrating this idea, one informant picked up a mangosteen, another a coconut, pointing out how "the whole fruit grows from the stem." This latter term is without a paired term to indicate the branch house. "Trunk" and "tip" here, rather than describing spatial relationships, are being used as a means of describing a diachronic relationship, of talking about time (cf. Traube 1989). The house sites, named and recalled within genealogies, form a sort of network, providing what is as much a geographical as a historical account of the settlement of the Toraja landscape, as people spread out to cultivate new areas.

A few sites are widely recognized (with local variations) as the oldest or most important ancestral houses. I am struck by the frequency with which these sites are identified with mountain tops, with no trace of any surviving house on them. This fact bears comparison with the situation in a number of other Indonesian societies, where origin sites or ceremonial centers are unoccupied or even vacant sites (not infrequently associated with mountains). As Traube (1989:329) has expressed it in relation to the Mambai, and the Tetum of Wehali (Timor), "Absence signifies original presence." Perhaps the most widely acknowledged and important site of all is Banua Puan in Mengkendek, where the ancestor Tangdilino' is said to have built the first carved *tongkonan* to have been consecrated with rituals. Tangdilino' lived before the arrival of the *to manurun* (ancestors supposedly descended from the sky) in Toraja—in one genealogy I collected, he is shown as two, in another as eight, generations removed from the first human couple on earth. The site at Banua Puan is not on a mountain top, but it is well remembered, even though it has not had a house on it for centuries. It has been kept clear by local descendants, although a church has been built close beside it. Most noble houses all over Toraja can trace an ultimate link to Banua Puan. Even though no material structure has existed here for so long, Banua Puan has kept its place in oral memory.

A number of other aristocratic houses have myths telling of founding ancestral couples described as *to manurun di langi'* (or "ones who descended from the sky") and *to kendek diomai liku* ("ones who rose out of a pool"), of whom the man is said to have descended from the sky on to a mountain top, and married a woman who rose out of a river pool. These supernatural ancestors give prestige to the houses they founded, which in the past were the loci of political power. It appears that these stories may have been borrowed from the Bugis, where legends of *to manurung*, supernatural beings who were received as local rulers, are told in court chronicles and seem to have served a legitimating function in the formation of lowland kingdoms during the thirteenth century. In southern districts of Toraja, Tamboro Langi' is the most prominent ancestor of this type, said to have descended on Mount Kandora. In the central Kesu' district, To Manurun Puang ri Kesu' ("Lord of Kesu' ") is often mentioned, while people of western districts claim Tamboro Langi' for themselves by insisting that he descended not on Kandora, but on Ullin, a peak in westerly Saluputti. Another *to manurun* of this region is Gonggang Sado'ko', said to have come down on a neighboring summit, Sado'ko'. Competition between the different districts over the details of these founding myths still continues at the present time, a fact which at first surprised me during my field work. But I came to see it as indicative of continued interests in issues of precedence in local politics; these mythical histories, then, still serve a purpose in the present.

Fentress and Wickham (1992), among others, have shown how in oral societies, history is commonly embedded in local landscapes, myths, and genealogies, and this is clearly true of the Toraja. One acquaintance, Pak Tandiruru of Alang-Alang, even made explicit the idea that the house served as a substitute for written history. Instead of the court chronicles which the Bugis and Makasar peoples recorded on strips of palm leaf (*lontara'*), Toraja people, he pointed out, had the *tongkonan*. The positions of houses in the landscape, the stories of their origins, their links to each other as founding and branch houses, their genealogies, have all been used as means for the transmission of a kind of history. Even certain ornamental elements added to the house structure itself add to this history, since they commemorate the holding of particular important rituals. History, here as everywhere, serves particular purposes; it was a prerogative of the aristocracy, who were the only ones permitted to build elaborately carved houses, and the only ones with an interest in remembering long genealogies. Both of these served as legitimating devices in the past, and to the extent that they continue to do so, the motivations still relate to claims of precedence, now sometimes having to do with the desire to enhance the status of one's own area as the most desirable and "authentic" destination for tourists visiting Toraja, with the attendant economic advantages that this may bring.

In the troubled times of the 1950s and 1960s, few origin houses were being rebuilt in Tana Toraja, but with economic recovery and development since the 1970s, there has been a marked resurgence of architectural activity. The continuity of this tradition can now be seen to be vigorous, a fact that contrasts only too markedly with many other areas of Indonesia where the survival of indigenous vernacular traditions is in question. Continuity does not imply stasis, however; Kis-Jovak and colleagues (1988) have vividly documented the transformation of the Toraja house, whose oldest surviving forms, rapidly becoming extremely rare, are far smaller than the standard model of today, and with only the slightest curve to the roof. As the form of the house has been pushed to its upward and outward limits, the usable interior space has if anything become reduced in proportion to the whole, even as the exterior has become more and more impressive in conveying the message of social status and power.

Nowadays, the majority of carpenters seem to be centralized in the town of Rantepao, and house forms have become correspondingly standardized, while local variations in the characteristic design and coloring of house carvings are at the same time lost. One curious new hybrid style has become popular since the early 1980s. It consists of a spacious, square first story, in Bugis style, with large door and windows, topped by a second-story *tongkonan* complete with carving and curved, extended roof. This composite seems to meet the felt need for more and lighter living space, while satisfying the equally important need to express status through the traditional shape of the *tongkonan*. *Tongkonan* shapes can be seen everywhere in modern buildings such as offices, banks, restaurants, and hotels.

Many of those who help to fund the renewal of origin houses will never live in them; in fact, the houses themselves may remain uninhabited, coming to life only when some ceremony draws descendants to gather there. Most remarkably, a plan is currently mooted for the resurrection of Tangdilino''s house at Banua Puan. In theory this could be easily accomplished, because so many people can trace descent from it that there is a huge number of potential financial contributors, who would need to give only small amounts to make up the sum required. But the logistical problems of controlling these funds may prove insuperable. However, some novel suggestions have been put forward as to what should be the functions of this house if it is rebuilt. One member of an

association which represents surviving adherents of *Aluk to Dolo*, the indigenous religion, has proposed that the house should be run by adherents of *Aluk
to Dolo* as "a place of prayer and a site for tourism and research into Toraja
history and ancestors." This suggests that Banua Puan would become a shrine
of sorts rather than a dwelling; given that the indigenous religion has never had
any form of temple or fixed place of worship, such a combination of modern
functions would be a new departure indeed. Control by a faction loyal to the
Aluk would doubtless be contested, however, by others who prefer the idea of
a Christian identity for modern Toraja and who look forward to what they
regard as the inevitable demise of the old religion. Either way, Banua Puan
offers a special potential as a self-conscious expression of ethnic identity. Its
reconstruction after so long a historical lapse would provide dramatic proof of
the immortality of the Toraja house, as well as the possibilities it offers for the
expression of new ideas.

CONCLUSION

I have sketched here some of the themes which continue to make the house a
focus of social relations for the Toraja—the idea of the house as alive, the
interweaving of its "life history" with those of its inhabitants, the part played by
the house within systems of hierarchy and precedence, its role as a vehicle for
memory and connections with place and with ancestors, and its ability to be
reborn in new guises. I have deliberately dwelt on a diachronic perspective,
which enables us to see the significance of houses to their owners in a number
of ways. Until recently, the influence of structuralism was responsible for a
more purely synchronic style of spatial analysis in anthropology. But the passage of time is equally fundamental to the meaning of place. It is an essential
element in assessing the importance of the "house" as a focal institution. Analyzing the development and alteration of buildings over time has always been
an important concern of archaeologists. But perhaps anthropologists, in re-
directing their attention to the diachronic dimension, can still offer some fresh
insights into ways of tracing the biographies of built forms. Southeast Asia is
only one area where we have begun to consider in detail the implications of the
house society concept. Perhaps some of these ideas about the house may suggest new interpretations of archaeological data in the various locations which,
thanks to Lévi-Strauss, we are beginning to re-evaluate as house societies.

My fieldwork in Tana Toraja was carried out over a period of 18 months in
1978–79 with the help of a grant from the Social Science Research Council of

the UK, and for nine months in 1982–83 with the aid of grants from the British Academy and the Cambridge University Evans Fund. I am very grateful to these bodies for their support, and also to LIPI, the Indonesian Institute of Sciences, which gave its permission for the research. I visited Tana Toraja again in 1994 and 1996.

10
Heirlooms and Houses
Materiality and Social Memory

Rosemary A. Joyce

Rosemary Joyce examines the use of objects to materialize memory, the basis for the identity and perpetuity of the house. She begins with several ethnographic case studies: Schneider's study of the Yapese, a major focus for his critique of classificatory approaches to kinship; Parmentier's analysis of the physical marking of social relationships in the landscape; and Kroeber's original ethnography of the Yurok, one of the exemplars of Lévi-Strauss's original explication of house societies. She draws on these ethnographic cases to demonstrate that, like the curation of skeletal remains as a form of ancestral veneration, the caching of valuable objects within houses or their associated tombs, some of them curated for centuries prior to their deposition, is an archaeological correlate of the ethnographic practice of retaining heirlooms and creating histories for them. In the case of the prehispanic Maya, valuable goods, usually costume ornaments, were not simply wealth objects cached to be taken out of circulation for ritual purposes, as these are usually interpreted. Instead, they were curated heirlooms, virtually all of which were deposited long after they were first made as markers of house prestige. Maya hieroglyphic inscriptions added to identify the "owners" of these objects allow a tentative start to writing the biography of Maya noble houses through the valuables that preserved the house in social memory, from their manufacture to their final deposition centuries later. Her discussion highlights important material domains of the house and its manifest utility for linking interdisciplinary research on culture and society.

Summed up in *The Way of the Masks* as "a corporate body holding an estate made up of both material and immaterial wealth, which perpetuates itself through the transmission of its name, its goods and its titles down a real or imaginary line, considered legitimate as long as this continuity can express itself in the language of kinship or of affinity and, most often, of both" (Lévi-Strauss 1982:174), the house stands as a model social formation that is distinguished by its attention to a number of material domains. Among these, land, the dwelling, and heirloom wealth items are the material embodiment of the continuity of the house. They are the focus of strategies for conservation and transmission on the part of members contending for position within the house, and for prominence of the house over neighboring houses or distant allied rivals.

The concept of the house provides a way to link the interests of ethnographers attentive to the role of material goods in creating relationships between social actors, with the goals of archaeologists concerned with the ways histories accrue in material things, and through their anchorage in those things, facilitate the continuity of particular forms of social relations. In the pages that follow, I explore connections between the anthropological critique of kinship and the model of house societies, and contrasts between the investment of social memory in the stable locus of the house building and in transactable heirlooms, in order to illuminate how the house can provide a site for productive intradisciplinary discussion that combines concerns with material culture, history, and social reproduction by active agents constantly negotiating and renegotiating their place in the world.

SOCIAL RELATIONS AND THE HOUSE

The house offers a useful alternative to other ways of talking about the social relations usually subsumed under the term kinship, an alternative that bridges concerns both ethnographers and archaeologists have had with traditional concepts of corporate kinship groups. Lévi-Strauss (1982, especially pp. 172–74, 1987:151–96) originally developed the concept of house societies as a means to categorize societies which presented problems for his kinship analyses. Thus the house, according to Lévi-Strauss, was a combination of lineal and consanguineal kin and affines. But while a rhetoric of relationship is commonly employed in house societies, the material grounding for relationship is not blood, but common investment in the house estate. This alternative way of looking at social relations, as the product of common activity, rather than a reflection of some essence, aligns the model of the house with contemporary anthropological approaches concerned with agency and the negotiation of social reproduction.

To pursue this point, I begin with the anthropological critique of kinship studies. David Schneider (1984:165–77) characterized "kinship" as an anthropological reification of a European folk concept of essential blood ties. His redescription of his original ethnography of Yapese society, while not explicitly framed in terms of house societies, provides an excellent and unusually detailed analysis of the workings of house persistence over time (1984:21–34; see also Sandstrom, this volume).

Schneider (1984:21) identified the Yapese term *gidi rog,* which may be literally translated as "my people," as the label for "a group of people living together who have different ties to the same land— perhaps a man who holds the land, the woman who lives with him, and the children she bears and they (or one of them) adopt." The dwelling of these people may be called *tabinau,* whether the reference is to the house, the plot of land on which it is located, or the co-resident group of people related through ties to land. "If there are no people, land alone does not constitute a *tabinau.* And people without a relationship through land cannot constitute a *tabinau*" (Schneider 1984:27). Neither birth nor residence alone is sufficient for *tabinau* membership, which is based on carrying out obligations to senior members of the *tabinau.*

Schneider (1984:57–92) demonstrated that what he originally explained as facts of biological relations providing the framework for kinship are better viewed as expressions of relative rights in landed estates physically marked by building platforms and fields. Rather than having an innate right to membership in the group by blood, Yapese must perform particular kinds of service for those in authority over the estate to which they have relative claims, in order to earn their place in the estate; in particular, they provide agricultural labor (1984:29–30). "The land of the *tabinau* was made, and it took work, *magar,* to make it what it is"; "people exchange their work for their rights in the *tabinau*" (1984:27–28). The *tafen,* or head of the *tabinau,* has the authority to allocate land and also to dispossess members of their rights to the land and its products (1984:27).

The major signs of rights in the estate granted to junior members are names, which are property of the estate and are subject to revocation for poor performance of expected duties (Schneider 1984:21–23). Each *tabinau* "is a distinct unit with its own name, made up of a collection of plots of land, that holds a more or less distinctive set of personal names for both men and women. These names are given to the children of women who marry men of the *tabinau.* And of course those who are now dead but were living members of the *tabinau* (called *thagith*) have these names too" (1984:21). Names are maintained by their use by new members, and are *tabinau* property. Those adopted into the *tabinau* are given names from its store.

The *tabinau* as described by Schneider clearly falls into the category of a house, and Yap can be characterized as a house society. While the specific duties owed and privileges earned by members of the *tabinau* are unique to Yap, the relationships described between claiming and validating house membership are typical of other house societies. The Northwest Coast Tlingit mortuary ceremonies described by Sergei Kan (1989:168–74, 213–18) exemplify the public performance of expected duties as a means to claim names and titles, solidify association with the house, and assert individual claims to the right to use such names—in this case, by performance of duties related to deceased house members.

In Yap, the ongoing presence of formerly living members of the *tabinau* was central to its continuity (Schneider 1984:21, 23, 31). The spirits of these deceased members of the *tabinau*, the *thagith*, live in the house platform and intercede with other spirits on behalf of the *tabinau*. The *thagith* explicitly include those who died while resident in the *tabinau*, including in-married women, and excluding women living away from their natal *tabinau*. While the land itself holds the names and titles that make up house identity, it is the dwelling platform, where the ancestral spirits remain, that physically marks the association of the *tabinau* with this land.

This house platform, the *daiv*, is a raised rock and coral foundation on which the dwelling is built, located on a special plot of land, normally that holding the highest-ranking names or titles of the *tabinau* (Schneider 1984:21, 23). Co-existing with the *daiv* on their high-ranking plots of land is a network of shrines sacred to particular mythical female ancestors (*nik*), whose descendants (*genung*) cross-cut the *tabinau* as a result of the normal movement of women from their natal *tabinau* to the *tabinau* in which they and their children earn rights through labor (1984:24–25). Connections between *tabinau* created through women are anchored in the *genung* shrine on its special plot of land. Similarly, other plots of land materially embody various leadership positions: "certain plots contain the offices of elder of the *binau*, chief of the *binau*, chief of the young men of the *binau*, or leader of various kinds of communal fishing and so on. Other plots have the office of those who deal with the spirits (*tamerong*) inherent in them" (1984:23). In a sense, the continuity of the *tabinau* is more generally marked by the built facilities with which former members are credited, and which new members must work to maintain: "those who hold the land today say they are indebted to those who came before for the work they did," including the construction of "paved paths, fitted stone house platforms and houses, terraced gardens, landfill out from the shoreline, the great stone platforms built out into the water from the shoreline on which the *faliu* (the young men's house) stand," taro pits, and stone fish traps (1984:27–28).

The physical anchoring of similar social units has been explored in more

detail by Richard Parmentier (1987), in his study of another Western Microne-
sian island, Belau. His analysis adds a critical connection between the physical
markers of social relations on the landscape and the representation of these
physical features in the reproduction of social memory through oral tradition.

Belau, like Yap, can be characterized as a house society. "In Belau political relations among villages are dominated by the actions of chiefly titlehold-
ers residing in high-ranking houses (*blai*). . . . Each principal house in a village
has belonging to it a male title . . . Each title is a named office which exists independently from the person holding the position at any one time" (Parmentier
1987:66, 67). Membership in a house can be traced through either male or
female links, but the title of the house passes through the women of the house,
even though women normally move to the dwelling of their husband and raise
their children there (1987:66–68). The titles held by high-ranking houses are
inherent in the land, just as they are in Yap (1987:215, 222). Succession to
titles gave the elder member of the house the right to a named seat in the
meetinghouse, where the assembled title-holders conducted village politics
(1987:70–73).

The existence of houses and the titles they held was materially lodged
in stone features on the landscape. Primary among these were "residential
houses (*blai*) and club and chiefly meetinghouses (*bai*), all built upon elaborate
stone foundations and linked together by elevated stone pathways which fan
out from a central paved square," where the backrest stones (*btangch*) of the
high-ranking title-holders were located (Parmentier 1987:56). The stone paths
led from the courtyard to the taro fields that had been constructed by ancestors
of the contemporary residents of the houses.

These stone features, and others, were historicized through oral narratives. Central to the construction of such histories were *olangch*, "permanent
signs which function as present evidence of a significant past" (Parmentier
1987:11–15, 308). Belauan people designated a wide variety of things as
olangch: names, titles, carved narrative pictures, and oral narratives, as well as
practices and objects described in oral narratives, including named ceramic
and glass valuables, anthropomorphic stone monoliths, stone grave pavements, and the prescribed seating patterns represented by sacred stones in the
village meetinghouse and courtyard.

Olangch anchor "mythological narratives in perceived experience" (Parmentier 1987:135–37). Some narratives suggest that the power of *olangch* was
enhanced when they were lodged in a material practice or object. For example, a gift of a name, made in payment for assistance during a building project,
was received with the statement, "We have no real *olangch* of this"; a metal
gong used during the building project, sounded for joy when the name was

presented, was added as an additional *olangch* (1987:283). Stone features were particularly significant *olangch* because of their permanence: "a stone (*bad*) cannot die, it remains forever" (1987:270; compare 2–3, 164–70).

As in Yap, in Belau the most permanent features that served as testimony to the truth of social memory contained in oral narratives were the constructions made by members of houses: the dwelling, taro pits, stone burial pavements, seats for titled house members, and the paths that linked them. In Yap, the work required to make these signs of history was the acknowledged legacy that house members received from their deceased predecessors, constituting a responsibility to continue to work to maintain the house estate. Parmentier shows that the "work" required to maintain a house estate also includes discursive practices: events require "being recorded in narratives, depicted in rafter carvings, commemorated in stones of various kinds, and labeled by names of places, groups, and persons. . . . For future generations, knowledge of the past is entirely mediated by these historical markers . . . and, more specifically, by the politically motivated actions of sign creators and preservers—the carving of a stone, the composition of a chant, the institution of a deferential protocol, or the presentation of an exchange valuable" (Parmentier 1987:307). The work of the house enters history through its transcription in material form, ideally the metonymical form of the house building itself.

HOUSE BUILDINGS AND NAMES: THE CASE OF THE YUROK

Common to house societies is the ability to define a physical estate through which members conceptualize themselves as a single group. The physical expression of house unity is usually, although not always, a building, a house, the dwelling or ceremonial residence of the house elders, or sometimes of the spirits of the ancestors. While the house has perhaps best been illustrated by ethnographers working in Indonesia and in Oceania, Lévi-Strauss's original formulation was based on societies of the Northwest Coast of the United States and other native American groups, and he also applied the model to Africa, feudal Japan, and medieval Europe.

Pivotal in his argument was the case of the Yurok of the Klamath River valley in Northwestern California. After laying out puzzling contradictions in the ethnology of the Kwakiutl *numayma*, Lévi-Strauss (1982:171–73) turned to the Yurok to identify the new social concept that would allow understanding: "At last the word is out; the same word, as a matter of fact, as the Yurok use to designate these, in principle perpetual, establishments": the house. Almost as quickly as he introduced this pivotal case—pivotal because Kroeber described the Yurok as lacking any political or social organization, and because the social organization the house provided was so strong among the Yurok—Lévi-Strauss (1982:174–187) moved on to an extended discussion of European historical examples.

The critical importance of the Yurok to Lévi-Strauss's development of the concept is underlined in his first lectures about house societies, from 1976–77, in which he stated that the Yurok suggested the "answer to the questions posed" (Lévi-Strauss 1987:151). He completely rejected consideration of the dwelling, despite recognizing that Yurok houses, "taken by anthropologists as mere buildings, are the actual bearers of rights and duties. The Yurok house cannot be reduced to a dwelling place. Its hereditary occupants, agnates or cognates, to whom are attached more distant relatives, affines and occasionally clients, exert control over material and immaterial goods" (1987:152). But what is it that the persons exerting control over goods occupy, if not a physical dwelling? In the background of Lévi-Strauss's formulation of house societies is the largely unarticulated case of the Yurok. An examination of the ethnographic literature on the Yurok consulted by Lévi-Strauss demonstrates a profound concurrence with the patterns evident in Yap and Belau, and allows a more explicit examination of the way house buildings themselves became materializations of house continuity and identity, in a setting where early ethnographers denied the presence of social, political, or even symbolic institutions that could have ensured the continuity of the Yurok.

Kroeber (1925:11) stated that "Yurok houses, or their sites, had names descriptive of their position, topography, size, frontage, or ceremonial functions. Many of the designations reappear in village after village. The names of abandoned houses were remembered for at least a lifetime, perhaps nearly as long as the pit remained visible. If a family grew and a son or married-in son-in-law erected a new dwelling adjacent to the old, the original name applied to both houses. Sweat houses were usually but not always called by the same name as the house to whose master they belonged, and seem normally to have been built close by." He reiterated the association of the name with the site: "The habit of naming *house sites* . . . is but one instance of many of the localizations of life in this region, of its deep rooting in the soil" (Kroeber 1925:11–12; emphasis added).

While insisting that there was no political unit among the Yurok, Kroeber did admit that social relationships between houses cross-cut the region (Kroeber 1925:13–14, 21–22, 28–32). He was forced to acknowledge the reality of ties between members of houses in considering property transactions and what he recognized as the operations of traditional law. While frustrated by what he saw as the tenuous nature of Yurok kinship, he noted that men linked through "full and dignified marriage" (distinguished from "half-marriage" by exchange of an acceptable amount of valuables) recognized strong ties to each other; that the husband living with his wife's father in the case of "half-marriage," and the children born of such a union, were linked socially and legally to the man in whose house they lived; and that a married woman's natal house continued to have quantifiable economic interests and legal rights in her and her offspring (compare Waterman and Kroeber 1934).

The monetary expression of Yurok house interests in its members was most obvious to Kroeber. In addition to marriage exchanges, payments were required for each house that had experienced a death during the year before the sacred dances could be held, or if someone inadvertently spoke the name of a deceased person, and these payments went to the house where the person had resided at death, not the natal house (Kroeber 1925:38). The ban on speaking the name of the dead person ended, after a year had passed, with the presentation of the name to a child of the house. Until they inherited a name in this fashion, Yurok children had no formal name, and were addressed by informal designations, sometimes until they were six or seven years old; through the recycling of house names, they might be formally presented with several names during their lives (Kroeber 1925:49). The effects of this practice were to guarantee that a child was a permanent resident of the house before endowing it with a house name, and to ensure the perpetuation of house names by assigning them to children of the house.

The presence of a limited number of house names given to multiple buildings is the historical sign of the social relationships that Kroeber found so diffuse but presented as eminently concrete. Waterman (1920:209) recorded 107 unique names applied to 219 distinct buildings, among them names referring to location within a village or a role in ceremonies, or descriptive of the house building itself. The social memory of names on the landscape was keyed to visible features, like the pit from an abandoned house. Erik Erikson (1943:273–74) described an elderly Yurok pointing to a house pit "like a European nobleman pointing to the castle of his ancestors. . . . What the old Yurok meant in saying he belonged to the pit was that, being born there, he participated in the name which the pit would keep as long as it was visible, and often much longer." Even when no human history could be associated with a pit, it might be interpreted as the remains of the house site of a predecessor spirit, or *wo'ge*: "Old village sites, where the Indian recognizes house pits or natural depressions resembling housepits but about which he has no information, are referred to as *wo'ge* towns . . . these *wo'ge* were so real [to one informant] that he sometimes bewildered me, making me think he was referring to real people. He would point out a 'house pit', for example, and tell me about the structure (which way the door faced, how big it was, etc.) and would then remark, incidentally, that the people who lived in it were immortals" (Waterman 1920:200).

As in Yap, the structures belonging to the house were the result of the work of past house members. Houses were built by kin who were fed, but not paid, for the service, even if they provided cut planks for use (Kroeber 1925:39). A traveler described Yurok houses (*mahlämath*) in 1851 as

constructed of planks, obtained either from ships which have stranded on the seashore, or made by themselves of split [redwood] trees. The floor dimensions of the [houses] are approximately sixteen by twenty feet, the height of the walls is four to six feet, and the height of the gable ten to fifteen feet. In one corner is the door, if the two-feet wide hole through which the inhabitants crawl in and out can be so designated. . . . In the middle of the floor, which is dug out several feet is the fireplace, over which in the roof is a hole that can be closed by means of a cover, which serves the double purpose of a flue and a window. . . . The [Yurok] sit and sleep around the fire, always with the seniors nearest to the fire. . . . The space in front of the [house] is kept very clean and the courtyard is sometimes paved . . . the *mahlämath* stand in straight lines next to each other two to four feet apart, surrounded by a mound of earth. (Meyer 1971 [1855]:265; compare Kroeber 1925:78–80; Jacknis 1995:9–13)

Dwellings of great houses were distinguished visually by having the top plank of the side wall projecting as much as four to five feet beyond the face of the front wall (Pilling 1989:426–28). This unusual architectural feature echoed projecting architectural elements in ceremonial buildings described as reaching "to the end of the world" (Kroeber and Gifford 1949:92). The doors of about one-third of the dwellings Kroeber recorded were decorated with geometric carving (Jacknis 1995:11). The number of roof ridges was an indication of the size of the dwelling, and thus the wealth of the house (Kroeber 1925:78).

Adjacent to about one-third of the Yurok dwellings mapped by Waterman (1920) were sweat houses. The sweat house was a roofed pit house with an interior floor paved with stone slabs or planks and a recessed square stone-lined fire box. A carved wooden pillow was the only furniture used in the sweat house, as men stayed close to the floor for fresh air (Jacknis 1995:11–13). A stone pavement outside the main entrance, placed on one of the long sides, faced the water, while a second smaller exit door was placed on one of the narrow sides of the building. The sweat house was the usual sleeping place of the men of a house, and contained seven named and ranked sleeping places (Kroeber 1925:80–82).

It appears that houses were considered in some ways the equivalent of persons (Jacknis 1995:37). The carved wooden pillow was called the "heart of the sweat house" (Driver 1939:386). The beams, ridgepole, and center post of a ceremonial building used in dances in four Yurok communities were replaced at least every six years, and were "several times treated as if they were a corpse": the ritual specialist said "I will bury you here" and left these six timbers overnight in a shallow grave, with their tip pointing downriver, just as the head of a dead person faced downstream (Kroeber and Gifford 1949:5, 91– 94). This description recalls the treatment of buildings as living beings recorded for other house societies. The Tlingit used body part terms to refer to the house, describing the door as its mouth and the beams and posts forming the frame as the eight long bones that were the permanent part of the human body: "boxes, houses, and human bodies were all containers of such valuables as property, knowledge, and human inhabitants" (Kan 1989:63 64). Similarly, the Yurok sweat house and dwelling house were containers for the people, goods, and nonmaterial property that made up the house estate, and conservation of this estate was the primary focus of the social activities Kroeber witnessed.

The house was the site of everyday life, and its interior was crowded with dried fish, stored acorns, and house valuables. Primary among the prized possessions of the house was dentalium shell money, which was stored in elaborately carved elk horn purses (Kroeber 1925:22–25, 93; Jacknis 1995:19). Other valuables were dance regalia, large obsidian bifaces, woodpecker scalps, and deer skins, stored in special carved wooden boxes (Kroeber 1925: 26–27, 92; Jacknis 1995:19–20). Yurok households also owned elaborate carved spoons and mush paddles (Jacknis 1995:16–17). The carved elk horn spoons were used during dance feasts by male guests, whose presence was also marked by formal deference by women and children toward the male visitors and men of the house (Jacknis 1995:16, 1998, Kroeber 1925:93).

Sacred dances were an opportunity for wealthy Yurok houses to display their valuables in competition with other houses (Kroeber 1925:54–61; Kroeber and Gifford 1949). The dance regalia, woodpecker scalps, deer skins, and obsidian bifaces were normally kept enclosed in carved boxes in the dwelling. Kroeber (1925:55) described the climax of sacred dances as marked by the presentation of "the most famous treasures." Elder men of wealthy houses entrusted to the dancers the valuables of their own house, as well as those of other houses to which they could claim ties of friendship or kinship, and it was the right to equip a dance party that was owned by named houses (Kroeber and Gifford 1949:126).

Kroeber (1925:4–5) noted that all Yurok rituals, including dances, featured what he called "formulas," narrative descriptions of the acts of spirits that were precedents for the ritual, owned by ritual specialists: "the recital of this

former action and its effect is believed to produce the identical effect now."
Erik Erikson (1943:270), quoting a Yurok ritual specialist, put it more clearly:
" 'Every story should have a foundation,' R says, meaning a foundation in
historical fact; 'explain where something began and came from. . . .' Every
magic formula of theirs is an account of the historical event occurring when the
formula was first used." The central action of Yurok ceremonies was a circuit of
places named in formulas (e.g., Kroeber and Gifford 1949:67–68, 76–80).

The specialists who owned the formulas required for sacred dances lived
for the duration of the dances in a sacred house and spent the nights in its associated sweat house. These buildings were "believed to have stood since the
time when there were no men in the world; the planks, it is true, are replaced,
but the structures occupy the identical spot" (Kroeber 1925:53–54). Every
dance was associated with a building, whether it was "a dwelling actually
inhabited at other times; or a sweathouse also used under less publicly sacred
circumstances; or a special structure hybrid between house and sweathouse in
its size and shape and used or entered only for the ceremony" (Kroeber and
Gifford 1949:3; compare Jacknis 1995:11). Dances at four Yurok towns were
actually performed inside dwellings named "Great" or "Big" House, preceded
by singing in a special building named "ancient sweathouse," understood to
have been established at the same place at the beginning of time, whose six
main timbers were regularly replaced as part of the ceremony (Kroeber and
Gifford 1949:86–98, 101–3). Kroeber noted that during these four dances the
"symbolic magic of renewal is most fully expressed in the rebuilding of the
sacred ritual structure . . . These ritual buildings represent the focus of an
impulse toward localization which pervades the system and in fact the whole
culture. Everything that is prescribed must be done only at a specified spot. . . .
the inner, verbal part of each ceremony is attached to an ordained structure or
group of structures in a settlement, and to a series of prayer and offering spots
about or near the town . . . the privilege and responsibility of providing the
equipment for a set of dancers is claimed as right by the descendants of certain
houses" (Kroeber and Gifford 1949:3).

The Yurok landscape was marked by such built features, and by other
places mentioned in oral traditions that were focal points for ritual practice.
Women called to become shamans sought "pains" at "mountaintop half-
enclosures of stone" called "seats" in English (Spott and Kroeber 1971[1942]:
533). The men who recited the formulas necessary for sacred dances to be
effective did so at "rocks or spots that mark the abode of these spirits" (Kroeber
1925:53). Yurok parents also reportedly used rocks as mnemonics for stories
about ancient beings recited to instruct children (Erikson 1943:287). The stone

features associated with links to oral tradition did not need to be large or in their original geological location. The Yurok ritual practitioner who carried out the ceremonies for building a dam to trap salmon used four stones to pound in stakes, identified as the same ones used by spirits in building the original dam, that "were preserved from year to year, being buried by the shaman. It is said that if they were thrown aside when the dam was finished they would return of their own accord to the hiding place" (Waterman and Kroeber 1938:53).

Stone is a particularly important medium for materially anchoring history in many house societies. The Tlingit valued stone as the "hardest, most stationary, and the longest-lasting object in the Tlingit universe. No wonder matrilineal groups indicated their ownership of certain bodies of water and beaches by leaving their marks on large rocks," and considered these stones transformed spirit beings from another time (Kan 1989:56). Place and its history have precedence: Yurok sacred dances were "made at a particular site that has caused the nameless and colorless spirit referred to in the formula to be associated with it, and not the reverse" (Kroeber 1925:55).

Nancy Munn's discussion of the relationship between the *dala*, the house of Melanesian Gawa, and the ancestral fertility lodged in its land, is pertinent. Each *dala* "has separate origin traditions frequently referring to its arrival on Gawa and acquisition of lands . . . the *dala* is physically represented in the land by stones expected to remain when the land is not being gardened. . . . Key garden stones mark the boundaries of *dala*-owned land tracts and cannot be moved" (Munn 1986:27–28). Gardens should be heavy: "the heaviness of the garden is not maintained simply by the crops rooted inside it, but most importantly by stones (*dakula*) that epitomize both heaviness and durability. Stones are hard (*matuwo*) objects that remain inside the land irrespective of whether it is being cleared, burned off, and planted that year or whether it has returned to bush. The most important stones—those that should remain in the land and become visible again when a garden is cleared—mark boundaries and corners of land tracts, junctures of major plot divisions or the center of a given garden. . . . At least one stone or stone cluster in a garden may contain the spirit (*balouma*) of a dala ancestor" (Munn 1986:80–81). The physical markers of the garden serve to materially anchor it, just as the material features recounted in Yurok ritual formulae, and referred to in myth as the signs of the actions of ancient spirits, ensure the same outcomes today as those that happened in the mythical past (compare Parmentier 1987:270).

Yurok houses sustained their claims to economic rights through reference to material features that linked contemporary ceremonies with their mythical precedents. All good hunting land along the rivers in Yurok territory was owned by individual houses, and all fishing spots along the rivers were also owned in perpetuity (Kroeber 1925:33–34). Some ceremonies were tied explicitly to fishing privileges (Kroeber 1925:60–61). A major ceremony was performed at the mouth of the river to initiate the salmon harvest (Waterman and Kroeber 1938:52). It was the property of a house named for two steatite pipes that it held as closely guarded valuables; this house was described in an origin tradition as a living being that helped to bring the salmon (Kroeber and Gifford 1949:99, 122). Although Kroeber was unable to find an eyewitness to its performance, a sacred dance was supposed to have been property of the same house, a claim asserted by his informants and supported by an origin myth.

Sacred dances held in conjunction with the annual construction of a salmon-fishing weir upstream, involving the use of a particular sacred house and sweat house, were the property of another great house (Kroeber 1925:58–60; Kroeber and Gifford 1949:81–85; Pilling 1989:423; Waterman and Kroeber 1938). The origin story for this fish trap and its associated ceremonies told of the destruction of an earlier dam downriver, that sparked its spirit owners into coming in protest to the new dam site, where a clump of redwood trees was identified as the still visible bodies of these spirits (Kroeber and Gifford 1949:114–15; Waterman and Kroeber 1938:69). These redwood trees were propitiated for the use of their twigs in the building of the fish traps through a ceremony in which the participants from downriver communities—the direction of the original dam destroyed in the origin myth—enacted a mock exchange of a woman and stones representing obsidian marriage valuables, along with rights to a fishing place and a spring, to a person playing the part of a redwood spirit mourning the loss of his wife, culminating in dance performances in which twigs and branches were used instead of real ornaments (Waterman and Kroeber 1938:59–60, 66, 69). Like the *olangch* of Belau, these redwood trees, steatite pipes, and other features mentioned in oral traditions were signs of the history of Yurok houses.

Central to house societies is a complex relationship between oral traditions and enduring material features. Erik Erikson (1943:270) noted that "the Yurok indicate that, to them, to tell history means to do something real to the present." The permanent features on the landscape—plots of land, house sites, dwellings, shrines, sweat houses, dance houses, built stone features, and even unmodified rocks and trees—are all containers of the social memory of the house. The dwelling itself serves as an ideal marker of social memory because it can contain the bodies of house members (and in some cases, the physical or spiritual remains of deceased members), the knowledge that these individuals have of traditional claims of the house, and the valuables the house safeguards that serve as concrete and transactable testimony to house traditions.

NAMES, SOCIAL MEMORY, AND HEIRLOOMS

Yurok dwellings contained the people who made up the house and their property. Elaborately carved spoons and mush paddles, carved boxes containing dance regalia, and incised elk horn purses containing dentalium shell money joined the more mundane food, baskets, and cooking utensils as evidence of the wealth of a house (Jacknis 1995:34). But house estates are "made up of both material and immaterial wealth": in addition to such forms of property as agricultural land, heirloom valuables, and the house building, houses may own rights to perform particular ceremonies, to produce particular craft goods, including regalia used in ceremonies, and, most important, to employ particular names and titles. The Yurok house was no exception. "Each great house owned a major dance, a ritual, or a ritual prayer" (Pilling 1989:423). Its immaterial property included distinctive basket designs, ritual formulas, rights to dance regalia, and a stock of names that were assigned to the living members of the house when previous users of the names died (Pilling 1989:423–26, 431–32).

In house societies, the transmission of house names often involved public ceremonies in which valuables played an important role. Through the transmission of house names members of a house are publicly marked as part of the group, and through their actions the names of the house continue to be manifest (Lévi-Strauss 1982:174–75). As part of the Tlingit potlatch held to commemorate a deceased member of the house, new names were given to the surviving house members, and if a new building was constructed, it was named at the same time (Kan 1989:45–46). House songs describing the immaterial crests of the house were sung, and valuables were presented to those from the allied houses attending the ceremony, sources of past in-married spouses, who had performed the necessary mortuary rites. Physical signs of changed status, such as ear-piercing and tattooing, were also bestowed as part of Tlingit naming ceremonies (Kan 1989:46, 88–89). Such naming ceremonies, if held separately from memorial potlatches, were marked by similar feasts and distributions of gifts. In the Trobriand Islands, newborn children were given house names by both mother and father. But the name given by the father was only "loaned," and when needed by the father's house, was reclaimed in a ceremony that included the exchange of women's valuables, decorated red skirts (Weiner 1976:126–27).

Personal naming ceremonies are not the only context in which house histories become lodged in valuables. Any occasion on which one house enters into transactions with another may call for an exchange of valuables. Ceremonies recognizing sexual relationships or commemorating deceased house members are equally prominent settings for the circulation of named valuables between allied houses (Kan 1989:236–46; McKinnon 1991:144–61; Munn 1986:124–38; Parmentier 1987:90, 92, 93–94). Through the use of valuables in ceremonies associated with named persons, specific valuables come to be associated with the histories of house names or titles. A Yurok woman retained a grinding stone from the building used by one of the houses in which she claimed membership, used in the ceremonies associated with the fish dam, and a special dress associated with ceremonies of a second house from which she claimed descent (Pilling 1989:423). Valuables can extend the knowledge of named persons far from the living holder of a name, both in space and in time. Through their permanence, valuables become repositories for the "fame" of members of the house, and of the house itself insofar as it contains these names (Munn 1986:105–9, 111–14; compare McKinnon 1991:99, 243–50; Parmentier 1987:37; Weiner 1976:181). Retained as "inalienable possessions" through strategies of close circulation among permanently allied houses, some valuables serve as house heirlooms, physical evidence of the long-term continuity of the house despite the requirements of external transactions (Weiner 1992; compare McKinnon 1991:91, 95–97, 227–58; Parmentier 1987:77–78).

In Prehispanic Mesoamerican societies costume ornaments were one of the major classes of valuables exchanged in marriage negotiations and incorporated in mortuary offerings (Gillespie and Joyce 1997; Joyce 1999). Some durable stone costume ornaments were conserved over long periods of time and can appropriately be referred to as heirlooms. Jade objects created circa 700–500 B.C. have been recovered archaeologically from caches in the Aztec Great Temple, dating between 1400 and 1520 A.D. (Matos Moctezuma 1996). Equally early jade costume ornaments were deposited in Maya caches and burials of the Classic period (ca. 250–1000 A.D.), and a stylistically similar ornament is depicted on a monument from the Classic Maya city of Piedras Negras (Andrews 1986; Friedel and Sabloff 1984:103–4; Proskouriakoff 1974; Schele and Miller 1986:219).

Retention of costume ornaments as heirlooms was not unique to such very early pieces. A pendant from Kendall, Belize, carved in a style dating to before 150 A.D., was recovered from a burial dating between 250 and 400 A.D. (Schele and Miller 1986:81). An incised peccary skull from Copan that apparently was part of a headdress, recovered from a tomb with pottery vessels

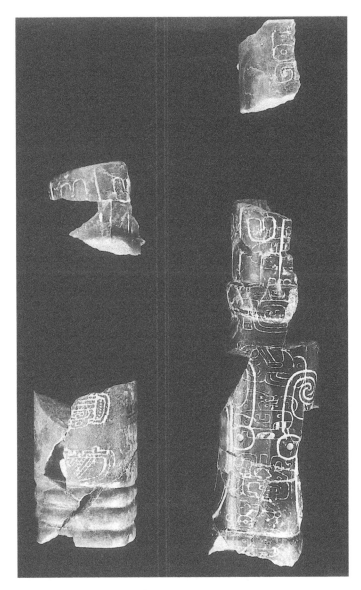

Figure 10-1. Fragments of bar pectoral ornaments recovered from the *cenote* at Chichen Itza. Each would have been suspended horizontally when in used. Incised texts are legible only when turned 90° from their proper orientation. The last four glyphs on the right-hand pendant are a name phrase written in Early Classic style. Other, later carving partially effaces this inscription. The pendants were most likely deposited after 800 A.D., several centuries later than the text inscribed on them. Peabody Museum, catalog 10-78-20/C6125; 63-32-20/C2001. Photo by Steve Burger, Peabody Museum Photographic Archive, negative 32904, © President and Fellows of Harvard College. By permission of the Peabody Museum, Harvard University.

typical of the period after 650 A.D., had a hieroglyphic date several centuries earlier (Coggins 1988:104–6; Baudez 1994:8–9). Undoubtedly many other examples of conservation of earlier valuables are not recognized because they do not differ as obviously in style from the later materials with which they were finally deposited.

Mesoamerican heirloom ornaments often traveled far from their point of origin as well. A shell ornament crafted by Classic Maya artists between 600 and 800 A.D. was recovered from the Central Mexican site of Tula, Hidalgo, whose principal occupation was several centuries later (Schele and Miller 1986:78). At least 21 pieces of jade plaques that originally were pendants from belt ornaments created by Early Classic Maya artists, cut and reworked as new pendants, were deposited in Costa Rican sites after 600 A.D. (Late Classic), and one has been reported from El Salvador (Houston and Amaroli 1988; Lange 1993:284).

Like their ethnographic analogues, the costume ornaments kept as heirlooms by Mesoamerican peoples were unique valuables that could acquire specific histories. The Maya used writing to inscribe historical texts directly on some of these valuables (Figure 10-1). Some texts were clearly added long after the original creation of the ornament. A pendant that probably was produced on the Mexican Gulf Coast sometime between 800 and 500 B.C. carries a low-relief incised figure and inscription on the reverse, in a style typical of the Maya writing system of around 50–250 A.D. (Coe 1966; Schele and Miller 1986: 119). The text records the "seating" in office of a named ruler, and the figure incised next to it is shown in the same seated position wearing regalia of this office.

Other Maya heirloom costume ornaments incised with specific notations of political ceremonies were recovered from much later contexts. The incised jade belt pendant known as the Leiden Plaque was found near the mouth of the Motagua River in Guatemala, with objects suggesting a date after 800 A.D. (Morley and Morley 1938). One side depicts an image of a standing figure wearing a belt ornamented with sets of three plaques hanging from ornamental masks. The text refers to a "seating" that took place at the Maya city, Tikal, sometime before 400 A.D. (Mathews 1985:44, Schele and Miller 1986:118, 120–21). This belt ornament circulated from its original place of creation, probably near the inland settlement named in its text, for at least 400 years before being carefully deposited with other valuables by later Maya people of the coast.

The texts and images incised on costume ornaments reinforced the effectiveness of the ornaments as material signs of the achievement of particular titles by condensing the use of an ornament with its historical precedent. A pendant recovered from a natural well (*cenote*) at Chichen Itza, apparently deposited sometime after 800 A.D., exemplifies this multiple layering of reference (Proskouriakoff 1974). In form, the ornament is a tubular jade bead that would have been oriented with its long axis horizontal when worn. Perpendicular to this orientation are carvings on two sides, one a text, the other an image of a young man standing with a heel raised in the Classic Maya stylization of movement. The figure wears a complex costume ornament on the chest, with a central tubular bead pendant like that on which the image is inscribed as the most prominent feature. The text refers to events in the life of a young Palenque noble, who lived between 650 and 800 A.D., related to his assumption of noble titles. One clause literally described him as "taking a step into" or "entering" the succession of rulers, the action mirrored in the image incised on this ornament.

A second example of an heirloom jade ornament incised with its history was also recovered from the *cenote* at Chichen Itza. This three-dimensional pendant portrait head was incised on the reverse and top surfaces with a single continuous text (Grube 1992b:494–95; Proskouriakoff 1944). The text records the completion of 13 calendrical cycles as lord of Piedras Negras, far south and west of Chichen Itza, by an unnamed ruler. It is fixed in time through a second clause, which makes a rare use of the future tense to state that in 7 cycles it will be the end of the first 20-cycle period as ruler of the site of this individual, whose personal name or titles, largely eroded, end the text. The event recorded was the adoption of the title of *ahaw* (lord) by the ruler. The ornament itself, a frontal human face, is the iconic version of *ahaw* and mimics the textual sign for this title. Its peculiar shape required that it be mounted on the front of a socketed armature, stabilized by cords passed through holes in the back of the chin, and it most likely served as the front ornament of a headdress that signified the right to the *ahaw* title, like those depicted in other Maya images (Fields 1991; Freidel 1993:154–59).

Both the Piedras Negras and the Palenque pendants were burned and broken before being thrown into the sinkhole pool at Chichen Itza, and were laboriously pieced together from fragments by archaeologists. Their recovery raises the question of the degree to which incised heirloom ornaments recovered from secondary locations can be considered to have had continued significance as repositories of social memory. Most students of the circulation of such inscribed Maya ornaments have regarded their reuse as evidence of recycling of raw material (especially commonly cited for the Costa Rican practice of cutting up Maya belt ornaments) or of looting of earlier sites. But the structured nature of the practices in which these items were used is a strong argument against such assumptions. Materials recovered from the cenote at

Chichen Itza present evidence of a formal sequence of ritual disposal of valued objects according to a set procedure of great antiquity within Classic Maya culture (Coggins and Shane, eds. 1984; Garber 1993:170). Tatiana Proskouriakoff (1974, 1993:87) suggested that these jades were looted from burials in antiquity, but was troubled by the inconsistency between this interpretation and her own identification of the probable burial of the ruler named on the Piedras Negras ornament with an undisturbed tomb. Grube (1992b:494), among others, suggests that these items were carried to the *cenote* by descendants of the ruler for whom they were manufactured, and who had conserved them as heirlooms of great value.

Even at their furthest remove from their sources of origin, Mesoamerican heirloom items continued to be used in ways consistent with their history as house valuables and repositories of powerful histories. Different forms of ornaments, all of which apparently reached Central America after 500 A.D., were treated in distinct ways. Incised "clam shell" pendants created before 500 B.C. were generally conserved unaltered or deliberately terminated in the same fashion as that used by the Maya (Guerrero 1993:193; Hirth and Grant Hirth 1993:186–87; but see Lange 1993:284 for a different view). Incised slate mirror backs with Maya texts dating to circa 250–400 A.D. were generally preserved intact as well (Baudez and Coe 1966; Stone and Balser 1965). In contrast, the belt pendant plaques that reached Costa Rica were always cut, but in a uniform fashion, either split in half lengthwise, or further divided into squares, a deliberate dismembering that recognizes the previous markings by systematically distorting them (Graham 1993:23).

Not all heirloom valuables were recovered at great distances from their sites of origin. They tended to be deposited in burials of nobles within the sites where they were made, and often the inscriptions seem to record persons other than the deceased individual. For example, shell plaques from a male burial at Piedras Negras record the names of a woman (Proskouriakoff 1993:84–87; Stuart 1985). The burial was located within a building that formed part of a group associated with the monuments of the same ruler commemorated on the jade ornament recovered from the *cenote* at Chichen Itza. The woman named in the inscriptions on the shells was also mentioned in monuments detailing events in the life of that ruler. The inscription on the shells records the birth of the noble woman in the territory of the Piedras Negras ruler. Dated shortly before the accession of the next ruler of the site, the final action recorded on the shells is described as taking place in the territory of the noble woman, perhaps implying a period of political authority between the male rulers.

Alternatively, Classic Maya inscribed heirlooms may name the *object* as property of a specific historical person, and reinforce the role of text in creating histories for objects. These "name-tag" texts take the form of possessive state-ments: "his or her [object type], name and titles of a person" (Houston and Taube 1987; see also Joyce and Shumaker 1995:46; Justeson 1983). A jade carving collected in Comayagua, Honduras, in the nineteenth century is a good example (Grube 1992a; Schele and Miller 1986:81–82). The ornament is a modeled portrait head that would have served as the centerpiece of a belt, supporting a set of three pendant plaques. Incised on the reverse of the portrait is a partially eroded text that refers to a lord of Palenque. The actions it records appear to be those involved in sacralizing the belt head itself.

These texts served to fix the use of the ornament at a particular point in time; they inscribe a specific history for and on the object. This is a history of being used by specific persons, and so the names of human beings are given permanent material form in the heirlooms. This history is necessarily carried along as the object is transmitted from person to person. By placing heirloom valuables with inscribed histories in tombs, Classic Maya nobles took them out of circulation and transformed them from transactable media into permanent points of historical reference.

The casual nature of much of the information available for heirloom orna-ments makes it difficult in most cases to document the patterns of circulation of these valuables. The extraordinarily well-documented excavations of Altun Ha, a Classic Maya site in northern Belize, provide an unusual opportunity for a fine-grained examination of such practices. While only a fraction of the site has been excavated, a number of chronologically related deposits containing inscribed heirloom valuables were recovered. They illustrate all the patterns discussed so far: the use of text to annotate items in ways that were invisible when the ornaments were worn; the incorporation of genealogical, social, and descriptive information that reinforces the practice-based associations of the object and its imagery; and the disjunction between the identity of the buried individual and of others named in the text, suggesting that these are not simply personal, but house property.

A pair of obsidian ear ornaments from the tomb of a male noble, dated to approximately 550 A.D., was incised with a single continuous inscription sty-listically typical of the period between 250 and 400 A.D. (Mathews 1979). The text would have been invisible, obscured by the ear, when the ornaments were worn. It consists of the possessive phrase, "his/her ear spool" followed by the titles of the owner. Although originally interpreted as a male name, the text begins with the title marking noble women's names, followed by a personal name. The text continues on the second ear spool with a new clause, intro-duced by a possessive that can be paraphrased "his/her mother," followed by two titles, one referring to junior members of a house, the second to a set of patron deities.

A pin carved from deer antler from a second burial also carries a reference to a noble woman's relationship to a noble man, not recognized originally. Again, the text is in the style of the period before 400 A.D., but was found in a burial dating to circa 600 A.D. (Mathews, cited in Pendergast 1982:63–64). The text is brief: a personal name is followed by the sign "child of a woman" which introduces the name of the mother, written with two signs—"noble woman" and a partly obliterated animal head. Mathews noted close parallels with a stylistically later text on a jade ornament from the same burial. This ornament carries a woven mat design, symbolic of seats of power, on one side, and a brief text on the reverse. The text may be glossed "noble woman, his mother, the young noble man," a genealogical claim entirely composed of honorific titles. The burial itself, like the tomb containing the incised ear spools, was lavishly stocked with durable wealth, including the largest single carved jade known from the Maya world, but also offered an unusual indication of the importance of soft valuables usually not preserved in the tropical environment. Pendergast (1982:65) notes that "virtually the entire crypt appears to have been draped in cloth . . . a bolt of cloth or a stack of pieces, lay on the southwest corner of the platform . . . much of the preserved cloth is coloured red . . . that appears to be the result of dyeing. . . . it appears the walls may have been draped with textiles . . . at least two separate objects, and possibly three or more, were represented in the lot from the southeast corner."

A longer text was preserved on a bead pendant in a third tomb, dated to circa 650 A.D.. At right angles to its orientation when worn, this pendant was carved with an enthroned male noble on one side and a long text on the opposite side (Mathews, cited in Pendergast 1982:84–87). Two dates contained in the text refer to days in the years 569 and 584 A.D., making the pendant only slightly older than the tomb in which it was laid. The text records a ritual action that took place at a location in the territory of a named title-holder on the earlier date, and the assumption of a noble title by the ruler of Altun Ha on the later date. Named by title, this ruler is referred to as the child of a named noble woman and the offspring of a male person referred to only by title as a 20-cycle lord (see also Mathews and Pendergast 1979).

Separated by periods of approximately one lifetime each, these three noble burials present a frozen image of the transaction of named valuables through time in the context of mortuary ceremonies. Each burial included abundant wealth items, many unique in their imagery, most used as costume items worn, according to the testimony of contemporary images, for social and political ceremonies. The costume ornaments with incised texts could not have been displayed for their historical content, since that content was largely obscured when they were in use. But the inscriptions on these ornaments, each of them at least slightly out of time in its final resting place, could have served as mnemonic scripts for recitations of house claims to authority and kin relationships. Such a use of previously inscribed ornaments would account for the disjunction between the sex of those buried and the actors named in texts, as heirs of houses conserved the valuables they gained through alliance along with the historical knowledge of those alliances that these valuables literally contained.

The self-referentiality of ornaments inscribed with texts is most obvious, but other Maya heirlooms subject to recirculation and ultimate deposition in the *cenote* at Chichen Itza also historicized their own presentation on the bodies of powerful nobles. The jade pendants in what Proskouriakoff (1974) called Nebaj style show seated rulers in elaborate costume, wearing pendants of the same general size and shape. With or without written exegesis incorporated on them, these Classic Maya ornaments made the occasions of their own use concrete and served as permanent references to specific historical events claimed as precedents by members of the houses that owned and used them.

CONCLUSION

The apparently transactable, but actually fixed, media provided by heirloom valuables with attached histories exemplify the resources strategically employed by members of house societies in competition with other houses. In house societies, a core of residents related through a combination of descent, marriage, and patron-client links cooperate in pursuit of the economic and social persistence of the house (e.g., McKinnon 1991:134–62, 199–226). Each individual's work advances the interests of the house as a whole. At the same time, each individual is a potential member of a contending faction within the house, when individual interests clash with those of the group. James Boon (1990b:215) describes houses as "ranked both internally and externally by birth order, by anisogamy, and by other indices of differential transmissions of estates, heirlooms, titles, prerogatives, and renown." Hierarchy is contested and negotiated through alliances and exchanges, where individual and house interests may part ways (McKinnon 1991:259–76).

David Schneider's reanalysis of Yap describes the core relationship in the *tabinau*, that of *citamangen* and *fak*, as inherently embodying hierarchy within the house. Glossed in his earlier description as the relationship between senior kin in a male line and junior kin, fathers and children, these terms are redescribed as senior and junior positions with respect to rights in the land (compare Schneider 1984:12–13, 29–30). *Citamangen* give care and protection, guidance, and authority to their *fak*, who reciprocate by obeying the *citamangen* and working on *tabinau* land.

As Susan McKinnon (1991) demonstrates, the boundary between high- and low-ranking houses is fluid and subject to different representations, as lower-ranking houses strive to formally recognize sexual alliances that noble houses choose to ignore. Among the Yurok, "even when basic circumstances interrupted the continuity of male lineage, the basic point of view was reaffirmed that the desirable and moral course was to pay fully for one's wife and to keep her and one's children at one's natal home. Only thus were the best standards upheld. The matter of residence might be adjusted, and so might the amount; but every compromise reaffirmed the standards" (Waterman and Kroeber 1934:3; compare Kroeber 1925:28–32). Such differences do not simply represent adoption of emic and etic perspectives; they reflect real, and interesting, divergence between asserted status and wealth. Where the consummation of marital alliances requires economic exchanges, there will be a relationship between wealth and status, between the fluidity of the boundary demarcating high-ranking houses and the inability of high-ranking houses to concentrate control of wealth in their own hands.

But wealth alone is not enough; and here the physical signs of the truth of historical claims to status are crucial. In Belau, "political rank thus depends in part on the control of historicizing *olangch* (narratives as well as stones)" (Parmentier 1987:257). The process is recursive, and changes in meaning can lead to changes in the form of durable signs of historical truth: "the receiving generation is not confined, however, to the automatic or neutral transmission of these records to its heirs, but it also capable of actively shaping the course of the historicizing process . . . historical signs can even be rendered mute: sacred stones are thrown into the lagoon or remain hidden beneath underbrush, exchange valuables are locked in banks, and rafter beams are left to rot when the meetinghouse decays or is blown down by a typhoon. More interesting, though, are cases in which these signs themselves become engaged in social activity because of their representational function and become thereby modified, either physically through alteration in their semiotically relevant properties or conceptually through the sedimenting potential inherent in contexts of action to contribute a subtle revaluation to the sign's meaning" (Parmentier 1987:307–8).

In the negotiation of status that typifies house societies, wealth and history serve as validations of each other, permanence in place is transformed into authority over place, and material displays are evidence of the rights to the immaterial property claimed through such display (Kan 1989:69–70, 94–95, 223, 246).

Taken to the extreme—as it was among the Yurok—the negotiation of status through practice in house societies can result in unresolvable conflicts as equally strong claims are advanced and cannot be reconciled (for example, Kroeber 1925:58; Kroeber and Gifford 1949:70–71). It is perhaps in this regard, finally, that the Yurok provided Lévi-Strauss with the original clue to the solution of his problem, and in this way that they epitomized house societies: "The Yurok procedure is simplicity itself. Each side to an issue presses and resists vigorously, exacts all it can, yields when it has to, continues the controversy when continuance promises to be profitable or settlement is clearly suicidal, and usually ends in compromising more or less. Power, resolution and wealth give great advantages; justice is not always done; but what people can say otherwise of its practices? The Yurok, like all of us, accept the conditions of their world, physical and social; the individual lives along as best he may; and the institutions go on" (Kroeber 1925:22).

I gratefully acknowledge comments on an earlier version of this essay by John S. Henderson, and irreplaceable guidance on the ethnography of the Yurok provided by Ira Jacknis.

Notes

1. Because "house" is a common word with many referents, it has become difficult to distinguish the house as defined by Lévi-Strauss and other scholars, as a specific social configuration, from its meaning as a dwelling or residential structure. One common solution has been to capitalize House when it refers to the Lévi-Straussian social group (e.g., Errington 1989:234; Hugh-Jones 1993; Rivière 1993; Schrauwers 1997); Sellato (1987a:196) further restricted the capitalized word for the dominant or ruling Houses of stratified societies. However, this solution becomes unworkable when the word begins the sentence or when it is translated into languages, such as German (*Haus*), that have different capitalization rules. It also introduces an analytical separation between the social group and the house that is the focus for its definition and identity, a distinction that is not always useful.

2. This notion also takes us back to the foundation of anthropology as evidenced in the last book by Lewis Henry Morgan, *Houses and House-Life of the American Aborigines* (1965 [1881]).

3. Lévi-Strauss presented his definition of the house in part as an attempt to understand societies which tend more toward ambilaterality than unilineality (1982). His conception of the house is similar in some respects to Paul Kirchhoff's (1959) earlier characterization of "conical clans." Kirchhoff, like Lévi-Strauss, sought to use this concept to "bridge the still existing gulf between the facts of anthropology and those of early European history" (1959:377).

4. Historical investigations include Schrauwers's (1997) study of proto-houses in South Sulawesi and Waterson's (1995a) examination of Japanese documentary information; see also Boon's (1977) earlier work on Balinese optional ancestral groups.

CHAPTER 2. *MAISON* AND *SOCIÉTÉ À MAISONS*

1. Kroeber's study of the Yurok cited by Lévi-Strauss was published in 1925. Kroeber (1938) later foreshadowed subsequent critiques of lineage theory in suggesting that the kinship principle was secondary and epiphenomenal to other, primary phenomena for the organization of groups, such as place of residence (see also Kuper 1982:78). The dialectic of residence and kinship lies at the core of understanding the Yurok and other house societies.

2. Another means by which the Kwakiutl and many other societies added to their estates was not discussed by Lévi-Strauss and is rarely mentioned by other scholars investigating house societies because it is outside the realm of kinship proper, but it deserves further study—conquest or captive-taking in war. As Mauss (1985[1938]:8–9) briefly mentioned for the Kwakiutl, by killing an enemy, or at least seizing his ritual regalia, a man could inherit thereby "his names, his goods, his obligations, his ancestors, his 'person' [*personne*], in the fullest sense of the word."

3. Mauss (1985[1938]:4ff), in his discussion of this same phenomenon among the Kwakiutl, Zuñi Pueblo, the Winnebago, and other groups in North America and elsewhere, referred to these named positions within a clan or a secret society as permanent "characters" or "roles" (*personnages*) occupied or embodied by specific individuals and thus came close to realizing the importance of the house: "What is at stake in all this is thus more than the prestige and the authority of the chief and the clan. It is the very existence of both of these and of the ancestors reincarnated in their rightful successors, who live again in the bodies of those who bear their names, whose perpetuation is assured by the ritual in each of its phases. The perpetuation of things and spirits is only guaranteed by the perpetuating of the names of individuals, of persons" (1985:8).

4. Cécile Barraud (1990:228) later observed, "What is indeed striking in Indonesia is the mutual identification of person and house, not as independent units, but as sets of permanent relationships."

5. A similar understanding of the house as a socio-economic unit was reached by an anthropologically influenced historian who investigated household economy and ideology from the eighteenth- and nineteenth-century court records of Neckarhausen, Germany (Sabean 1990). This research demonstrated how taxonomic approaches to households, which treat them as things classifiable into types each having its own quantifiable characteristics, lack utility because they neglect the within-house relationships that are "at the heart of social processes" (1990:100). The Neckarhausen *Haus* was an important indigenous concept used in everyday situations, but historical records re-

vealed that this noun was actually extremely rare. In contrast, the verb *hausen*, referring to the economic and physical aspects of a married couple living and working together in a household, was quite frequent. Sabean (1990:101) summarized the indigenous view of the house as "a central idiom for expressing values, making claims, allocating blame, and struggling over resources . . . its use was always strategic and continually touched on issues of hierarchy, exchange, reciprocity, right, and obligation." This *Haus* was not a house in the Lévi-Straussian sense, however, for it did not perpetuate itself or maintain an estate across generations.

6. A symposium on the house held in Oslo in 1996 was briefly reported on (Sparkes 1997a, b) but has not yet been published. It, too, focused on the house in Southeast Asia, looking at its relationship to the built environment and to social, economic, and political organization, especially as many of these societies are undergoing profound demographic and economic changes. I am indebted to Clark Cunningham for calling this symposium to my attention.

7. Headley's (1987:214) further remarks make clear that rather than dealing with independent sociopolitical systems, his examples of the "weak" house refer to peasant village-dwellers within a larger complex system that may include "strong" (true) houses. What becomes of interest is why the strategies these peoples pursue and the ideology of the house they have adopted are different from those of groups organized in true houses within the same sociopolitical system. A key difference seems to be the referent that objectifies the house—the concentrated and perpetuated estate in true (high-ranked) houses versus the transitory personification of a family's "siblings" in lower-ranked groups (1987:214; see McKinnon 1991:32 for the similar contrast between "named" and "unnamed" houses in Tanimbar, Indonesia).

8. The "fetish" notion of the house was thus broadened beyond Lévi-Strauss's original usage. In her Malaysian example, Janet Carsten (1987:166) carefully separated her use of the term "fetish" from Lévi-Strauss's discussion. His examples considered the literal objectification of the house as an elaborate physical structure, whereas she envisions a "phantasmagoric" or "shadow" house as a metaphysical phenomenon. Furthermore, the house as fetish or representation has been applied to both extremes of sociopolitical hierarchy, the "strong" as well as the "weak" ends of the spectrum. In highly stratified states, the royal palace is metaphorically extended to encompass the entire polity as a similar fetishistic image, but on a much larger scale (Sellato 1987a: 202–3; also Errington 1989; see Headley 1987 for a slightly different perspective on the royal house as representation rather than institution).

9. Stephen Hugh-Jones (1993) observed a similar problem for the Amazonian Tukanoans, but took a very different perspective on the utility of the

house concept from that of James Fox (1987), one more along the lines that Lévi-Strauss (1987:158) had argued for the Balinese *dadia* (see above). Hugh-Jones noted there is "considerable ambiguity as to precisely at what level—longhouse, sib, sib-set, endogamous group—the notion of House applies and ambiguity too concerning who represents whom and who owns what. In one sense this is a non-issue for the Tukanoan House is an ideal, ritual construct . . . But on a more practical level, these issues . . . are the very essence of traditional Tukanoan politics. . . . Demographic fluctuations, the adoption of individuals and sometimes whole sibs from one group to another, and transfers of ritual wealth by both ceremonial exchange and illicit theft and borrowing, have left a situation in which, though all subscribe to the same ideal picture, not everyone agrees as to how this ideal maps onto current reality" (Hugh-Jones 1993:110).

10. Schrauwers (1997:376) drew the parallel between this situation and the relationship between the Shan and Kachin described by Leach (1965) for highland Burma: "the *santina* is to the Luwu' *kapolo* what the [Kachin] *gumsa* polity is to the Shan state. The *santina*, like the *gumsa* realm, appears to unsuccessfully 'emulate' the more highly stratified bordering state; it is unsuccessful in translating itself into a ranked House, however, because the very means by which it establishes its 'Household'—a secondary funeral—dissipates its centre, its shared inheritance which objectifies its marriage alliances. Its inheritance spent, the *santina* tends to disperse under the weight of genealogical amnesia, giving rise to an oscillation not unlike that between *gumsa* and *gumlao*."

CHAPTER 3. NAHUA TOPONYMIC GROUPS AND HOUSE ORGANIZATION

1. Despite the relative neglect of social organization in Mesoamerican research, a few excellent studies of Nahua kinship have appeared over the years (examples include Arizpe-Schlosser 1972a, b, 1973; Dehouve 1978; Murphy 1976; Nutini 1967, 1968, 1976; Taggart 1972, 1975a, b, 1976). In 1993, Eileen Mulhare organized a symposium at the American Anthropological Association meetings on supra-domestic social organization in Mesoamerica. The papers from this symposium were published as a special issue of the journal *Ethnology* 35,2 (Spring 1996), 3 (Summer 1996).

2. See Kuznar (1997) for a summary of the postmodern critique and a strong argument to return to a more scientific anthropology.

3. Sandstrom 1991:157–92; see also Stresser-Péan 1979 for a brief description of this fascinating region, and Sandstrom 1995 for a summary description of Nahua culture.

4. Nahuas name their kin using a combination of Eskimo and Hawaiian

terminological systems that is compatible with their bilateral type of descent (Sandstrom 1991:159–66). Interestingly, Lévi-Strauss writes that the cousin designation in Eskimo and Hawaiian systems "allows the . . . freedom to disguise social or political maneuvers under the mantle of kinship" (Lévi-Strauss 1982:176). In other words, the term "cousin" or the equation of siblings with cousins allows people to manipulate social groups for political ends. House societies exemplify this type of social manipulation, and the Nahuas are no exception.

5. Cognatic systems such as we find among the Nahuas are often seen by anthropologists as being too inclusive to form functioning descent groups. Lévi-Strauss reverses this common view by writing that cognatic systems actually function to constrict the number of kinsmen in a given setting: "what seems to be operating here in the kindred is a sort of selection procedure, operating in such a way that some elements come to reinforce the agnatic lineage, whereas others are definitely excluded from it" (Lévi-Strauss 1987:164). In other words, cognatic systems are designed to distance certain kinsmen from agnatic cores.

6. Interestingly, part of this rivalry is vividly expressed in Nahua oral narrations that portray the father, who actually plays a significant positive role in the socialization of his children, as a self-serving and negative personage (Taggart and Sandstrom 1996).

7. The concept of house society also has the potential to resolve a long-standing debate in Mesoamerican anthropology about the nature of the Aztec *calpulli*. The *calpulli* ("great house") functioned as a unit of land tenure, a focus of ritual activity, a productive unit, a means of separating classes within estates (see Nutini 1995), a kinship unit, a military unit, and a political and administrative division (Hunt and Nash 1967:260). All these features are, for the most part, congruent with house society as outlined by Lévi-Strauss. The use of the house society concept to further understanding of the *calpulli* is an approach calling for further research.

CHAPTER 5. TEMPLES AS "HOLY HOUSES"

1. Firth himself makes this point clearly: "In Tikopia view the origin of the temples was quite clear—they were former dwelling places in which ancestors had been buried and which had been abandoned for domestic life accordingly as the site became too heavily charged with spirit potential for comfort" (1970:114).

2. There is a hint, in the writings of the nineteenth-century Hawaiian sage Samuel Kamakau, of temples being constructed on ground made sacred

through former use. He writes that *Heiau* "could not be built just anywhere, but only upon sites formerly built on by ka po'e kahiko [people of old]" (1976:132).

CHAPTER 6. THE CONTINUOUS HOUSE

1. "Neolithic" here refers to the whole period of prehistory in Southeast Europe which covers the seventh to the fourth millennium B.C., which in the local literature is broken down into a Neolithic-Early Eneolithic-Late Neolithic sequence (Tringham 1991b).

2. Details of the archaeological project of the Opovo site may be found in Tringham (1994b; Tringham et al. 1985, 1992, 2000).

3. Details of the 1960s excavation of this site may be found in Mellaart (1967, 1972). Those of the more recent 1993–present excavations may be found in Hodder (1997, Hodder, ed. 1997) and the Çatalhöyük Web page (www.catal.arch.cam.ac.uk/catal/catal.html). In the latter are also the reports of the BACH team (Berkeley Archaeologists @ Çatalhöyük).

CHAPTER 7. MAYA "NESTED HOUSES"

1. Carsten and Hugh-Jones (1995:2) described the house not just as a container but as "an extension of the person, like a second skin, carapace or second layer of clothes, it serves as much to reveal and display as it does to hide and protect"; see also Errington (1979).

2. Keane (1995:104); see, e.g., Carsten and Hugh-Jones (1995), Cunningham (1994), Ellen (1986), Fox, ed. (1993), Waterson (1990, 1993); see Lok (1987) for a Mexican example.

3. For detailed descriptions of traditional Maya house construction, including names of house parts, see, e.g., Breton (1984:167–77), Gann (1918: 26–27), La Farge (1947:30–31), Redfield and Villa Rojas (1962[1934]:33–35), Thompson (1930:91–92, Pl. X), Tozzer (1907:63–64), Villa Rojas (1945:51–52), Vogt (1969:71–83), and Wisdom (1940:119–28).

4. See John Chance's (1996) description of a fundamental social unit of central Mexico, the *teccalli*, "lord-house" or "noble house," following on the work of Pedro Carrasco (1976:21–22). Although Chance did not make reference to the literature on house societies, his explanation of the organizing principles of the *teccalli* match the expectations of a house. See also Sandstrom's (this volume) comment on the Aztec *calpulli*, "great house."

5. Attempts to understand Maya social organization, according to the pervasive assumption that they were organized in patrilineages, have been beset by some of the same problems encountered by ethnographers and histo-

rians that are highlighted by Lévi-Strauss in his discussion of house societies (in Chapter 2; Gillespie 1995). For example, high-ranking persons acknowledged links to their uterine relatives, including inheritance of titles, as recorded in both ethnohistoric (Roys 1940:38) and earlier epigraphic texts (e.g., Marcus 1983:470). In the Classic period, women were prominently displayed and named in some of the monumental artworks, and high-ranking females were the recipients of elaborate mortuary ritual (McAnany 1995:61, 123). Furthermore, shared residence was as important a determinant of social group membership as common descent (Carmack 1981:62; Farriss 1984:137).

6. See, e.g., Alfredo López Austin (1993) and Alan Sandstrom (1991) for descriptions of this animating force. Waterson's (1990:115–16) discussion of *semangat* in Indonesia demonstrates that it, too, is conceived and treated as both a personalized and impersonalized force.

7. Such shrines are not unique to Palenque. For example, a miniature house (with an inside height of 2 feet) was built against the back wall inside the temple atop Pyramid A-I, Uaxactun, Guatemala (Smith 1934:5, Pl. I).

8. To interpret this Palenque usage, Stephen Houston (1996:139) turned to the symbolic importance of the sweat house among the Mam Maya of Chimaltenango in highland Guatemala (in Wagley 1949). In this community, families did not have household altars; instead, the family sweat house was the focal point for the ritual continuity of family membership. The afterbirth was buried in the father's sweat house, and this action was considered to bind an individual to the patrilateral extended family. Adults carried out ritual activities at the sweat house in which their afterbirth was buried (Wagley 1949:23–24, 54). See also Waterson (1990:198) for a brief discussion of the "intimate association of the individual with the placenta (which is widely regarded as a sort of twin), and the house where it is buried" as a notable feature in many Indonesian societies.

9. The sarcophagus's hollow interior gives the impression of a cave within the earth (Benson 1985:185). Caves and sweat houses are likened to earth-wombs in Mesoamerican cosmology. They represent a point of transition and the transcendence of life and death; the dead are placed within the earth, and the newly born emerge from sweat houses in which their mothers gave birth. The usual interpretation of the scene on the sarcophagus cover (Figure 7-3) is the descent of Pakal into the underworld at the moment of death, falling into a cave-like earth-entrance formed by profile skeletal serpent heads (Robertson 1983:57). However, Pakal can also be seen as a seed being planted in the typical fashion—dropped into a hole in the ground made by a digging stick (the ceiba tree behind him?); the juxtaposition of fertility with funerary symbolism is widely known (Bloch and Parry 1982). As noted above, there is

ethnohistorical exegesis that the ancestors emerged from the earth at the roots of a ceiba tree. In the lowland Maya languages used in the hieroglyphs, Yucatec and Cholan, *pak'* means "to plant" (Kaufman and Norman 1984:128), and in Yucatec *pak'al* is an orchard or a tree in the orchard (Barrera Vásquez et al. 1980:624–25). The fruit trees juxtaposed behind each of Pakal's ancestors on the sarcophagus's four sides create an enclosing orchard around Pakal, like the orchards planted in the yard around the house. A different but related interpretation of this imagery can be made by referring to colonial Tzotzil *pakal*, signifying a bench, chair, or seat (Laughlin 1988:278), and by extension a foundation, a place of immobility and concentrated power.

10. David Stuart (1998:393–94) suggests that Classic Period hieroglyphic texts concerning rituals involving burning incense that were apparently used to dedicate structures, an event that can be glossed as "fire-entering," may be much earlier manifestations of this type of ceremony.

11. More such information is becoming available as epigraphers now recognize that many of the hieroglyphic texts that occur on or adjacent to buildings recorded dedications and similar rituals focused on those structures and their spaces (Stuart 1998:375).

12. See also Wisdom's (1940:119) description of Chorti house compounds in a forest clearing. Similarly, the Nahua-speaking people of the village of Amatlan, Veracruz, Mexico built their residences in clusters of two to eight houses, usually but not always belonging to patrilineally related males, in a cleared area of the forest. These cleared areas, connected by trails, formed the basic settlement pattern of the village until a gridded road system was recently introduced. It is the group of houses in the clearing that is referred to as *caltinej*, "houses." Such individual clearings are named, and the resulting toponyms locate not only spatial units where individuals reside but also the individuals themselves within the social organization, for they often take their identifying names or nicknames from the name of their *caltinej* (Sandstrom 1991:107; see Sandstrom, this volume).

13. An additional important component to the nestedness of the house that links it to the body is the notion that the house is a womb. Waterson (1990:196–97) observed that while the concept of house as womb may be universal, an "irreducibly 'natural' symbol," its implications may vary considerably from one society to the next and are especially dependent on gender relationships and ideology. Maya notions of gender complementarity are similar to those of Southeast Asia described by Waterson. The house is like a "mother"—and in Yucatec Maya *na* (house) is homophonous with *na'* (mother) (Barrera Vásquez et al. 1980:545)—but the reference is not simply to the fe-

male gender. "Mother" represents the joining of female and male as procreator, and thus signifies origins and the source of life; hence *na*, "mother," is also the word for origin (Barrera Vásquez et al. 1980:545; see Gillespie and Joyce 1997).

CHAPTER 8. THE TANIMBARESE *TAVU*

An earlier version of portions of this chapter appeared as "The House Altars of Tanimbar: Abstraction and Ancestral Presence," *Tribal Art* (Bulletin of the Musée Barbier-Mueller, Geneva) 1 (1987): 3–16. Reprinted by permission.

1. See Fox (1971) for an analysis of plant metaphors used in relation to kinship among the Rotinese, and Traube (1980, 1986, 1989) for explorations of the meaning of the "trunk and tip" metaphors among the Mambai of East Timor. Both Fox (1993) and Waterson (1993, 1995a) explore these metaphors across the Austronesian world more generally.

2. Photographs of *tavus* may be found in *Art of the Archaic Indonesians* (1982), Barbier (1984), *Budaya-Indonesia* (1987), Drabbe (1940), Geurtjens (1941), Heine-Geldern (1966), McKinnon (1987), McKinnon (1991), and van Nouhuys (1924).

3. The cervical vertebrae (*nit botun*) and the small wooden statues (*walut*) of the ancestors were often carried by men in a small pouch (*luvu*) to ensure efficacy in the hunt, on fishing expeditions, and in warfare, as well as in the practice of various trades such as house building, boat building, and metal work (Drabbe 1940:84–101, 105–14; Forbes 1885:324; Geurtjens 1917:67, 1941:20; de Hoog 1959:59). Not uncommonly, the small ancestor statues came as a male-female pair—tied together into a single unit (Geurtjens 1941: 20; de Hoog 1959:59).

4. The four languages spoken in the Tanimbar archipelago are, in order of number of speakers, Yamdenan, Fordatan, Selaruan, and Seluwasan. The Yamdenan word for the ancestor altar panel is *lamngatabu* (see Drabbe 1932b: 55, 103).

5. Drabbe wavers in his thoughts on the meaning of the word, suggesting that *tavu* is "from the general Indonesian word *tabu*, prohibited, although it could also be the word *tavu*, which means base" (1928:151). It should be noted that the Fordatan language has both the root *tabu* (as in *ntabu teri*, "forbids, hinders, blocks, prohibits") as well as the word *tavun* "beginning, starting point, base, root."

6. The conceptual connection between specific architectural (ritual) parts of the house and the past is noted by Cunningham (1973:220) for the

Atoni of Timor, where the words for roof thatch, the "head mother post" (the main ritual post), the "eldest" and the "distant past" are cognate in various Atoni languages.

7. In other areas of Indonesia and Polynesia, the pathways along which the ancestors and gods descend take other forms, such as house posts and cloth (see, e.g., Adams 1974:336; Barnes 1974:74–75; Sahlins 1981:118; Traube 1986:165, 266).

8. This can also be seen in the fact that—because the names for eldest sons repeat in alternate generations—the head of the house (who sat in front of the *tavu*) and his deceased father (whose skull rested on top of the *tavu* and whose spirit descended to sit alongside him) together represented the totality of a dual identity. At any given time that totality was manifest; only the relative positions alternated in the cycling of time.

9. Sometimes this hierarchical relationship is conceptualized as the difference between those who occupy named and unnamed houses, and sometimes it is conceptualized as the difference between those who occupy a house and those who do not (see McKinnon 1991:97–98).

10. These long-established *lolat* rows also have traveling along them a steady stream of named and unnamed valuables, which move from house to house in bride wealth exchanges. This again marks the concentration of value along the rows that is not possible along more recently formed exchange pathways (McKinnon 1991).

11. The term "master of the house" (*rahan duan*) also refers to the head of a house, the traditional wife-givers of the house, as well as to the brothers of a house—as opposed to the sisters, who are referred to as "strangers" (*mangun*), since they are destined to marry out of their natal house and become members of the houses of their husbands.

12. Carvings of valuables also appear on certain house beams in at least some areas of Sumba. Adams notes that on "the upper part of the sacred pillar, on the beam (*woaharu*) extending toward the back of the men's side are carvings of plants and various gold ornaments" (1974:336). Leach also reports sacrificial altars with drawings of wealth objects on them among the Kachin (1965:118).

13. Drabbe had the following to say about the valuables carved on the Ditilebit *tavu*: "On the *tavu* are represented all the valuables of the house, to begin with the golden breast pendant Koramuku which the [carved] head wears in relief around the neck. . . ; further, [there are] the two earthenware armbands (*diti*), of which the right one is called Sengi and the left one is called Bati. Further, [there are] the earrings of which one of the pair is out (*af*), with the name Ngarotuk and Wol Nafrenar" (translation mine: quoted in the notes

to Series 392, No.5 in the files of the Koninklijk Instituut voor de Tropen, Amsterdam).

Because such detailed notes are rare, and because I happen to be particularly well acquainted with the history of the Ditilebit house, it is perhaps worthwhile to offer an extended commentary on Drabbe's notes. The single *loran* named Wol Nafrenar ("S/he Does Not Hear")—which is carved into the center of the right hand armband—is still thought of as one of the heirloom valuables of the Ditilebit house, even though it was stolen many years ago and sold to a Chinese merchant. Drabbe's comments suggest that Wol Nafrenar's absent odd-matched pair is Ngarotuk (actually Ngarutut), which is not represented on the *tavu*. However, Ngarutut is the name of a full pair of *loran* that, in 1983, was held by one of Ditilebit's traditional wife-givers, and I have never heard that the three pieces ever belonged together. The golden breast pendant that Drabbe refers to as Koramuku is a mystery. The heirloom breast pendant held now—as well as during the time of Drabbe (1940:151)—by the Ditilebit house is not Koramuku, and among the dozens of named breast pendants I have taken note of, I have never heard Koramuku mentioned, certainly not as an heirloom valuable, or even as a circulating valuable held for a time by Ditilebit. The representation of the armbands on this *tavu* poses an interesting problem. Shell armbands (*sislau*), which are always composed of ten individual bands lashed together, are not usually kept as heirloom valuables. Curiously enough, Drabbe refers to the single bands shown on the Ditilebit *tavu* as *diti*. *Diti* are the dark earthenware, coconut shell, or Venetian glass bands that are lashed onto the top of a particularly valuable set of shell bands. While it is possible that, at the time the *tavu* was carved, the Ditilebit house held a pair of armbands called Sengi and Bati, it is also possible that their representation on the *tavu* is a play on the house name Ditilebit. If this were the case, the armbands here would play much the same role as the animals shown on other *tavu*—that is, as a visual mnemonic reference to the name and history of the house.

14. Waterson—in reviewing the common association, throughout Indonesia, of immobility, fertility, centers, and high rank—notes: "Immobility thus is utilized as a way of representing a concentration of creative, supernatural or political power" (1993:230).

15. Affiliation to a house is not given by descent, but must be achieved through exchange (McKinnon 1991, 1995). The most highly valued form of affiliation and residence is patrilateral and virilocal/patrilocal, but matrilateral affiliation and uxorilocal/matrilocal residence is also possible, depending upon the type of marriage and exchange relations.

16. Among the Lio of Flores, by contrast, the panels that are in an analo-

gous position to the Tanimbarese *tavus* are most often unambiguously female. "These may represent the ancestral couple of the House, or more commonly just a female figure or pair of breasts, thus graphically denoting the female quality of Houses" (Howell 1995:159).

17. I am grateful to Roy Wagner for suggesting an interpretation along these lines.

CHAPTER 9. HOUSE, PLACE, AND MEMORY IN TANA TORAJA

1. Toraja have terms for first, second, third cousin, etc. and prefer marriage between cousins categorized as "distant" (fourth cousin and beyond); but in everyday speech they prefer to avoid stressing distance and instead refer to all cousins as "siblings." To ask about degrees of cousinhood without giving offense, I learned to say, "Where do your houses join?" An answer to this question would immediately be forthcoming, explaining which house had been the birthplace of shared ancestors.

2. See Kopytoff (1986).

3. A comparison may be drawn here with the Mambai of Timor (Traube 1986:73, 1989).

References Cited

Adams, Marie J.
1974   Symbols of the Organized Community in East Sumba, Indonesia. *Bij-dragen tot de Taal-, Land- en Volkenkunde* 130:324–47.
Adams, Richard E. W.
1970   Suggested Classic Period Occupational Specialization in the Southern Maya Lowlands. *Monographs and Papers in Maya Archaeology,* W. R. Bullard, Jr., ed. Papers of the Peabody Museum of Archaeology and Ethnology 61, 487–98. Cambridge, Mass.: Peabody Museum, Harvard University.
Ames, Kenneth M.
1995   Chiefly Power and Household Production on the Northwest Coast. In Price and Feinman, eds. (1995), 155–87.
Andrews, E. Wyllys IV and E. Wyllys Andrews V
1980   *Excavations at Dzibilchaltun, Yucatan, Mexico.* Middle American Research Institute Publication 48. New Orleans: Tulane University.
Andrews, E. Wyllys V
1986   Olmec Jades from Chacsinkin, Yucatan, and Maya Ceramics from La Venta, Tabasco. In *Research and Reflections in Archaeology and History: Essays in Honor of Doris Stone,* Andrews V, ed., 11–49. Middle American Research Institute Publication 57. New Orleans: Tulane University.
Andrews, E. Wyllys V and Barbara W. Fash
1992   Continuity and Change in a Royal Maya Residential Complex at Copan. *Ancient Mesoamerica* 3:63–88.
Arizpe-Schlosser, Lourdes
1972a   Nahua Domestic Groups: The Developmental Cycle of Nahua Domestic Groups in Central Mexico. In *!Kung* (special issue produced by I. Green, M. Hill, M. J. Schwartz, T. Selwyn, J. Webster, and J. Winter): 40–46. *Magazine of the L.S.E. Anthropology Society* (London).
1972b   Zacatipan Kinship Terminology: A Dual Approach. *Canadian Review of Sociology and Anthropology* 9(3):227–37.
1973   *Parentesco y economía en una sociedad nahua.* Mexico City: Instituto Nacional Indigenista y Secretaría de Educación Pública.

Art of the Archaic Indonesians
1982   Dallas, Tex.: Dallas Museum of Fine Arts.

Ashmore, Wendy and Richard R. Wilk
1988   House and Household in the Mesoamerican Past: An Introduction. In
            Wilk and Ashmore, eds. (1988), 1–28.

Bailey, Douglass
1990   The Living House: Signifying Continuity. In Samson, ed. (1990), 19–48.
1993   The Looting of Bulgaria. *Archaeology* (March/April):26–27.
1997   Impermanence and Flux in the Landscape of Early Agricultural South-
            eastern Europe. In *Landscapes in Flux,* J. Chapman and P. Dolukhanov,
            eds., 39–56. Colloquenda Pontica. Oxford: Oxbow.

Banning, E. B. and Brian F. Byrd
1989   Renovations and the Changing Residential Unit at 'Ain Ghazal, Jordan.
            In MacEachern, Archer, and Garvin, eds. (1989), 525–33.

Barbier, Jean Paul
1984   *Indonesian Primitive Art.* Dallas: Dallas Museum of Art.

Barnes, J. A.
1962   African Models in the New Guinea Highlands. *Man* 62:5–9.

Barnes, Robert H.
1974   *Kédang: A Study of the Collective Thought of an Eastern Indonesian
            People.* Oxford: Clarendon Press.

Barnes, Ruth
1989   *The Ikat Textiles of Lamahera: A Study of an Eastern Indonesian Weaving
            Tradition.* Leiden: E. J. Brill.

Barraud, Cécile
1979   *Tanebar-Evav: une société de maisons tournée vers le large.* Cambridge:
            Cambridge University Press; Paris: Editions de la Maison des Sciences de
            l'Homme.
1990   Wife-Givers as Ancestors and Ultimate Values in the Kei Islands. *Bij-
            dragen tot de Taal-, Land- en Volkenkunde* 146:193–225.

Barrera Vásquez, Alfredo, Juan Ramón Bastarrachea Manzano, William Brito Sansores,
Refugio Vermont Salas, David Dzul Góngora, and Domingo Dzul Poot
1980   *Diccionario Maya Cordemex: Maya-Español, Español-Maya.* Merida,
            Mexico: Ediciones Cordemex.

Baudez, Claude
1994   *Maya Sculpture of Copan: The Iconography.* Norman: University of Okla-
            homa Press.

Baudez, Claude and Michael Coe
1966   Incised Slate Disks from the Atlantic Watershed of Costa Rica: A Com-
            mentary. *American Antiquity* 31:441–43.

Beaglehole, J. C., ed.
1967   *The Journals of Captain James Cook on His Voyages of Discovery.* Vol-

ume III, in Two Parts, *The Voyage of the* Resolution *and* Discovery, *1776–1780.* Cambridge: Cambridge University Press.

Bellwood, Peter, James J. Fox, and Darrell Tryon
1995   The Austronesians in History: Common Origins and Diverse Transforma-
            tion. In *The Austronesians: Historical and Comparative Perspectives,*
            P. Bellwood, J. J. Fox, and D. Tryon, eds., 1–16. Canberra: Australian
            National University.

Bender, Barbara, ed.
1998   *Stonehenge: Making Space.* Oxford: Berg.

Benjamin, David N. and David Stea, eds.
1995   *The Home: Words, Interpretations, Meanings, and Environments.* Al-
            dershot: Avebury.

Benson, Elizabeth P.
1985   Architecture as Metaphor. In *Fifth Palenque Round Table, 1983,* M. G.
            Robertson and V. M. Fields, eds., 183–88. San Francisco: Pre-Columbian
            Art Research Institute.

Berger, John
1972   *Ways of Seeing.* London: BBC and Penguin Books.
1979   *Pig Earth.* New York: Pantheon.

Biggs, Bruce
n.d.   POLLEX: The Comparative Polynesian Lexicon. Computer-based lexical
            database. University of Auckland.

Blanton, Richard
1994   *Houses and Households: A Comparative Study.* New York: Plenum.

Bloch, Maurice
1995a   Questions Not to Ask of Malagasy Carvings. In Hodder et al., eds. (1995),
            212–15.
1995b   The Resurrection of the House Amongst the Zafimaniry of Madagascar.
            In Carsten and Hugh-Jones, eds. (1995), 69–83.

Bloch, Maurice and Jonathan Parry
1982   Introduction: Death and the Regeneration of Life. In *Death and the Re-
            generation of Life,* Bloch and Parry, eds., 1–44. Cambridge: Cambridge
            University Press.

Blom, Frans and Oliver La Farge
1926–27   *Tribes and Temples.* Middle American Research Institute Publication 1,
            2 vols. New Orleans: Tulane University.

Bogucki, Peter
1988   *Forest Farmers and Stockherders: Early Agriculture and Its Consequences
            in North-Central Europe.* Cambridge: Cambridge University Press.

Boon, James A.
1977   *The Anthropological Romance of Bali, 1597–1972: Dynamic Perspec-
            tives in Marriage and Caste, Politics, and Religion.* Cambridge: Cam-
            bridge University Press.

1990a   *Affinities and Extremes: Crisscrossing the Bittersweet Ethnology of East Indies History, Hindu-Balinese Culture, and Indo-European Allure.* Chicago: University of Chicago Press.

1990b   Balinese Twins Times Two: Gender, Birth Order, and "Household" in Indonesia/Indo-Europe. In *Power and Difference: Gender in Island Southeast Asia,* J. M. Atkinson and Shelly Errington, eds., 209–33. Stanford, Calif.: Stanford University Press.

Bourdieu, Pierre

1973   The Berber House. In *Rules and Meanings: The Anthropology of Everyday Knowledge,* M. Douglas, ed., 98–110. Harmondsworth: Penguin.

1977   *Outline of a Theory of Practice.* Richard Nice, trans. Cambridge: Cambridge University Press.

1990   *The Logic of Practice.* Richard Nice, trans. Cambridge: Cambridge University Press.

Breton, Alain

1984   *Bachajón: organización socioterritorial de una comunidad Tzeltal.* Mexico City: Instituto Nacional Indigenista.

British Columbia

1914   Royal Commission on Indian Affairs, West Coast Agency. Evidence from Hearings. National Archives of Canada, Gg 10, Vol.11025, File AH13. Microfilm Copy on file (Reel B-5640), British Columbian Provincial Archives, Victoria.

Budaya-Indonesia

1987   *Budaya-Indonesia: Kunst en cultuur in Indonesië.* Amsterdam: Tropenmuseum.

Bunzel, Ruth

1952   *Chichicastenango: A Guatemalan Village.* Publications of the American Ethnological Society 22. Locust Valley, N.Y.: J. J. Augustin.

Caldwell, Ian

1991   The Myth of the Exemplary Centre: Shelly Errington's *Meaning and Power in a Southeast Asian Realm. Journal of Southeast Asian Studies* 22(1):109–18.

Canada

1881   Census Returns, Province of British Columbia, District No. 191, West Coast Agency, Nootka Tribe. National Archives of Canada, Microfilm C-13285. Microfilm copy on file (Reel B-390), British Columbia Provincial Archives, Victoria.

1891   Census Returns, Province of British Columbia, District No. 3, Sub-district No. 20, West Coast from Cape Cook to Port San Juan. National Archives of Canada. Microfilm copy on file (Reel B-7041), British Columbia Provincial Archives, Victoria.

1913   Royal Commission on Pelagic Sealing. Public Hearings, Victoria, Indian Claims, December 1913. Volumes 8 and 9, Royal Commission on Pelagic Sealing, L.A. Audette Commissioner. Xerox copy, Ethnology Division, Royal British Columbia Museum, Victoria.

Carlsen, Robert S. and Martin Prechtel

1991   The Flowering of the Dead: An Interpretation of Highland Maya Culture. *Man* 26:23–42.

Carmack, Robert M.

1981   *The Quiché Mayas of Utatlán: The Evolution of a Highland Guatemalan Kingdom.* Norman: University of Oklahoma Press.

Carrasco Pizana, Pedro

1976   Los linajes nobles del México antiguo. In *Estratificación social en la Mesoamérica prehispánica*, Carrasco Pizana et al., eds., 19–36. Mexico City: Instituto Nacional de Antropología e Historia.

Carsten, Janet

1987   Analogues or Opposites: Household and Community in Pulau Langkawi, Malaysia. In Macdonald, ed. (1987), 153–68.

1995a   Houses in Langkawi: Stable Structures or Mobile Homes? In Carsten and Hugh-Jones, eds. (1995), 105–28.

1995b   The Substance of Kinship and the Heat of the Hearth: Feeding, Personhood, and Relatedness Among Malays in Pulau Langkawi. *American Ethnologist* 22:223–41.

1997   *The Heat of the Hearth: The Process of Kinship in a Malay Fishing Community.* Oxford: Clarendon Press.

Carsten, Janet and Stephen Hugh-Jones

1995   Introduction: About the House—Lévi-Strauss and Beyond. In Carsten and Hugh-Jones, eds. (1995), 1–46. Cambridge: Cambridge University Press.

Carsten, Janet and Stephen Hugh-Jones, eds.

1995   *About the House: Lévi-Strauss and Beyond.* Cambridge: Cambridge University Press.

Chamoux, Marie-Noelle

1981   *Indiens de la Sierra: la communauté paysanne au Mexique.* Paris: Éditions l'Harmattan.

Chance, John K.

1996   The Barrios of Colonial Tecali: Patronage, Kinship, and Territorial Relations in a Central Mexican Community. *Ethnology* 35:107–39.

Chapman, John

1989   The Early Balkan Village. In *Neolithic of Southeastern Europe and Its Near Eastern Connections,* ed. S. Bökönyi, vol. 2, 33–55. Varia Archaeologica Hungarica 2. Budapest: Institute of Archaeology of the Hungarian Academy of Sciences.

1990a   Regional Study of the North Sumadija Region. In *Selevac: A Neolithic Village in Yugoslavia,* R. Tringham and D. Krstič, eds., 13–44. Monumenta Archaeologica 15. Los Angeles: Institute of Archaeology, UCLA.

1990b   Social Inequality on Bulgarian Tells and the Varna Problem. In Samson, ed. (1990), 49–92.

Chiang, Bien

1992   House in Paiwan Society. Paper presented at the International Symposium on Austronesian Studies Relating to Taiwan, Institute of History and Philology, Academia Sinica, Taipei.

Childe, V. G.

1951   *Social Evolution*. New York: Meridien.

Coe, Michael D.

1966   *An Early Stone Pectoral from Southeastern Mexico*. Studies in Pre-Columbian Art and Archaeology 1. Washington, D.C.: Dumbarton Oaks.

Coggins, Clemency Chase

1988   On the Historical Significance of Decorated Ceramics at Copan and Quirigua and Related Classic Maya Sites. In *The Southeast Classic Maya Zone*, E. H. Boone and G. R. Willey, eds., 95–124. Washington, D.C.: Dumbarton Oaks.

Coggins, Clemency Chase and Orrin C. Shane III, eds.

1984   *Cenote of Sacrifice: Maya Treasures from the Sacred Well at Chichen Itza*. Austin: University of Texas Press.

Collier, Jane Fishburne and Sylvia Junko Yanagisako, eds.

1987   *Gender and Kinship: Essays Toward a Unified Analysis*. Stanford, Calif.: Stanford University Press.

Connerton, Paul

1991   *How Societies Remember*. Cambridge: Cambridge University Press.

Cook, Garrett

1986   Quichean Folk Theology and Southern Maya Supernaturalism. In *Symbol and Meaning Beyond the Closed Community: Essays in Mesoamerican Ideas*, G. H. Gossen, ed., pp. 139–53. Albany: Institute for Mesoamerican Studies, State University of New York.

Cornejo Cabrera, Ezequiel

1964   La habitación desde el punto de vista sociológico, entre los ejidatarios veracruzanos. *Revista Mexicana de Sociología* 26(1): 253–85.

Crockford, Cairn E.

1991   *Changing Economic Activities of the Nuu-chah-nulth of Vancouver Island, 1840 to 1920*. B.A. Honours Essay, Department of History, University of Victoria, Victoria.

Croes, Dale R. and Jonathan O. Davis

1977   Computer Mapping of Idiosyncratic Basketry Manufacture Techniques in the Prehistoric Ozette House, Cape Alava, Washington. In *The Individual in Prehistory: Studies of Variability in Style in Prehistoric Technologies*, J. N. Hill and J. Gunn, eds., 155–65. New York: Academic Press.

Cuisenier, Jean
1991   *La maison rustique: logique sociale et composition architecturale.* Paris: Presses Universitaires de France.
Cunningham, Clark E.
1964   Order in the Atoni House. *Bijdragen tot de Taal-, Land- en Volkenkunde* 120:34–68.
1965   Order and Change in an Atoni Diarchy. *Southwestern Journal of Anthropology* 21:359–82.
1970   Thai "Injection Doctors": Antibiotic Mediators. *Social Science and Medicine* 4:1–24.
1973   Order in the Atoni House. In *Right & Left: Essays on Dual Symbolic Classification,* R. Needham, ed., 204–38. Chicago: University of Chicago Press.
Davenport, William H.
1959   Nonunilinear Descent and Descent Groups. *American Anthropologist* 61:557–72.
Dawley, Walter T.
n.d.   W. T. Dawley Papers. Add Mss 1076. Archives and Records Service of British Columbia, Victoria.
Deal, Michael
1987   Ritual Space and Architecture in the Highland Maya Household. In *Mirror and Metaphor: Material and Social Constructions of Reality,* D. W. Ingersoll, Jr., and G. Bronitsky, eds., 171–98. Lanham, Md.: University Press of America.
Dehouve, Danièle
1978   Parenté et mariage dans une communauté Nahuatl de l'état de Guerrero. *Journal de la Société des Américanistes* n.s. 65:173–208.
Devereux, F. A.
1893   Original Survey Notebooks, Indian Reserves, Vancouver Island, Volume 32. Victoria: British Columbia Ministry of Attorney General, Land Title Office.
Dewhirst, John
1980   The Indigenous Archaeology of Yuquot, a Nootkan Outside Village. In *The Yuquot Project,* vol. 1, W. J. Folan and J. Dewhirst, eds. History and Archaeology 39. Ottawa: Parks Canada.
1990   Mowachaht Ownership and Use of the Salmon Resources of the Leiner River and Upper Tahsis Inlet, Nootka Sound, British Columbia. Unpublished report prepared by Archeo Tech Associates, Victoria.
Drabbe, Petrus
1925   Dood en begrafenis en spiritisme op Tanimbar. *Tijdschrift van het Koninklijk Nederlandsch Aardrijkskundig Genootschap* 42:31–63.
1928   Het Tanimbareesche Huis. Rahan Tnebar. *Volkenkundige Opstellen* 2:145–61.

1932a   Woordenboek der Fordaatsche taal. *Verhandelingen van het Konink-
               lijk Bataviaasch Genootschap van Kunsten en Wetenschappen* 71(2):1–
               118.
1932b   Woordenboek der Jamdeensche taal. *Verhandelingen van het Koninklijk
               Bataviaasch Genootschap van Kunsten en Wetenschappen* 71(3):1–122.
1940   *Het leven van den Tanémbarees: Ethnograpfische studie over het Taném-
               bareesche volk.* Supplement to vol. 38 of *Internationales Archiv für Eth-
               nographie.* Leiden: E. J. Brill.

Driver, Harold E.
1939   *Northwest California.* Culture Element Distributions 10. University of
               California Anthropological Records 1, no. 6. Berkeley: University of Cal-
               ifornia Press.

Drucker, Philip
1951   *The Northern and Central Nootkan Tribes.* Bureau of American Ethnol-
               ogy Bulletin 144. Washington, D.C.: Smithsonian Institution.

Drummond, Lee
1996   *American Dreamtime: A Cultural Analysis of Popular Movies and Their
               Implications for a Science of Humanity.* Lanham, Md.: Littlefield Adams.

Duff, Wilson
1964   *The Indian History of British Columbia.* Vol. 1, *The Impact of the White
               Man.* Anthropology in British Columbia Memoir 5. Victoria: British Co-
               lumbia Provincial Museum.

Earle, Duncan M.
1986   The Metaphor of the Day in Quiche: Notes on the Nature of Everyday
               Life. In *Symbol and Meaning Beyond the Closed Community: Essays in
               Mesoamerican Ideas,* G. H. Gossen, ed., 155–72. Albany: Institute for
               Mesoamerican Studies, State University of New York.

Ellen, Roy
1986   Microcosm, Macrocosm and the Nuaulu House: Concerning the Reduc-
               tionist Fallacy as Applied to Metaphorical Levels. *Bijdragen tot de Taal-,
               Land- en Volkenkunde* 142:1–30.

Emory, Kenneth P.
1943   Polynesian Stone Remains. In *Studies in the Anthropology of Oceania
               and Asia,* C. S. Coon and J. M. Andrews IV, eds. Papers of the Peabody
               Museum of American Archaeology and Ethnology 20, 9–21. Cambridge,
               Mass.: Peabody Museum, Harvard University.

Erikson, Erik H.
1943   *Observations on the Yurok: Childhood and World Image.* University of
               California Publications in American Archaeology and Ethnology 35, no.
               10. Berkeley: University of California Press.

Errington, Shelly
1979   The Cosmic House of the Buginese. *Asia* 1(5):8–14.
1983a   Embodied Sumangé in Luwu. *Journal of Asian Studies* 42:545–70.

1983b   The Place of Regalia in Luwu. In *Centers, Symbols, and Hierarchies: Essays on the Classical States of Southeast Asia.* L. Gesick, ed., 194–241. Yale University Southeast Asia Monographs 26. New Haven, Conn.: Yale University.

1987   Incestuous Twins and the House Societies of Island Southeast Asia. *Cultural Anthropology* 2:403–44.

1989   *Meaning and Power in a Southeast Asian Realm.* Princeton, N.J.: Princeton University Press.

Evans-Pritchard, E. E.

1940   *The Nuer: A Description of the Modes of Livelihood and Political Institutions of a Nilotic People.* Oxford: Oxford University Press.

Farriss, Nancy M.

1984   *Maya Society Under Colonial Rule: The Collective Enterprise of Survival.* Princeton, N.J.: Princeton University Press.

Feld, Steven and Keith H. Basso

1996   Introduction. In *Senses of Place,* Feld and Basso, 3–11. Santa Fe, N.M.: School of American Research Press.

Fentress, James and Chris Wickham

1992   *Social Memory.* Oxford: Blackwell.

Fields, Virginia

1991   The Iconographic Heritage of the Maya Jester God. In *Sixth Palenque Round Table, 1986,* M. G. Robertson and Fields, 167–74. Norman: University of Oklahoma Press.

Firth, Raymond W.

1936   *We, the Tikopia: A Sociological Study of Kinship in Primitive Polynesia.* New York: American Book Co.

1961   *History and Traditions of Tikopia.* Polynesian Society Memoir 33. Wellington, N.Z.: Polynesian Society.

1967   *The Work of the Gods in Tikopia.* 2nd ed. New York: Humanities Press.

1970   *Rank and Religion in Tikopia: A Study in Polynesian Paganism and Conversion to Christianity.* Boston: Beacon Press.

1985   *Tikopia-English Dictionary: Taranga Fakatikopia ma Taranga Fakainglisi.* Auckland, N.Z.: Auckland University Press.

1989   Fiction and Fact in Ethnography. In *History and Ethnicity,* E. Tonkin, M. McDonald, and M. Chapman, eds., 48–52. London: Routledge.

Folan, William J.

1972   *The Community, Settlement and Subsistence Patterns of the Nootka Sound Area: A Diachronic Model.* Ph.D. dissertation, Southern Illinois University, Carbondale.

Folan, William J., Joyce Marcus, Sophia Pincemin, María del Rosario Domínguez Carrasco, Loraine Fletcher, and Abel Morales López

1995   Calakmul: New Data from an Ancient Maya Capital in Campeche, Mexico. *Latin American Antiquity* 6:310–34.

Forbes, Henry O.
1885   *A Naturalist's Wanderings in the Eastern Archipelago.* London: Sampson
            Low, Marston, Searle and Rivington.

Forth, Gregory
1991   *Space and Place in Eastern Indonesia.* Centre of South-East Asian Studies
            Occasional Paper 16. Canterbury: University of Kent at Canterbury.

Fox, James J.
1971   Sister's Child as Plant: Metaphors in an Idiom of Consanguinity. In *Rethink-
            ing Kinship and Marriage,* R. Needham, ed., 219–52. Association for So-
            cial Anthropologists Monograph 11. London: Tavistock Publications.
1980   Introduction. In Fox, ed. (1980), 1–18.
1987   The House as a Type of Social Organization on the Island of Roti. In
            Macdonald, ed. (1987), 171–91.
1993   Comparative Perspectives on Austronesian Houses: An Introductory Es-
            say. In Fox, ed. (1993), 1–28.
1994   Reflections on "Hierarchy" and "Precedence." *History and Anthropol-
            ogy* 7(1–4):87–108.
1995   Origin Structures and Systems of Precedence in the Comparative Study of
            Austronesian Societies. *Austronesian Studies* (August): 27–57.

Fox, James J., ed.
1980   *The Flow of Life: Essays on Eastern Indonesia.* Cambridge, Mass.: Har-
            vard University Press.
1993   *Inside Austronesian Houses: Perspectives on Domestic Designs for Liv-
            ing.* Canberra: Research School of Pacific Studies, Australian National
            University.

Freidel, David A.
1993   The Jade Ahau: Toward a Theory of Commodity Value in Maya Civiliza-
            tion. In Lange, ed. (1993), 149–65.

Freidel, David A. and Jeremy Sabloff
1984   *Cozumel: Late Maya Settlement Patterns.* New York: Academic Press.

Freidel, David A. and Linda Schele
1989   Dead Kings and Living Temples: Dedication and Termination Rituals
            Among the Ancient Maya. In *Word and Image in Maya Culture: Explora-
            tions in Language, Writing, and Representation,* W. F. Hanks and D. S.
            Rice, eds., 233–43. Salt Lake City: University of Utah Press.

Freidel, David A., Linda Schele, and Joy Parker
1993   *Maya Cosmos: Three Thousand Years on the Shaman's Path.* New York:
            William Morrow.

Gann, Thomas
1918   *The Maya Indians of Southern Yucatan and Northern British Honduras.*
            Bureau of American Ethnology Bulletin 64. Washington, D.C.: U.S. Gov-
            ernment Printing Office.

Garber, James
1993   The Cultural Context of Jade Artifacts from the Maya Site of Cerros, Belize. In Lange, ed. (1993), 166–72.
García Salazar, Heriberto
1975   Kaltokayotl: Estructura y función de la familia extensa entre los nahuas de la Huasteca. In *XIII Mesa Redonda,* vol. 3, 265–68. Mexico City: Sociedad Mexicana de Antropología.
Geertz, Hildred and Clifford Geertz
1975   *Kinship in Bali.* Chicago: University of Chicago Press.
Geurtjens, H.
1917   Reisindrukken van de Tenimber-eilanden, III. *Annalen van Onze Lieve Vrouw van het Heilig Hart* 35:66–69.
1941   *Zijn Plaats onder de Zon.* Roermond: J. J. Romen.
Gibbs, P.
1987   *Building a Malay House.* Singapore: Oxford University Press.
Gibson, Thomas
1995   Having Your House and Eating It: Houses and Siblings in Ara, South Sulawesi. In Carsten and Hugh-Jones, eds. (1995), 129–48.
Gillespie, Susan D.
1994   Ancestral Altars and Heirloomed Headdresses: A "House" Interaction Model for Mesoamerica. Paper presented to the Department of Anthropology, University of Kentucky.
1995   The Role of Ancestor Veneration in Maya Social Identity and Political Authority. Paper presented at the 94th Annual Meeting of the American Anthropological Association, Washington, D.C.
1999   Olmec Thrones as Ancestral Altars: The Two Sides of Power. In *Material Symbols: Culture and Economy in Prehistory,* J. E. Robb, ed., 224–53. Center for Archaeological Investigations Occasional Paper 26. Carbondale: Southern Illinois University.
Gillespie, Susan D. and Rosemary A. Joyce
1997   Gendered Goods: The Symbolism of Maya Hierarchical Exchange Relations. In *Women in Prehistory: North America and Mesoamerica,* C. Claassen and Joyce, eds., 189–207. Philadelphia: University of Pennsylvania Press.
1998   Deity Relationships in Mesoamerican Cosmologies: The Case of the Maya God L. *Ancient Mesoamerica* 9:279–96.
Gimbutas, Marija
1991   *Civilization of the Goddess.* San Francisco: Harper and Row.
Godelier, Maurice, Thomas R. Trautmann, and Franklin E. Tjon Sie Fat
1998   Introduction. In *Transformations of Kinship,* Godelier, Trautmann, and Tjon Sie Fat, eds., 1–26. Washington, D.C.: Smithsonian Institution Press.

Goodenough, Ward H.
1955   A Problem in Malayo-Polynesian Social Organization. *American Anthropologist* 57:71–83.

Gottlieb, Alma
1992   *Under the Kapok Tree: Identity and Difference in Beng Thought.* Bloomington: Indiana University Press.

Graham, Mark Miller
1993   Displacing the Center: Constructing Prehistory in Central America. In *Reinterpreting Prehistory of Central America,* Graham, ed., 1–38. Niwot: University of Colorado Press.

Gray, Robert F., and P. H. Gulliver, eds.
1964   *The Family Estate in Africa: Studies in the Role of Property in Family Structure and Lineage Continuity.* London: Routledge and Kegan Paul.

Green, Roger C.
1996   From Proto-Oceanic **Rumaq* to Proto-Polynesian **Fale:* A Significant Reorganization in Austronesian Housing. Paper presented at the 95th Annual Meeting of the American Anthropological Association, San Francisco.

Grinker, Roy Richard
1996   Reconstructing the House in Anthropology. *American Anthropologist* 98:856–58.

Grube, Nikolai
1992a   Catalogue Number 153: Porträtmaske. In *Die Welt der Maya: archäologische Schätze aus drei Jahrtausenden,* E. Eggebrecht, A. Eggebrecht, and Grube, eds., 488–89. Mainz am Rhein: P. von Zabern.
1992b   Catalogue Number 156: Anhänger. In Eggebrecht, Eggebrecht, and Grube, eds., 494–95.

Grube, Nikolai, and Linda Schele
1990   Royal Gifts to Subordinate Lords. *Copán Note* 87. Honduras: Copán Mosaics Project and the Instituto Hondureño de Antropología.

Gudeman, Stephen, and Alberto Rivera
1990   *Conversations in Colombia: The Domestic Economy in Life and Text.* Cambridge: Cambridge University Press.

Guerrero M., Juan Vicente
1993   The Context of Jade in Costa Rica. In Lange, ed. (1993), 191–202.

Haggarty, James C.
1982   *The Archaeology of Hesquiat Harbour: The Archaeological Utility of an Ethnographically Defined Social Unit.* Ph.D. dissertation, Washington State University, Pullman.

Hammel, Eugene and Peter Laslett
1974   Comparing Household Structure over Time and Between Cultures. *Comparative Studies in Society and History* 16:73–109.

Hammond, Norman, Gair Tourtellot, Sara Donaghey, and Amanda Clarke
1996   Survey and Excavation at La Milpa, Belize, 1996. *Mexicon* 18:86–91.
Hanks, William F.
1989   Elements of Maya Style. In *Word and Image in Maya Culture: Explorations in Language, Writing, and Representation,* Hanks and D. S. Rice, eds., pp. 92–111. Salt Lake City: University of Utah Press.
1990   *Referential Practice: Language and Lived Space Among the Maya.* Chicago: University of Chicago Press.
Harris, David
1978   Settling Down: An Evolutionary Model for the Transformation of Mobile Bands into Sedentary Communities. In *The Evolution of Social Systems,* J. Friedman and M. Rowlands, eds., 401–18. London: Duckworth; Pittsburgh: University of Pittsburgh Press.
Harris, Marvin
1975   Why a Perfect Knowledge of All the Rules That One Must Know in Order to Act like a Native Cannot Lead to a Knowledge of How Natives Act. *Journal of Anthropological Research* 30:242–51.
Haviland, William A.
1968   *Ancient Lowland Maya Social Organization.* Middle American Research Institute Publication 26:93–117. New Orleans: Middle American Research Institute, Tulane University.
1981   Dower Houses and Minor Centers at Tikal, Guatemala: An Investigation of Valid Units in Settlement Hierarchies. In *Lowland Maya Settlement Patterns.* W. Ashmore, ed., 89–117. Albuquerque: University of New Mexico Press.
1988   Musical Hammocks at Tikal: Problems with Reconstructing Household Composition. In Wilk and Ashmore, eds. (1988), 121–34.
1992   Status and Power in Classic Maya Society: The View from Tikal. *American Anthropologist* 94:937–40.
Headley, Stephen C.
1987   The Idiom of Siblingship: One Definition of "House" in Southeast Asia. In Macdonald, ed. (1987), 209–18.
Heine-Geldern, Robert
1966   Some Tribal Art Styles of Southeast Asia: An Experiment in Art History. In *The Many Faces of Primitive Art,* D. Fraser, ed., 165–221. Englewood Cliffs, N.J.: Prentice-Hall.
Helliwell, C.
1993   Good Walls Make Bad Neighbours: The Dyak Longhouse as a Community of Voices. In Fox, ed. (1993), 220–35.
Helmig, Thomas
1997   The Concept of Kinship on Yap and the Discussion of the Concept of Kinship. *Journal of Anthropological Research* 53(1):1–15.

Helms, Mary
1999   Why Maya Lords Sat on Jaguar Thrones. In *Material Symbols: Culture and Economy in Prehistory.* J. E. Robb, ed., 56–69. Center for Archaeological Investigations, Occasional Paper No. 26. Carbondale: Southern Illinois University.

Hendon, Julia A.
1991   Status and Power in Classic Maya Society: An Archaeological Study. *American Anthropologist* 93:894–918.

Hicks, David
1976   *Tetum Ghosts and Kin: Fieldwork in an Indonesian Community.* Palo Alto, Calif.: Mayfield.

Hirsch, Eric and Michael O'Hanlon, eds.
1995   *The Anthropology of Landscape: Perspectives on Place and Space.* Oxford: Clarendon Press.

Hirth, Kenneth G., and Susan Grant Hirth
1993   Ancient Currency: The Style and Use of Jade and Marble Carvings in Central Honduras. In Lange, ed. (1993), 173–90.

Hodder, Ian
1991a   *Reading the Past: Current Approaches to Interpretation in Archaeology.* 2nd ed. Cambridge: Cambridge University Press.
1991b   *The Domestication of Europe.* Oxford: Basil Blackwell.
1997   Always Momentary, Fluid and Flexible: Towards a Reflexive Excavation Methodology. *Antiquity* 71(273):691.

Hodder, Ian, ed.
1989   *The Meanings of Things: Material Culture and Symbolic Expression.* London: Unwin Hyman.
1996   *On the Surface: Catalhoyuk 1993–95.* Cambridge: British Institute of Archaeology at Ankara and McDonald Institute for Archaeological Research.

Hodder, Ian et al., eds.
1995   *Interpreting Archaeology: Finding Meaning in the Past.* London: Routledge.

Hoog, J. de
1959   Nieuwe methoden en inzichten ter bestudering van de funktionele beteknis der beelden in het Indonesisch-Melanesisch kultuurgebied. *Kultuurpatronen: Bulletin van het Delfts Etnografisch Museum* 1:1–98.

Hopkins, Nicholas A.
1988   Classic Mayan Kinship Systems: Epigraphic and Ethnographic Evidence for Patrilineality. *Estudios de Cultura Maya* 17:87–121.

Hoskins, Janet
1998   *Biographical Objects: How Things Tell the Stories of People's Lives.* New York: Routledge.

Houston, Stephen D.

1996   Symbolic Sweatbaths of the Maya: Architectural Meaning in the Cross
            Group at Palenque, Mexico. *Latin American Antiquity* 7:132–51.

Houston, Stephen and Karl Taube

1987   Name-Tagging in Classic Mayan Script. *Mexicon* 9(2):38–41.

Houston, Stephen and Paul Amaroli

1988   *The Lake Güija Plaque.* Research Reports in Ancient Maya Writing 15.
            Washington, D.C.: Center for Maya Research.

Howay, F. W., ed.

1941   *Voyages of the "Columbia" to the Northwest Coast 1787–1790 and
            1790–1793.* Boston: Massachusetts Historical Society.

Howell, Signe

1990   Husband/Wife or Brother/Sister as the Key Relationship in Lio Kinship
            and Sociosymbolic Relations. *Ethnos* 55:248–59.

1995   The Lio House: Building, Category, Idea, Value. In Carsten and Hugh-
            Jones, eds. (1995), 149–69.

Huelsbeck, David R.

1988   Faunal Remains and the Identification of Social Groups in the Archae-
            ological Record. In *Recent Developments in Environmental Analysis in
            Old and New World Archaeology,* R. E. Webb, ed., 131–49. BAR Inter-
            national Series 416. Oxford: BAR.

1989   Food Consumption, Resource Exploitation and Relationships Within and
            Between Households at Ozette. In MacEachern, Archer, and Garvin, eds.
            (1989), 157–67.

Hugh-Jones, Stephen

1993   Clear Descent or Ambiguous Houses? A Re-Examination of Tukanoan
            Social Organisation. *L'Homme* 126–28, 33(2–4):95–120.

1995   Inside-Out and Back-to-Front: The Androgynous House in Northwest
            Amazonia. In Carsten and Hugh-Jones, eds. (1995), 226–52.

Hunt, Eva

1977   *The Transformation of the Hummingbird: Cultural Roots of a Zinacantan
            Mythical Poem.* Ithaca, N.Y.: Cornell University Press.

Hunt, Eva and June Nash

1967   Local and Territorial Units. In *Social Anthropology,* M. Nash, ed., 253–
            82. *Handbook of Middle American Indians,* R. Wauchope, general ed.,
            vol. 6. Austin: University of Texas Press.

Inglis, Richard I. and James C. Haggarty

1986   Pacific Rim National Park, Ethnographic History. Calgary: Unpublished
            report to Parks Canada.

Ingold, Tim

1995   Building, Dwelling, Living: How Animals and People Make Themselves
            at Home in the World. In *Shifting Contexts: Transformations in Anthropo-
            logical Knowledge,* M. Strathern, ed., 57–80. London: Routledge.

Jacknis, Ira
1995   *Carving Traditions of Northwest California.* Berkeley: Phoebe Apperson
                Hearst Museum of Anthropology, University of California.
in press   Notes Toward a Culinary Anthropology of Native California. In *Food in
                California Indian Culture.* Berkeley: Phoebe Apperson Hearst Museum
                of Anthropology, University of California.
Janowski, Monica
1995   The Hearth-Group, the Conjugal Couple and the Symbolism of the Rice
                Meal Among the Kelabit of Sarawak. In Carsten and Hugh-Jones, eds.
                (1995), 84–104.
Jewitt, John R.
1976 [1807]   *A Journal Kept at Nootka Sound by John R. Jewitt, One of the Surviving
                Crew of the Ship Boston of Boston, John Salter, Commander, Who Was
                Massacred on 22nd of March 1803, Interspersed with some Account of
                the Natives, their Manners and Customs.* New York: Garland.
Jonaitis, Aldona
1988   *From the Land of the Totem Poles.* New York: American Museum of
                Natural History.
Jones, Chief Charles and Stephen Bosustow
1981   *Queesto, Pacheenaht Chief by Birthright.* Nanaimo, B.C.: Theytus Books.
Jones, Laurie
1991   *Nootka Sound Explored: A Westcoast History.* Campbell River, B.C.: Ptar-
                migan Press.
Joyce, Rosemary A.
1992   Ideology in Action: The Rhetoric of Classic Maya Ritual Practice. In *An-
                cient Images, Ancient Thought: The Archaeology of Ideology, Papers
                from the 23rd Chac Mool Conference,* A. S. Goldsmith, S. Garvie,
                D. Selin, and J. Smith, eds., 497–506. Calgary: Department of Archaeol-
                ogy, University of Calgary.
1996   Social Dynamics of Exchange: Changing Patterns in the Honduran Ar-
                chaeological Record. In *Chieftains, Power, and Trade: Regional Interac-
                tion in the Intermediate Area of the Americas.* C. H. Langebaek and
                F. Cardenas-Arroyo, eds., 31–45. Bogotá: Departamento de Antropolo-
                gía, Universidad de los Andes.
1999   Social Dimensions of Pre-Classic Burials. In *Social Patterns in Pre-Classic
                Mesoamerica,* D. C. Grove and R. A. Joyce, eds., 15–47. Washington,
                D.C.: Dumbarton Oaks.
Joyce, Rosemary A. and Susan A. M. Shumaker
1995   *Encounters with the Americas.* Cambridge, Mass.: Peabody Museum,
                Harvard University.
Justeson, John
1983   Mayan Hieroglyphic "Name-Tagging" of a Pair of Rectangular Jade
                Plaques from Xcalumkin. In *Recent Contributions to Maya Hieroglyphic*

Decipherment, No. 1. S. D. Houston, ed., 40–43. New Haven, Conn.: Human Relations Area Files, Inc.

Kaiser, T. and B. Voytek
1983   Sedentism and Economic Change in the Balkan Neolithic. *Journal of Anthropological Archaeology* 2:323–53.

Kamakau, Samuel Manaiakalani
1976   *The Works of the People of Old: Na Hana a ka Poʻe Kahiko.* Bernice P. Bishop Museum Special Publication 61. Honolulu: Bishop Museum Press.

Kan, Sergei
1989   *Symbolic Immortality: The Tlingit Potlatch of the Nineteenth Century.* Washington, D.C.: Smithsonian Institution.

Kaufman, Terrence S. and William M. Norman
1984   An Outline of Proto-Cholan Phonology, Morphology and Vocabulary. In *Phoneticism in Mayan Hieroglyphic Writing,* J. S. Justeson and L. Campbell, eds., 77–166. Albany: Institute for Mesoamerican Studies, State University of New York.

Keane, Webb
1995   The Spoken House: Text, Act, and Object in Eastern Indonesia. *American Ethnologist* 22:102–24.

Keesing, Roger M.
1970   Shrines, Ancestors, and Cognatic Descent: The Kwaio and Tallensi. *American Anthropologist* 72:755–75.

Kennedy, Donald G.
1931   *Field Notes on the Culture of Vaitupu, Ellice Islands.* Memoirs of the Polynesian Society 9. New Plymouth, N.Z.: T. Avery.

Kent, Susan, ed.
1989   *Farmers as Hunters: The Implications of Sedentism.* Cambridge: Cambridge University Press.
1990   *Domestic Architecture and the Use of Space: An Interdisciplinary Cross-Cultural Study.* Cambridge: Cambridge University Press.

Kent, Susan and Helga Vierich
1989   The Myth of Ecological Determinism—Anticipated Mobility and Site Spatial Organization. In Kent, ed., 96–130.

Kenyon, Susan M.
1980   *The Kyuquot Way: A Study of a West Coast (Nootkan) Community.* Canadian Ethnology Service Paper 61. Ottawa: National Museums of Canada.

Kipling, Rudyard
1951 [1906]   *Puck of Pook's Hill.* London: Macmillan.

Kirch, Patrick Vinton
1984   *The Evolution of the Polynesian Chiefdoms.* Cambridge: Cambridge University Press.
1985   *Feathered Gods and Fishhooks: An Introduction to Hawaiian Archaeology and Prehistory.* Honolulu: University of Hawaii Press.

1990   Monumental Architecture and Power in Polynesia Chiefdoms: A Com-
            parison of Tonga and Hawaii. *World Archaeology* 22:206–22.
1996   Tikopia Social Space Revisited. In *Oceanic Culture History: Essays in
            Honour of Roger Green,* J. Davidson, G. Irwin, F. Leach, A. Pawley and
            D. Brown, eds., 257–74. Dunedin: New Zealand Journal of Archaeology
            Special Publication.
1997   *The Lapita Peoples: Ancestors of the Oceanic World.* Oxford: Blackwell.
Kirch, Patrick V. and Roger C. Green
1987   History, Phylogeny, and Evolution in Polynesia. *Current Anthropology*
            28:431–56.
in press   *Hawaiki: Ancestral Polynesia: An Essay in Historical Anthropology.*
            Cambridge: Cambridge University Press.
Kirch, Patrick Vinton, and D. E. Yen
1982   *Tikopia: The Prehistory and Ecology of a Polynesian Outlier.* Bernice P.
            Bishop Museum Bulletin 238. Honolulu: Bishop Museum Press.
Kirchhoff, Paul
1959   The Principles of Clanship in Human Society. In *Readings in Anthropol-
            ogy,* vol. 2, *Cultural Anthropology,* Morton H. Fried, ed., 259–70. New
            York: Thomas Y. Crowell.
Kis-Jovak, J., H. Nooy-Palm, R. Schefold, and U. Schulz-Dornberg
1988   *Banua Toraja: Changing Patterns in Architecture and Symbolism among
            the Sa'dan Toraja, Sulawesi, Indonesia.* Amsterdam: Royal Tropical In-
            stitute.
Kolb, Michael
1994   Ritual Activity and Chiefly Economy at an Upland Religious Site on
            Maui, Hawai'i. *Journal of Field Archaeology* 21:417–36.
Kopytoff, I.
1986   The Cultural Biography of Things. In *The Social Life of Things: Com-
            modities in Cultural Perspective,* Arjun Appadurai, ed., 64–91. Cam-
            bridge: Cambridge University Press.
Kroeber, A. L.
1925   The Yurok. *Handbook of Indians of California.* Bureau of American
            Ethnology, *Bulletin* No. 78, 1–97. Washington, D.C.: Smithsonian
            Institution.
1938   Basic and Secondary Patterns of Social Structure. *Journal of the Royal
            Anthropological Institute of Great Britain and Ireland* 68:299–309.
Kroeber, A. L. and Edward Winslow Gifford
1949   *World Renewal, a Cult System of Native Northwest California.* Univer-
            sity of California Anthropological Records 13. Berkeley: University of
            California Press.
Kroll, E. M. and T. G. Price, eds.
1991   *The Interpretation of Archaeological Spatial Patterning.* New York:
            Plenum.

Kuper, Adam
1982   Lineage Theory: A Critical Retrospect. *Annual Review of Anthropology*
            11:71–95.
1993   The "House" and Zulu Political Structure in the Nineteenth Century.
            Journal of African History 34:469–87.
Kuznar, Lawrence
1997   *Reclaiming a Scientific Anthropology.* Walnut Creek, Calif.: Altamira Press.
La Farge, Oliver
1947   *Santa Eulalia: The Religion of a Cuchumatán Indian Town.* Chicago:
            University of Chicago Press.
Landa, Diego de
1982 [c. 1566] *Relación de las cosas de Yucatán.* 12th ed. Mexico City: Editorial Porrúa.
Lange, Frederick W.
1993   Formal Classification of Prehistoric Costa Rican Jade: A First Approxima-
            tion. In Lange ed. (1993), 269–88.
Lange, Frederick W., ed.
1993   *Precolumbian Jade: New Geological and Cultural Interpretations.* Salt
            Lake City: University of Utah Press.
Las Casas, Bartolomé de
1967 [1555– *Apologética historia sumaria.* Edmundo O'Gorman, ed. 3rd ed. 2 vols.
59]   Mexico City: Universidad Nacional Autónoma de México.
Laughlin, Robert M.
1988   *The Great Tzotzil Dictionary of Santo Domingo Zinacantan.* Vol. 1,
            Tzotzil-English. Smithsonian Contributions to Anthropology 31. Wash-
            ington, D.C.: Smithsonian Institution.
Lawrence, Denise L. and Setha M. Low
1990   The Built Environment and Spatial Form. *Annual Review of Anthropol-
            ogy* 19:453–505.
Lea, Vanessa
1995   The Houses of the Mẽbengokre (Kayapó) of Central Brazil—A New Door
            to Their Social Organization. In Carsten and Hugh-Jones, eds. (1995),
            206–25. Cambridge: Cambridge University Press.
Leach, Edmund R.
1965   *Political Systems of Highland Burma.* Boston: Beacon Press.
1968   *Pul Eliya: A Village in Ceylon: A Study of Land Tenure and Kinship.*
            Cambridge: Cambridge University Press.
León-Portilla, Miguel
1988   *Time and Reality in the Thought of the Maya.* 2nd ed. Norman: University
            of Oklahoma Press.
Lévi-Strauss, Claude
1969 [1949] *The Elementary Structures of Kinship.* Rev. ed. J. H. Bell, J. R. von Stur-
            mer, and R. Needham, trans., R. Needham. Boston: Beacon Press.
1979a   *La Voie des masques.* Rev. ed. Paris: Plon.

1979b   Nobles sauvages. In *Culture, science et développement: contribution à une histoire de l'homme: mélanges en l'honneur de Charles Morazé,* 41–55. Toulouse: Privat.

1982   *The Way of the Masks.* S. Modelski, trans. Seattle: University of Washington Press.

1983   Histoire et ethnologie. *Annales: économies, sociétés, civilisations* 38(6): 1217–31.

1984   *Paroles données.* Paris: Plon.

1987   *Anthropology and Myth: Lectures 1951–1982.* R. Willis, trans. Oxford: Blackwell.

1991   Maison. In *Dictionnaire de l'ethnologie et de l'anthropologie,* P. Bonte and M. Izard, eds., 434–36. Paris: Presses Universitaires de France.

Lewis, E. Douglas
1988   *People of the Source: The Social and Ceremonial Order of the Tana Wai Brama on Flores.* Dordrecht: Foris.

Lewis, I. M.
1965   Problems in the Comparative Study of Unilineal Descent. In *The Relevance of Models for Social Anthropology,* M. Banton, ed., 87–112. London: Tavistock.

Lloyd, Seton
1980   *Ancient Architecture.* New York: Electa/Rizzoli.

Lok, Rossana
1987   The House as a Microcosm: Some Cosmic Representations in a Mexican Indian Village. In *The Leiden Tradition in Structural Anthropology: Essays in Honor of P. E. de Josselin de Jong,* R. de Ridder and J. A. J. Karremans, eds., 211–23. Leiden: Brill.

Lomnitz-Adler, Claudio
1992   *Exits from the Labyrinth: Culture and Ideology in the Mexican National Space.* Berkeley: University of California Press.

López Austin, Alfredo
1993   *The Myths of the Opossum: Pathways of Mesoamerican Mythology.* B. R. Ortiz de Montellano and T. Ortiz de Montellano, trans. Albuquerque: University of New Mexico Press.

Macdonald, Charles
1987   Histoire d'un projet: de la notion de "maison" chez Lévi-Strauss à la comparaison des sociétés en Asie du Sud-Est insulaire. In Macdonald, ed. (1987), 3–12.

Macdonald, Charles, ed.
1987   *De la hutte au palais: sociétés "à maison" en Asie du Sud-Est insulaire.* Paris: Centre National de la Recherche Scientifique.

S. MacEachern, S., D. J. W. Archer and R. D. Garvin, eds.
1989   *Households and Communities: Proceedings of the 21st Annual Con-*

ference of the Archaeological Association of Calgary. Calgary: University of Calgary Archaeological Association.

Marcus, Joyce
1983   Lowland Maya Archaeology at the Crossroads. *American Antiquity* 48:454–88.

Marshall, Mac, ed.
1981   *Siblingship in Oceania: Studies in the Meaning of Kin Relations.* Association for Social Anthropology in Oceania Monograph 8. Ann Arbor: University of Michigan Press.

Marshall, Yvonne M.
1989   The House in Northwest Coast, Nuu-Chah-Nulth, Society: The Material Structure of Political Action. In MacEachern, Archer, and Garvin, eds. (1989), 15–21.
1992   Mowachaht/Muchalaht Archaeology Project, Final Report, Victoria: Unpublished report prepared for the British Columbia Heritage Trust, Mowachaht/Muchalaht Band and the British Columbia Archaeology Branch.
1993a   Dangerous Liaisons: Maquinna, Quadra, and Vancouver in Nootka Sound, 1790–5. In *From Maps to Metaphors: The Pacific World of George Vancouver,* R. Fisher and H. Johnston, eds., 160–75. Vancouver: UBC Press.
1993b   A Political History of the Nuu-Chah-Nulth People: A Case Study of the Mowachaht and Muchalaht Tribes. Ph.D. dissertation, Department of Archaeology, Simon Fraser University.
1999   The Nuu-chah-nulth Potlatch House. In *Huupakwanum: Art, History and Culture of the Nuu-chah-nulth People.* A. Hoover, ed. Victoria: Royal British Columbia Museum.

Marshall, Yvonne M. and Alexandra Maas
1997   Dashing Dishes. *World Archaeology* 29(3):275–90.

Mathews, Peter
1979   The Glyphs from the Ear Ornament from Tomb A 1/1. In *Excavations at Altun Ha, Belize, 1964–1970,* D. Pendergast, ed., vol. 1, 79–80. Toronto: Royal Ontario Museum.
1985   Maya Early Classic Monuments and Inscriptions. In *Considerations of the Early Classic Period in the Maya Lowlands,* G. R. Willey and P. Mathews, eds., 5–54. Albany: Institute for Mesoamerican Studies, State University of New York.

Mathews, Peter and David Pendergast
1979   The Altun Ha Jade Plaque: Deciphering the Inscription. In *Studies in Ancient Mesoamerica,* IV., J. Graham, ed., 197–214. University of California Archaeological Research Facility Contributions 41. Berkeley: University of California Press.

Matos Moctezuma, Eduardo
1996   Catalogue Entry 94: Deity Mask. In *Olmec Art of Ancient Mexico.* E. P.

Benson and B. de la Fuente, eds., 252. Washington, D.C.: National Gallery of Art.

Mauger, Jeffrey E.
1991   Shed-Roof Houses at Ozette and in a Regional Perspective. In Samuels, ed. (1991), 29–174.

Mauss, Marcel
1985 [1938] A Category of the Human Mind: The Notion of Person; The Notion of Self. In *The Category of the Person: Anthropology, Philosophy, History,* M. Carrithers, S. Collins, and S. Lukes, 1–25. Cambridge: Cambridge University Press.

McAnany, Patricia A.
1995   *Living with the Ancestors: Kinship and Kingship in Ancient Maya Society.* Austin: University of Texas Press.

McCracken, Grant
1988   *Culture and Consumption: New Approaches to the Symbolic Character of Consumer Goods and Activities.* Bloomington: Indiana University Press.

McGee, R. Jon
1990   *Life, Ritual, and Religion Among the Lacandon Maya.* Belmont, Calif.: Wadsworth.

McKenzie, Kathleen H.
1974   *Ozette Prehistory—Prelude.* M.A. thesis, Department of Archaeology, University of Calgary.

McKinnon, Susan
1987   The House Altars of Tanimbar: Abstraction and Ancestral Presence. *Tribal Art* (Bulletin of the Barbier-Mueller Museum, Geneva) 1:3–16.
1991   *From a Shattered Sun: Hierarchy, Gender, and Alliance in the Tanimbar Islands.* Madison: University of Wisconsin Press.
1995   Houses and Hierarchy: The View from a South Moluccan Society. In Carsten and Hugh-Jones, eds. (1995), 170–88.
1996   Hot Death and the Spirit of Pigs: The Sacrificial Form of the Hunt in the Tanimbar Islands. In *For the Sake of Our Future: Sacrificing in Eastern Indonesia,* S. Howell, ed. 337–49. Leiden: Research School, CNWS, Leiden University.

McMillan, Alan D.
1996   Since Kwatyat Lived on Earth: An Examination of Nuu-chah-nulth Culture History. Ph.D. dissertation, Simon Fraser University.

Meares, John
1967   *Voyages Made in the Years 1788 and 1789 from China to the North West Coast of America to which are Prefixed, an Introductory Narrative of a Voyage in 1786, From Bengal, in the Ship Nootka; Observations on the Probable Existence of a North West Passage and some account of the Trade Between the North West Coast of America and China; and the Latter Country and Great Britain.* 2 vols. London: Logographic Press.

Mellaart, James
1967   *Çatal Hüyük: A Neolithic Town in Anatolia.* London: Thames and Hudson.
1972   A Neolithic City in Turkey. In *Old World Archaeology.* C. C. Lamberg-Karlovsky, ed., 120–31. San Francisco: W.H. Freeman.
1975   *The Neolithic of the Near East.* London: Thames and Hudson.
Metcalf, Peter
1982   *A Borneo Journey into Death: Berawan Eschatology from Its Rituals.* Philadelphia: University of Pennsylvania Press.
Métraux, A.
1940   *Ethnology of Easter Island.* Bernice P. Bishop Museum Bulletin 160. Honolulu: Bishop Museum Press.
Meyer, Carl
1971 [1855] The Yurok of Trinidad Bay, 1851. In *The California Indians: A Sourcebook,* 2nd ed. R. F. Heizer and M. A. Whipple, eds., 262–71. Berkeley: University of California Press.
Miller, Daniel and Christopher Tilley
1996   Editorial. *Journal of Material Culture* 1:5–14.
Monaghan, John
1995   *The Covenants with Earth and Rain: Exchange, Sacrifice, and Revelation in Mixtec Society.* Norman: University of Oklahoma Press.
1996   The Mesoamerican Community as a "Great House." In *Mesoamerican Community Organization: Barrios and Other Customary Social Units,* Part II, E. M. Mulhare, ed. Special issue of *Ethnology* 35(3):181–94.
Montoya Briones, José de Jesús
1964   *Atla: etnografía de un pueblo náhuatl.* Departamento de Investigaciones Antropológicas, Publicación No. 14. Mexico City: Instituto Nacional de Antropología e Historia.
Morgan, Lewis Henry
1965 [1881] *Houses and House-Life of the American Aborigines.* Chicago: University of Chicago Press.
Morley, Frances Louella and Sylvanus G. Morley
1938   *The Age and Provenance of the Leyden Plate.* Contributions to American Anthropology and History 24. Carnegie Institution of Washington Publication 509. Washington, D.C.: Carnegie Institution.
Moser, A. J.
1926   *Reminiscences of the West Coast of Vancouver Island.* Victoria: Acme Press.
Mulhare, Eileen M.
1996   Barrio Matters: Toward an Ethnology of Mesoamerican Customary Social Units. In *Mesoamerican Community Organization: Barrios and Other Customary Social Units,* Part I, Mulhare, ed. Special issue of *Ethnology* 35(2):93–106.

Munn, Nancy
1986   *The Fame of Gawa: A Symbolic Study of Value Transformation in a Mas-
            sim (Papua New Guinea) Society.* Durham, N.C.: Duke University Press.
Murdock, George Peter
1960   Cognatic Forms of Social Organization. In *Social Structure in Southeast
            Asia,* Murdock, ed., 1–14. Viking Fund Publication in Anthropology No.
            29. New York: Viking Fund.
Murphy, August
1957   Livelihood of Indians of Nootka. Manuscript, Archives Deschatelets, Ot-
            tawa: Typescript held in the Mowachaht/Muchalaht Band Office.
Murphy, Timothy D.
1976   Marriage and Family in a Nahuat-Speaking Community. In Nutini, Car-
            rasco, and Taggart, eds. (1976), 187–205.
Nash, June
1970   *In the Eyes of the Ancestors: Belief and Behavior in a Maya Community.*
            New Haven, Conn.: Yale University Press.
Needham, Rodney
1958   A Structural Analysis of Purum Society. *American Anthropologist* 60:75–
            101.
van Nouhuys, Jan Willem
1924   Verslag betreffende het Museum voor Land- en Volkenkunde en het Ma-
            ritiem Museum "Prins Hendrik" over het jaar 1923. In *Verslag omtrent
            den Toestand van het Museum voor Land- en Volkenkunde en Maritiem
            Museum "Prins Hendrik," te Rotterdam over het Jaar 1923.* Rotterdam.
Nutini, Hugo G.
1967   A Synoptic Comparison of Mesoamerican Marriage and Family Struc-
            ture. *Southwestern Journal of Anthropology* 23:383–404.
1968   *San Bernardino Contla: Marriage and Family Structure in a Tlaxcalan
            Municipio.* Pittsburgh: University of Pittsburgh Press.
1976   Introduction: The Nature and Treatment of Kinship in Mesoamerica. In
            Nutini, Carrasco, and Taggart, eds. (1976), 3–27.
1984   *Ritual Kinship: Ideological and Structural Integration of the Compa-
            drazgo System in Rural Tlaxcala.* Princeton, N.J.: Princeton University
            Press.
1995   *The Wages of Conquest: The Mexican Aristocracy in the Context of West-
            ern Aristocracies.* Ann Arbor: University of Michigan Press.
Nutini, Hugo G., Pedro Carrasco Pizana, and James M. Taggart, eds.
1976   *Essays on Mexican Kinship.* Pittsburgh: University of Pittsburgh Press.
Ohnuki-Tierney, Emiko
1990   Introduction: The Historicization of Anthropology. In *Culture Through
            Time: Anthropological Approaches,* Ohnuki-Tierney, ed., pp. 1–25.
            Stanford, Calif.: Stanford University Press.

Parmentier, Richard J.
1984   House Affiliation Systems in Belau. *American Ethnologist* 11:656–76.
1987   *The Sacred Remains: Myth, History, and Polity in Belau.* Chicago: University of Chicago Press.
Pendergast, David
1982   *Excavations at Altun Ha, Belize, 1964–1970,* vol. 2. Toronto: Royal Ontario Museum.
Pilling, Arnold
1989   Yurok Aristocracy and "Great Houses." *American Indian Quarterly* 13:421–36.
Plath, David W.
1990   My-Car-Isma: Motorizing the Showa Self. *Daedalus* 119:229–44.
Popol Vuh
1996   *Popol Vuh: The Mayan Book of the Dawn of Life.* Revised. D. Tedlock, trans. New York: Simon and Schuster.
Porteous, J. Douglas
1995   Domicide: The Destruction of Home. In Benjamin and Stea, eds. (1995), 151–61. Aldershot: Avebury.
Price, T. Douglas and James A. Brown
1985   Aspects of Hunter-Gatherer Complexity. In *Prehistoric Hunter-Gatherers, The Emergence of Cultural Complexity,* Price and Brown, eds., pp. 3–20. New York: Academic Press.
Price, T. Douglas and Gary M. Feinman, eds.
1995   *Foundations of Social Inequality.* New York: Plenum.
Proskouriakoff, Tatiana
1944   An Inscription on a Jade Probably Carved at Piedras Negras. *Notes on Middle American Archaeology and Ethnology* 2:142–47.
1963   *An Album of Maya Architecture.* Norman: University of Oklahoma Press.
1974   *Jades from the Cenote of Sacrifice, Chichen Itza, Yucatan.* Peabody Museum of Archaeology and Ethnology Memoirs 10, 1. Cambridge, Mass.: Peabody Museum, Harvard University.
1993   *Maya History.* Austin: University of Texas Press.
Rafferty, Janet
1985   The Archaeological Record on Sedentariness: Recognition, Development, and Implications. In *Advances in Archaeological Method and Theory,* M. Schiffer, ed., 8: 113–56. New York: Academic Press.
Rapoport, Amos
1969   *House Form and Culture.* Englewood Cliffs, N.J.: Prentice-Hall.
Rathje, William L.
1970   Socio-Political Implications of Lowland Maya Burials: Methodology and Tentative Hypotheses. *World Archaeology.* 1:359–75.

Ravicz, Robert
1967   Compadrinazgo. In *Social Anthropology,* M. Nash, ed., 238–52. *Hand-book of Middle American Indians,* R. Wauchope, general ed., vol. 6. Austin: University of Texas Press.

Redfield, Robert
1936   The Coati and the Ceiba. *Maya Research* 3:231–43.

Redfield, Robert and Alfonso Villa Rojas
1962 [1934]   *Chan Kom, a Maya Village.* Abridged. Chicago: Phoenix Books, University of Chicago Press.

Reyes García, Luis
1961   *Pasión y muerte del Cristo Sol: carnaval y cuaresma en Ixcatepec.* Xalapa, Mexico: Universidad Veracruzana.

Riedel, J. G. F.
1885   Eenige opmerkingen over de recente ethnologische, linguistische, geographische en ornithologische mededeelingen omtrent de Tanembar- en Timorlao-eilanden. *Tijdschrift Nederlands Aardrijkskundig Genootschap* 2d ser. 1:721–25.
1886   *De sluik- en kroesharige rassen tusschen Selebes en Papua.* The Hague: Martinus Nijhoff.

Rivière, Peter
1993   The Amerindianization of Descent and Affinity. *L'Homme* 126–28, 33(2–4):507–16.
1995   Houses, Places, and People: Community and Continuity in Guiana. In Carsten and Hugh-Jones, eds. (1995), 189–205.

Robertson, Merle Greene
1983   *The Sculpture of Palenque.* Vol. 1, *The Temple of the Inscriptions.* Princeton, N.J.: Princeton University Press.
1985   *The Sculpture of Palenque.* Vol. 3, *The Late Buildings of the Palace.* Princeton, N.J.: Princeton University Press.
1991   *The Sculpture of Palenque.* Vol. 4, *The Cross Group, the North Group, the Olvidado, and Other Pieces.* Princeton, N.J.: Princeton University Press.

Robichaux, David
1996   Localized Patrilineal Kin Groups in Mesoamerica: A Patrilineal Bias or Patrilineal Principles? Paper presented at the 95th Annual meeting of the American Anthropological Association, San Francisco.
1997a   Residence Rules and Ultimogeniture in Tlaxcala and Mesoamerica. *Ethnology* 36(2):149–71.
1997b   Un modelo de familia para el "México profundo." In *Espacios familiares: Ambitos de solidaridad,* 187–213. Mexico City: DIF.

Rosen, Arlene M.
1986   *Cities of Clay: The Geoarchaeology of Tells.* Chicago: University of Chicago Press.

Rousseau, Jerôme
1987   Débat sur le concept de maison. In Macdonald, ed. (1987), 179–91.
Routledge, K. S.
1919   *The Mystery of Easter Island*. London: Sifton, Praed and Co.
Roys, Ralph L.
1940   *Personal Names of the Maya of Yucatan*. Contributions to American An-
               thropology and History 31:31–48. Carnegie Institution of Washington
               Publication 523. Washington, D.C.: Carnegie Institution.
1967   *The Book of Chilam Balam of Chumayel*. Norman: University of Okla-
               homa Press.
Ruan, Xing
1996   Empowerment in the Practice of Making and Inhabiting: Dong Architec-
               ture in Cultural Reconstruction. *Journal of Material Culture* 1:211–37.
Ruz Lhuillier, Alberto
1968   *Costumbres funerarias de los antiguos mayas*. Mexico City: Universidad
               Nacional Autónoma de México.
1992   *El Templo de las Inscripciones, Palenque*. Mexico City: Fondo de Cultura
               Económica.
Sabean, David Warren
1990   *Property, Production, and Family in Neckarhausen, 1700–1870*. Cam-
               bridge: Cambridge University Press.
Sahagún, Bernardino de
1963 [c.   *Florentine Codex: General History of the Things of New Spain*. Book 11:
 1575–77]   *Earthly Things*. Trans. C. E. Dibble and A. J. O. Anderson. Santa Fe, N.M.:
               School of American Research and the University of Utah.
Sahlins, Marshall D.
1981   The Stranger-King; or, Dumézil Among the Fijians. *Journal of Pacific His-
               tory* 16(3):107–32.
Samson, Ross, ed.
1990   *The Social Archaeology of Houses*. Edinburgh: Edinburgh University
               Press.
Samuels, Stephan R.
1989   Spatial Patterns in Ozette Longhouse Floor Middens. In MacEachern,
               Archer, and Garvin, eds. (1989), 143–56.
1991   Patterns in Ozette Floor Middens: Reflections of Social Units. In Samuels,
               ed. (1991), 175–200.
Samuels, Stephan R., ed.
1991   *Ozette Archaeological Project Research Reports*. Vol. 1, *House Structure
               and Floor Midden*. Reports of Investigations 63. Pullman: Department of
               Anthropology, Washington State University.
Samuels, Stephan R. and Richard D. Daugherty
1991   Introduction to the Ozette Archaeological Project. In Samuels, ed.
               (1991), 1–28.

Sandstrom, Alan R.

1991   *Corn Is Our Blood: Culture and Ethnic Identity in a Contemporary Aztec Indian Village,* Civilization of the American Indian Series 206. Norman: University of Oklahoma Press.

1995   Nahuas of the Huasteca. In *Encyclopedia of World Cultures,* vol. 8. J. Dow and R. V. Kemper, vol. eds., pp. 184–87; D. Levinson, editor-in-chief. Boston: G. K. Hall-Macmillan; New Haven, Conn.: Human Relations Area Files, Yale University.

1996   Center and Periphery in the Social Organization of Contemporary Nahuas of Mexico. In *Mesoamerican Community Organization: Barrios and Other Customary Social Units,* Part II, E. M. Mulhare, ed. Special issue of *Ethnology* 35(3):161–80.

Sandstrom, Alan R. and Pamela Effrein Sandstrom

1986   *Traditional Papermaking and Paper Cult Figures of Mexico.* Norman: University of Oklahoma Press.

Sapir, Edward

n.d.   Census of Nootka Bands, 1920–21. Nootka Field Notebooks, Vols. I–XXIV. Boas Collection, W2a.18 #33 (pt. 1 & 2). American Philosophical Society Library, Philadelphia. Copy held by the Human History Division, Royal British Columbia Museum, Victoria.

Şaul, Mahir

1991   The Bobo "House" and the Uses of Categories of Descent. *Africa* 61:71–97.

Scheffler, Harold W.

1973   Kinship, Descent, and Alliance. In *Handbook of Social and Cultural Anthropology,* J. J. Honigman, ed., 747–93. Chicago: Rand McNally.

Schele, Linda and Mary Ellen Miller

1986   *The Blood of Kings: Dynasty and Ritual in Maya Art.* Fort Worth, Tex.: Kimbell Art Museum.

Schele, Linda and David Freidel

1990   *A Forest of Kings: The Untold Story of the Ancient Maya.* New York: William Morrow.

Schmid, Karl

1957   Zur Problematik von Familie, Sippe und Geschlecht, Haus und Dynastie beim mittelalterlichen Adel. Vorfragen zum Thema "Adel und Herrschaft im Mittelalter." *Zeitschrift für die Geschichte des Oberrheins* 105(1):1–62.

Schneider, David M.

1965   Some Muddles in the Models: Or, How the System Really Works. In *The Relevance of Models for Social Anthropology,* M. Banton, ed., 25–85. London: Tavistock.

1972   What Is Kinship All About? In *Kinship Studies in the Morgan Centennial Year,* P. Reining, ed., 32–63. Washington, D.C.: Anthropological Society of Washington.

1984   *A Critique of the Study of Kinship.* Ann Arbor: University of Michigan Press.

Schrauwers, Albert
1997   Houses, Hierarchy, Headhunting, and Exchange: Rethinking Political Relations in the Southeast Asian Realm of Luwu'. *Bijdragen tot de Taal-, Land- En Volkenkunde* 153:356–80.

Schryer, Frans
1990   *Ethnicity and Class Conflict in Rural Mexico.* Princeton, N.J.: Princeton University Press.

Sellato, Bernard
1987a   "Maisons" et organisation sociale en Asie du Sud-Est. In Macdonald, ed. (1987), 195–207.
1987b   Note préliminaire sur les sociétés "à maison" à Bornéo. In Macdonald, ed. 1987, 15–44.

Sendey, John
1977   *The Nootkan Indian—A Pictorial.* Alberni Valley Museum, Port Alberni, British Columbia.

Sewell, William H., Jr.
1992   A Theory of Structure: Duality, Agency, and Transformation. *American Journal of Sociology* 98:1–29.

Sharer, Robert J.
1994   *The Ancient Maya.* 5th ed. Stanford, Calif.: Stanford University Press.

Smith, Augustus Ledyard
1934   *Two Recent Ceramic Finds at Uaxactun.* Contributions to American Archaeology 2, no. 5. Carnegie Institution of Washington Publication 436. Washington, D.C.: Carnegie Institution.
1962   Residential and Associated Structures at Mayapan. In *Mayapan, Yucatan, Mexico* by H. E. D. Pollock, R. L. Roys, T. Proskouriakoff, and A. L. Smith, 165–319. Carnegie Institution of Washington Publication 619. Washington, D.C.: Carnegie Institution.

Sosa, John R.
1989   Cosmological, Symbolic and Cultural Complexity Among the Contemporary Maya of Yucatan. In *World Archaeoastronomy.* A. F. Aveni, ed., 130–42. Cambridge: Cambridge University Press.

Sparkes, Stephen
1997a   Anthropological Dominance in a Multidisciplinary Symposium: Reflection on "The House in Southeast Asia." *Newsletter of the Nordic Association for Southeast Asian Studies* 12:18–20.
1997b   The House in Southeast Asia: A Changing Social, Economic and Political Domain. *Newsletter of the Nordic Association for Southeast Asian Studies* 12:8–13.

Spott, Robert, and A. L. Kroeber
1971 [1942] Yurok Shamanism. In *The California Indians: A Sourcebook.* 2nd ed. R. F.

Heizer and M. A. Whipple, eds., 533–43. Berkeley: University of California Press.

Steadman, D. W., C. Vargas, and F. Cristino

1994 Stratigraphy, Chronology, and Cultural Context of an Early Faunal Assemblage from Easter Island. *Asian Perspectives* 33:79–96.

Stevanović, Mirjana

1996 *The Age of Clay: The Social Dynamics of House Destruction.* Ph.D. dissertation, University of California, Berkeley.

1997 The Age of Clay: The Social Dynamics of House Destruction. *Journal of Anthropological Archaeology* 16:334–95.

Stevanović, Mirjana and Ruth Tringham

1998 The Significance of Neolithic Houses in the Archaeological Record of Southeast Europe. In *Zbornik posvecen Dragoslavu Srejovicu*, Z. Mikič, ed. Belgrade: Balkanoloski Institut.

Stone, Doris Z. and Carlos Balser

1965 Incised Slate Disks from the Atlantic Watershed of Costa Rica. *American Antiquity* 30:310–29.

Strathern, Marilyn

1984 Domesticity and the Denigration of Women. In *Rethinking Women's Roles: Perspectives from the Pacific,* D. O'Brien and S. Tiffany, eds., 13–31. Berkeley: University of California Press.

Stresser-Péan, Guy

1979 Introduction. [to La Huasteca et la Frontière Nord-Est de la Mésoamérique]. *Actes du XLIIe Congrès International des Américanistes* (Paris, 2–9 September 1976), 9B: 9–11.

Stuart, David

1985 The Inscriptions on Four Shell Plaques from Piedras Negras. In *Fourth Palenque Round Table, 1980,* M. G. Robertson and E. P. Benson, eds., 175–83. San Francisco: Pre-Columbian Art Research Institute.

1998 "The Fire Enters His House": Architecture and Ritual in Classic Maya Texts. In *Function and Meaning in Classic Maya Architecture,* S. D. Houston, ed., 373–425. Washington, D.C.: Dumbarton Oaks.

Taggart, James M.

1972 The Fissiparous Process in Domestic Groups of a Nahuat-Speaking Community. *Ethnology* 11:132–49.

1975a *Estructura de los grupos domésticos de una comunidad nahuat de Puebla.* Mexico City: Instituto Nacional Indigenista y Secretaría de Educación Pública.

1975b "Ideal" and "Real" Behavior in the Mesoamerican Nonresidential Extended Family. *American Ethnologist* 2:347–57.

1976 Action Group Recruitment: A Nahuat Case. In Nutini, Carrasco, and Taggart, eds. (1976), 137–53.

Taggart, James M. and Alan R. Sandstrom
1996   The Nahua Father. Paper presented at the 95th Annual Meeting of the American Anthropological Association, San Francisco.
Taylor, Paul M., ed.
1994   Fragile Traditions: Indonesian Art in Jeopardy. Honolulu: University of Hawaii Press.
Tedlock, Barbara
1982   Time and the Highland Maya. Albuquerque: University of New Mexico Press.
Teljeur, D.
1990   The Symbolic System of the Giman of South Halmahera. Dordrecht: Foris.
Thomas, P.
1995   Gender, Space, and Temanambondro Houses: Refractions of the Domestic Domain in Southeast Madagascar. Paper presented at the ASEASUK Conference, University College, Durham.
Thompson, Donald E. and J. Eric S. Thompson
1955   A Noble's Residence and Its Dependencies at Mayapan. Carnegie Institution of Washington Current Reports 25. Washington, D.C.: Carnegie Institution.
Thompson, J. Eric S.
1930   Ethnology of the Mayas of Southern and Central British Honduras. Field Museum of Natural History Publication 274, Anthropological Series 17, no. 2. Chicago
1954   A Presumed Residence of the Nobility at Mayapan. Carnegie Institution of Washington Current Reports 19. Washington, D.C.: Carnegie Institution.
1970   Maya History and Religion. Norman: University of Oklahoma Press.
Tilley, Christopher, ed.
1993   Interpretative Archaeology. Providence, R.I.: Berg.
Título de Totonicapán, El
1983   El Título de Totonicapán. R. M. Carmack and J. L. Mondloch, trans. Mexico City: Universidad Nacional Autónoma de México.
Todorova, Henrietta, V. Vasiliev, I. Ianusevič, M. Koracheva, and P. Valev, eds.
1983   Ovcharovo. Sofia: Archaeological Institute of the Bulgarian Academy of Sciences.
Tourtellot, Gair
1988   Developmental Cycles of Households and Houses at Seibal. In Wilk and Ashmore, eds. (1988), 97–120.
Tozzer, Alfred Marston
1907   A Comparative Study of the Mayas and the Lacandones. New York: Macmillan.

Traube, Elizabeth G.
1980   Mambai Rituals of Black and White. In Fox, ed. (1980), 290–314.
1986   *Cosmology and Social Life: Ritual Exchange Among the Mambai of East Timor.* Chicago: University of Chicago Press.
1989   Obligations to the Source: Complementarity and Hierarchy in an Eastern Indonesian Society. In *The Attraction of Opposites: Thought and Society in the Dualistic Mode,* D. Maybury-Lewis and U. Almagor, eds., 321–44. Ann Arbor: University of Michigan Press.

Tringham, Ruth
1990   Conclusion: Selevač in the Wider Context of European Prehistory. In *Selevac, a Neolithic Village in Yugoslavia,* Tringham and D. Krstič, eds., 567–616. Los Angeles. Institute of Archaeology, UCLA.
1991a   Households with Faces: The Challenge of Gender in Prehistoric Architectural Remains. In *Engendering Archaeology: Women and Prehistory,* J. Gero and M. Conkey, eds., 93–131. Oxford: Blackwell.
1991b   In Anbetracht der Vinca-Plocnik-Phase der Vinca-Kultur: die Manipulierung der Zeit. In *Die Kupferzeit als historische Epoche,* J. Lichardus, ed., 271–86. Saarbrücker Beitrage zur Altertumskunde 55. Bonn: Dr. Rudolf Habelt GMBH.
1991c   Men and Women in Prehistoric Architecture. *Traditional Dwellings and Settlements Review* 3(1):9–28.
1994a   Constructing the Prehistories of a Place in Europe: Visual Imagery for a Feminist Archaeology. Paper presented at the 59th Annual Meeting of the Society for American Archaeology, Anaheim, California.
1994b   Engendered Places in Prehistory. *Gender, Place, and Culture* 1(2):169–203.
1995   Archaeological Houses, Households, Housework and the Home. In Benjamin and Stea, eds. (1995), 79–107.
1996   But Gordon, Where Are the People? Some Comments on the Topic of Craft Specialization and Social Evolution. In *Craft Specialization and Social Evolution: In Commemoration of V. Gordon Childe,* B. Wailes, ed., 233–39. University Museum Monograph 93. Philadelphia: University of Pennsylvania Museum of Anthropology and Archaeology.
2000   Southeastern Europe in the Transition to Agriculture in Europe: Bridge, Buffer or Mosaic. In *Europe's First Farmers,* T. D. Price, ed. New York: Cambridge University Press.

Tringham, Ruth, Bogdan Brukner, and Barbara Ann Voytek
1985   The Opovo Project: A Study of Socio-Economic Change in the Balkan Neolithic. *Journal of Field Archaeology* 12:425–44.

Tringham, Ruth et al.
1992   The Opovo Project: A Study of Socio-Economic Change in the Balkan Neolithic. Second Preliminary Report. *Journal of Field Archaeology* 19:351–86.

Tringham, Ruth, Mirjana Stevanovič, and Bogdan Brukner, eds.
n.d.   *Opovo: The Construction of a Prehistoric Place in Europe.* Berkeley:
                University of California Archaeological Research Facility Publications.

Villa Rojas, Alfonso
1945   *The Maya of East Central Quintana Roo.* Carnegie Institution of Wash-
                ington Publication 559. Washington, D.C.: Carnegie Institution.

Vogt, Evon Z.
1964   Ancient Maya Concepts in Contemporary Zinacantan Religion. *Proceed-
                ings of the Sixth International Congress of Anthropological and Ethno-
                logical Sciences* 2 (part 2), 497–502. Paris.
1969   *Zinacantan: A Maya Community in the Highlands of Chiapas.* Cam-
                bridge, Mass.: Harvard University Press.
1976   *Tortillas for the Gods: A Symbolic Analysis of Zinacanteco Rituals.* Cam-
                bridge, Mass.: Harvard University Press.

Vom Bruck, Gabriele
1997   A House Turned Inside Out: Inhabiting Space in a Yemeni City. *Journal of
                Material Culture* 2:139–72.

Voytek, Barbara Ann and Ruth Tringham
1988   Re-thinking the Mesolithic: The Case of Southeast Europe. In *The Meso-
                lithic in Europe: Papers Presented at the Third International Symposium,
                Edinburgh, 1985,* C. Bonsall, ed., 492–99. Edinburgh: John Donald, 1989.

Wagley, Charles
1949   *The Social and Religious Life of a Guatemala Village.* Memoir Series of
                the American Anthropological Association 71. Menasha, Wis.: Ameri-
                can Anthropological Association.

Watanabe, John M.
1990   From Saints to Shibboleths: Image, Structure, and Identity in Maya Re-
                ligious Syncretism. *American Ethnologist* 17:131–50.

Watanabe, Mas
1991   Mowachaht Band 50-year Population Projection Report, 1991–2041,
                Report 2. Unpublished report compiled for the Mowachaht/Muchalaht
                Band. Mowachaht/Muchalaht Band Office, Gold River, B.C.

Waterman, T. T.
1920   *Yurok Geography.* University of California Publications in American Ar-
                chaeology and Ethnology 16, no. 5, 177–314. Berkeley: University of
                California Press.

Waterman, T. T. and Alfred L. Kroeber
1934   *Yurok Marriages.* University of California Publications in American Ar-
                chaeology and Ethnology 35, no. 1, 1–14. Berkeley: University of Cal-
                ifornia Press.
1938   *The Kepel Fish Dam.* University of California Publications in American
                Archaeology and Ethnology 35, no. 6, 49–80. Berkeley: University of
                California Press.

Waterson, Roxana

1986   The Ideology and Terminology of Kinship among the Sa'dan Toraja. *Bij-dragen tot de Taal-, Land- en Volkenkunde* 142:87–112.

1988   The House and the World: The Symbolism of Sa'dan Toraja House Carvings. *RES: Anthropology and Aesthetics* 15:34–60.

1990   *The Living House: An Anthropology of Architecture in Southeast Asia.* Kuala Lumpur and Singapore: Oxford University Press.

1993   Houses and the Built Environment in Island South-East Asia: Tracing Some Shared Themes in the Uses of Space. In Fox, ed. (1993), 221–35.

1995a   Houses and Hierarchies in Island Southeast Asia. In Carsten and Hugh-Jones, eds. (1995), 47–68.

1995b   Houses, Graves and the Limits of Kinship Groupings Among the Sa'dan Toraja. *Bijdragen tot de Taal-, Land- en Volkenkunde* 151:194–217.

1997   The Contested Landscapes of Myth and History in Tana Toraja. In *The Power of Place,* J. J. Fox, ed. Canberra: Department of Anthropology, Research School of Asian and Pacific Studies, Australian National University.

Wauchope, Robert

1934   *House Mounds of Uaxactun, Guatemala.* Contributions to American Archaeology 2, no. 7, pp. 107–71. Carnegie Institution of Washington Publication 436. Washington, D.C.: Carnegie Institution.

1938   *Modern Maya Houses: A Study of Their Archaeological Significance.* Carnegie Institution of Washington Publication 502. Washington, D.C.: Carnegie Institution.

Webster, David

1989   The House of the Bacabs: Its Social Context. In *The House of the Bacabs, Copan, Honduras,* D. Webster, ed., 5–40. Studies in Pre-Columbian Art and Archaeology 29. Washington, D.C.: Dumbarton Oaks.

Weiner, Annette B.

1985   Inalienable Wealth. *American Ethnologist* 12:210–17.

1976   *Women of Value, Men of Renown: New Perspectives in Trobriand Exchange.* Austin: University of Texas Press.

1992   *Inalienable Possessions: The Paradox of Keeping-While-Giving.* Berkeley: University of California Press.

Welsh, W. Bruce M.

1988   *An Analysis of Classic Lowland Maya Burials.* BAR International Series 409. Oxford: BAR.

Wessen, Gary

1982   *Shell Middens as Cultural Deposits: A Case Study from Ozette.* Ph.D. dissertation, Department of Anthropology, Washington State University.

1988   The Use of Shellfish Resources on the Northwest Coast: The View from Ozette. In *Prehistoric Economies of the Pacific Northwest Coast.* B. L.

Issac, ed., pp. 179–207. Research in Economic Anthropology, Supplement 3. Greenwich, Conn.: JAI Press.

White, Brian Peter
1972   *The Settlement of Nootka Sound: Its Distributional Morphology 1900–1970.* M.A. thesis, Department of Geography, Simon Fraser University.

Whittle, Alasdair
1985   *Neolithic Europe: A Survey.* Cambridge: Cambridge University Press.
1996   *Europe in the Neolithic: The Creation of New Worlds.* Cambridge: Cambridge University Press.

Wilk, Richard R. and William Rathje
1982   Household Archaeology. In *Archaeology of the Household: Building a Prehistory of Domestic Life,* R. R. Wilk and W. Rathje, eds., 617–40. *American Behavioral Scientist* 25(6).

Wilk, Richard R., ed.
1989   *The Household Economy: Reconsidering the Domestic Mode of Production.* Boulder, Colo.: Westview Press.
1991   *Household Ecology: Economic Change and Domestic Life Among the Kekchi Maya in Belize.* Tucson: University of Arizona Press.

Wilk, Richard R. and Wendy Ashmore, eds.
1988   *Household and Community in the Mesoamerican Past.* Albuquerque: University of New Mexico Press.

Wilson, Peter J.
1988   *The Domestication of the Human Species.* New Haven, Conn.: Yale University Press.

Wisdom, Charles
1940   *The Chorti Indians of Guatemala.* Chicago: University of Chicago Press.

Wouden, F. A. E. van
1968 [1935]   *Types of Social Structure in Eastern Indonesia.* Trans. R. Needham, The Hague: Martinus Nijhoff.

Wylie, Alison
1992   The Interplay of Evidential Constraints and Political Interests: Recent Archaeological Research on Gender. *American Antiquity* 57:15–35.

Zvelebil, Marek
1989   On the Transition to Farming in Europe, or What Was Spreading with the Neolithic: A Reply to Ammerman. *Antiquity* 63:379–83.

Contributors

Clark E. Cunningham is Professor Emeritus, Department of Anthropology, University of Illinois, Urbana. His ethnographic research in Indonesia, particularly in Timor, includes one of the first studies to explicitly explore the relationship of dwellings and social organization.

Susan D. Gillespie is Assistant Professor, Department of Anthropology, University of Illinois, Urbana. She has conducted archaeological fieldwork in Mexico on Formative period archaeological sites in Oaxaca and the Gulf Coast. She is the author of the award-winning book *The Aztec Kings: The Construction of Rulership in Mexican History,* based on her extensive research on Aztec ethnohistory.

Rosemary A. Joyce is Associate Professor, Department of Anthropology, University of California, Berkeley. Her archaeological research on gender in prehispanic Mesoamerica complements ongoing fieldwork in the Ulua Valley of Honduras, where she has worked since 1979. She is the author of *Cerro Palenque: Power and Identity on the Maya Periphery,* and co-editor with Cheryl Claassen of *Women in Prehistory: North America and Mesoamerica.*

Patrick V. Kirch is Professor, Department of Anthropology, University of California, Berkeley. He has conducted fieldwork throughout the Pacific, with interests ranging from the earliest peopling of the region by the Lapita people to the societies of Hawaii at the time of European contact. He is the author of numerous books, among them the award-winning *Anahulu: The Anthropology of History in the Kingdom of Hawaii* (with Marshall Sahlins), and has been a Distinguished Lecturer of the Archeology Division of the American Anthropological Association.

Yvonne Marshall is Lecturer in Archaeology, University of Southampton, United Kingdom. Her research includes archaeological studies of both Oceania and the Northwest Coast, among them an early contribution to the archaeology of gender, "Who Made the Lapita Pots?"

Susan McKinnon is Associate Professor, Department of Anthropology, University of Virginia, Charlottesville, Virginia. She is the author of *From a Shattered Sun: Hierarchy, Gender, and Alliance in the Tanimbar Islands,* based on ethnographic work in Indonesia.

Alan R. Sandstrom is Professor, Department of Sociology and Anthropology, Indiana University-Purdue University, Fort Wayne. In addition to his ethnography of the social and economic organization of the Nahuas of Veracruz published as *Corn Is Our Blood: Culture and Ethnic Identity in a Contemporary Aztec Indian Village,* he is noted as the author of *Traditional Papermaking and Paper Cult Figures of Mexico* (with Pamela Sandstrom).

Ruth Tringham is Professor, Department of Anthropology, University of California, Berkeley. She is the author of *Hunters, Fishers and Farmers of Eastern Europe* and editor of *Man, Settlement and Urbanism* (with Peter Ucko and G. W. Dimbleby). She has conducted archaeological projects in Southeast Europe and is currently engaged in research at Çatalhüyük, Turkey. She has contributed to the development of ethnoarchaeological research, household archaeology, and the archaeology of gender. Currently she is engaged in the creation of new media for representing archaeological research, using the power of hypermedia to increase multivocality in archaeology.

Roxana Waterson is Senior Lecturer, Department of Sociology, National University of Singapore, Kent Ridge, Singapore. An ethnographer working in Indonesia, she is the author of *The Living House,* a pathbreaking study of domestic architecture and its meanings.

Index

Adams, Marie J., 222 n. 12
Africa: descent rules in, 28, 39–40; house studies in, 6, 38
Age stratification, 64
Agriculture, as basis of organization, 59, 61
Alliances. *See* House (social organization), between-house relationships of; Marriage
Altar: ancestor, 17, 147, 149, 161, 163–68, 169–70, 171, 221 n. 5; as bed, 146–47, 149, 151; as coffin, 151; in Guatemala, 17; house as, 139; inside house, 67, 139, 143, 144, 145, 163–70, 171; Maya, 17, 139, 143, 144, 145, 146–47, 149, 151, 157, 159; as miniature house, 146, 147; Nahua, 67; ornamented, 161; outside house, 157, 159; Tanimbarese, 163–68, 169–70, 171, 221 n. 5. *See also* Ritual
Amazonia, 35, 215–16 n. 9
Ancestors: altars as links to, 17, 147, 149, 161, 163–68, 169–70, 171, 221 n. 5; bones of, 165, 167, 169, 173; buried under houses, 104; founding couple as, 183, 184, 185; house legitimized by, 12, 17, 19–20, 50, 104, 135, 144, 150, 159, 161, 174, 180, 192; Maya, 140, 141, 144–45, 146–47, 149–50, 159; names of, 140, 222 n. 8; ritual role of, 149, 165, 167, 169, 170, 173; supernatural, 184–85, 186–87; Tanimbarese, 162, 163–70, 171, 173, 174–75, 221 n. 5, 222 n. 8; Toraja, 183, 184–85, 186–87; as unilinear, 141; veneration of, 12, 19–20, 140, 141, 144–45, 146–47, 149–50, 159, 163–70, 171, 221 n. 5
Architecture: house as, 7, 8, 121 (*see also* House (building)); Neolithic, 116–19; ritual, 106, 107–10, 112, 113

Asia, Southeast, house societies in, 13–14, 16, 35–39, 51, 105, 137, 215 n. 6. *See also* Indonesia
Austronesia: house (building) in, 180–81; house (social organization) in, viii–ix, 19, 104; kinship systems in, 28; plant metaphor in, 162; ritual structures in, 104, 106
Aztecs, 152–53, 203, 217 n. 7

Bailey, Douglass, 119
Bali, 31
Barraud, Cécile, 214 n. 4
Belau, 193–94, 211
Belize, 149, 208. *See also* Maya
Berbers, 179
Berger, John, 125
Biggs, Bruce, 111
Blenkinsop, 88
Bloch, Maurice, 49, 104–5, 180
Boas, Franz, 24, 26
Body: house as microcosm of, 143–44; as metaphor for house, 136–37, 198
Bones, of ancestors, 165, 167, 169, 173, 177
Boon, James, 32, 37, 42, 210
Borneo, 40
Bourdieu, Pierre, 31, 179
Bulgaria, 129, 132
Burials: of heirlooms, 207, 208–10; in or under houses, 13, 19, 103, 104, 105, 108, 112, 135, 140, 147, 149, 180, 182, 201; Maya, 140, 146, 147–49, 207, 208–9; near origin house, 182; of placentas, 177, 180, 182; Tanimbarese, 180; Tlingit, 192; Toraja, 177, 182
"Burned House Horizon," 116, 124, 131
Burning, of houses, 115, 116–17, 123–24, 127, 134

California. See Yurok
Carsten, Janet, 9, 13, 38, 57, 121, 215 n. 8, 218
    n. 1; on language of house, 46–47
Çatalhöyük, 117, 126–27, 129, 132
Caves, 219–20 n. 9
Ceiba tree, 145, 151, 154, 219–20 n. 9
Center, versus periphery, 13–14, 139, 156–57
Centre National de la Recherche Scientifique,
    35–37
Chance, John, 218 n. 4
Chapman, John, 129
Chichen Itza, 204, 206–7, 210
Childbirth rituals, 177, 180, 182, 219 n.8
Childe, V. Gordon, 129
Clans, 6
Clay, as house material, 115, 116–17, 121,
    123
Clearing, house includes, 54, 59, 61, 220 n. 12
Compounds: Maya, 141, 157; Nahua, 66
Connerton, Paul, 125
Construction, of house, 136, 183, 197
Containers: concentric, 158–59; house (build-
    ing) as, 17–18, 136, 146, 154, 198, 201–2;
    house (social organization) as, 136; Maya
    on, 146, 154, 158–59
Continuity: heirlooms mark, 203, 205–6; of
    house location, 15–16, 17, 73, 76–77, 79,
    115, 119–20, 121–23, 124–25, 127, 131,
    136, 177, 180–81, 195; house societies
    reflect, 12–14, 131, 191, 192; name marks,
    173; Neolithic, 121–23; rebuilding reflects,
    15–16, 115–34; ritual for, 154–55; and
    social memory, 121
Cook, Captain James, 82
Copan, 150, 158. See also Maya
Corpse, house as, 198
Cosmology: Aztec, 152–53; house link to, 105;
    Maya, 137, 139, 143, 144–46, 151–52, 153,
    158–59, 219–20 n. 9
Cousins, 60, 181, 216–17 n. 4
Creation myth. See Origin myth
Crockford, Cairn E., 90
Cross/tree symbolism, 145–46, 151, 153, 154,
    157

Dance, 198–99, 200, 201, 202
Dawley, Walter, 98
Dead, speaking of, 196
Dedication rituals, 144, 154, 155–56
Deities, 111, 153–54
Descent groups, 8, 12, 24, 25, 110–11; in
    Africa, 28, 39–40; bilateral, 59, 60, 63, 75;

house (building) traces, 183; house (social
    organization) compared to, viii, 7, 37, 74–
    75; Nahua, 59, 60, 63; names passed via,
    196; Nuu-chah-nulth, 74, 75; overlap in, 75;
    unilineal, 7, 39. See also Kinship
Devereux, F. A., 92, 99, 100
Drabbe, Petrus, 169, 172, 173, 174–75, 221
    n. 5
Drucker, Philip, 74, 79, 92, 94, 97
Durkheim, Emile, vii
Dwelling. See House (building)

Easter Island, 113
Economics: as basis of house (social organiza-
    tion), 88–89, 96, 129, 214–15 n. 5; rights, of
    house (social organization), 200–201
Egalitarian societies, 36–37, 43
Ellen, Roy, 137, 152
Erikson, Erik, 196, 199, 201
Errington, Shelly, 37, 156; on Southeast Asian
    societies, 13–14, 42, 43–44
Europe. See Neolithic Europe
Exchange, as basis of house relationships, 44,
    45, 60, 70–71, 203, 223 n. 15

Fentress, James, 185
Fertility, house associated with, 200
Fetish: house (building) as, 17, 22, 24, 30–31,
    36, 37–38, 48, 56, 66–67, 137, 158, 215
    n. 8; in house, 17; of marriage alliances, 24
Firth, Raymond, 19, 103, 178; on Tikopia,
    107–8, 109
Fishing privileges, 200–201
Forbes, Henry O. 168–69
Fox, Jim, 104, 112

Gawa, 200
Geertz, Hildred and Clifford, 31–32
Germany, house societies in, 214–15 n. 5
Geurtjens, H., 169
Gibson, Thomas, 10
Gillespie, Susan D., 17, 181
God pots, 153–54
Great house, 217 n. 7
Green, Roger C., 106, 110
Guatemala, 17, 140, 147. See also Maya

Hammel, Eugene, 121
Hanks, William, 155, 156
Haswell (eighteenth-century explorer), 83
Hawai'i, 112–13
Headley, Stephen, 36–37

Heirlooms: in burials, 207, 208–10; continuity marked by, 203, 205–6; curated, 19–20, 189; discarded or destroyed, 206–7, 208; as house wealth, 19–20, 172–73, 174, 177, 184, 189, 190, 198, 202, 203–10; in house, 19–20, 189; Maya, 19–20, 189, 203–10; ornaments as, 203–10; Tanimbarese, 172–73, 174; Toraja, 184

Helliwell, C., 179

Helmig, Thomas, 69

Hierarchies, 8, 12, 42, 43, 44–45, 49, 51, 181, 193, 195–96, 210; altars mark, 161; concentration v. dispersal of value and, 171; house (building) reflects, 81–82, 150–51, 161, 163, 182–83; Lévi-Strauss on, 9, 29–30, 33; marriage alliances and, 30, 211; Maya, 150–51; Nuu-chah-nulth, 81–82; Tanimbarese, 162–63, 170–73; Toraja, 182–83; weak versus strong houses in, 36–37; Yurok, 198, 211

History, 26; house embodies, 182; house substitutes for, 185; oral, 185; on ornaments, 203–10. See also Memory

Hodder, Ian, 116, 126, 132, 178

House (building), 6, 46, 47; as alive, 136, 187, 198; ancestors in, 17, 19–20, 144, 150, 159, 174, 180, 192; Austronesian, 180–81; Berber, 179; burials in or under, 13, 19, 103, 104, 105, 108, 112, 135, 140, 147, 149, 180, 201; of clay, 115, 116–17, 121, 123; in compounds, 66, 141, 157; construction of, 136, 140, 143, 183, 197; as container, 17–18, 136, 146, 154, 198, 201–2; continuity in, 15–16, 17, 73, 76–77, 79, 119–20, 121–23, 124–25, 127, 131, 136, 177, 180–81, 195; as corpse, 198; as cosmic model, 135, 137, 139, 143–46, 151–57, 158, 159; decorated or ornamented, 94–96, 102, 141, 161, 162, 177, 180, 182, 185, 197; dedicated, 144, 154, 155–56; deliberately or ritually destroyed, 16, 115, 116–17, 123–24, 127, 134, 183–84; descent traced via, 119, 183; as fetish, 17, 22, 24, 30–31, 36, 37–38, 48, 56, 66–67, 137, 158, 215 n. 8; function of changes, from dwelling to ritual center, 73, 76, 84, 90, 92–94, 104, 105–14, 175; hierarchical status reflected by, 81–82, 94–96, 102, 141, 150–51, 161, 163, 182–83, 185–86; history substituted by, 185; identity with, 16, 67, 124, 177, 180–81, 195; in Indonesia, 31, 177, 179, 180, 181–88; interiors of, 76, 77, 81–82, 140, 197; Kwakiutl, 74; Lévi-

Strauss on, 135, 136, 137; Maya, 19–20, 137–60; memory of, 124–26, 131, 177, 195, 196–97, 201–2; miniature, 153, 154, 158; Nahua, 58–59, 67–68; named, 173, 175, 182–83, 195, 196–97, 201, 202; in Neolithic Europe, 117, 121–23, 124–26, 129, 133; nested, 139, 158, 159; Nuu-chah-nulth, 75, 76–77, 79, 81–82, 84, 90, 92–94, 96, 101, 102; outbuildings of, 140, 157–58, 183; personified, 136–37, 175, 197–98; as physical expression of house (social organization), 48, 136, 174, 190, 193, 194–202; Polynesian, 103–14; rebuilt or rehabilitated, 15–16, 75, 115, 119–34, 177, 181, 183–84, 186, 194; rituals in, 16, 17, 47, 67–68, 76, 94, 102, 103, 104, 105–14, 135–36, 139, 144, 147, 149, 150, 155, 157, 159, 162, 163–68, 170, 174, 175, 177, 180, 182, 185, 192, 195, 197, 198, 199, 202; as second skin, 218 n. 1; Tanimbarese, 163–68, 170, 172–73, 174, 175; Toraja, 182–84, 185–86, 187; in Turkey, 117, 126–27, 129, 132; wealth of, 19–20, 172–73, 174, 177, 184, 189, 190, 198, 201, 202, 203–10; as womb, 179–80, 220–21 n. 13; Yap, 191, 192, 194; Yurok, 194–202

House (social organization): as abstraction, 45; in Africa, 6, 38; Amazonian, 35, 215–16 n. 9; ancestors' role in, 50, 104, 105, 135, 161, 174, 192; Austronesian, viii–ix, 19, 104; in Bali, 31; in Belau, 211; between-house relationships of, 9–10, 11, 29–30, 32, 33, 44, 45, 60, 70–71, 198, 202, 203, 223 n. 15; as center, 13–14, 156–57; as change agent, 33; clan as, 6; clearing as, 54, 59, 61, 220 n. 12; as container, 136; continuity of, 203, 205–6; as economic unit, 88–89, 96, 129, 214–15 n. 5; embryonic, 68; and fertility of land, 200; hierarchy within, 9–10, 42, 49, 81–82, 210; house (building) as physical expression of, 48, 136, 174, 190, 193, 194–202; as identity locator, 18, 20, 27, 45, 73–74, 135, 136, 157, 173; as idiom, 42; in Indonesia, 11, 30; as institution, 36, 37–38; in Japan, 26; kinship-based, viii, 7, 22, 23, 25, 27, 31, 34, 37, 39, 43–44, 50, 54–55, 59–60, 66, 74–75, 170, 173, 182, 190–94; Kwakiutl, 25, 26, 49; language of, 46–47, 142, 220–21 n. 13; Lévi-Strauss's model of, 1, 3, 6–9, 10, 12, 15, 17, 20, 22, 23, 24, 26, 27, 28–29, 30–33, 34–39, 40, 41, 42–43, 47, 48, 51, 54–55, 56–57, 67–68, 74, 103,

House (*cont.*)
   107, 135–36, 141–42, 158, 162, 189–90,
   213 n. 3; in literate societies, 26; as living,
   181–82; marriages link, 9–10, 11, 12, 26,
   30, 43–44, 171, 195–96, 211; Maya, 141–
   42, 157, 220–21 n. 13; Melanesian, 200;
   membership in not based on kinship, 12, 29,
   30, 39–40, 53, 56, 68–71, 73–74, 75, 190,
   191, 192, 223 n. 15; memory of, 184–85,
   189, 193–94, 201, 203–10; Nahua, 18, 59,
   60–61, 64–68, 71; named, 65, 105, 142,
   170–73, 191, 196, 201, 202, 203; Neolithic,
   16, 26, 116–34; Nuu-chah-nulth, 79–81,
   84–88, 89–90, 92, 96, 97–102; as patrilineal, 27; perpetuity of, 48–50; in regional
   society, 44–45; rituals of, 10, 13–14, 17, 19,
   59, 88, 96–97, 105, 111, 157, 174, 202;
   songs of, 202; in Southeast Asia, 16, 35–39,
   105, 215 n. 6; as symbol, 137; Tanimbarese,
   105, 170–73, 174, 223 n. 15; Tikopia, 103,
   107; title of, 193; Toraja, 182; as transition or
   hybrid, 33–34, 51; transmittal of property
   via, 50–51, 66, 162–63; unifies incompati-
   bles, 31–32, 36, 41, 42, 56, 64, 161, 162; in
   unilineal systems, 68; in village context, 31–
   32; wealth of, 12–13, 25–26, 31, 49, 50–
   51, 56, 66, 162–63, 171, 172–73, 174, 184,
   190, 191, 200–201, 202, 203–10; Yap, 194;
   Yurok, 25, 195, 198, 200–201, 202, 203–10
Household: as basis of house, 84–88, 89, 92,
   121, 129; head of, 175–76; as kinship unit,
   59–60; Nahua, 59–60; Nuu-chah-nulth,
   84–88, 89, 92; as social unit, 121, 129; Tanimbarese, 175–76
House societies, 1–3, 6–7, 15; architecture in,
   121; Austronesian, 19; in Belau, 193–94;
   continuity of, 12–14, 131, 191, 192; German, 214–15 n. 5; in Indonesia, 16, 17, 37,
   70; as intermediate or bridging form, 51;
   Kwakiutl, 74; Lévi-Strauss on, vii, ix, 23, 27–
   32, 55–56, 121, 181, 189, 190, 195, 210–
   11, 212, 213 nn. 1, 3; Malay, 38; marriage
   alliances in, 37; Mixtec, 70–71; Nahua as,
   53, 58–72; names transmitted in, 202; Neolithic, 115–21; Nuu-chah-nulth as, 18–19,
   73, 74; oral traditions in, 201–2; Polynesian,
   19; positions within, 8 26, 170, 211–12;
   relations between houses in, 9–10, 29–30,
   36–37, 43, 44–45, 170–73, 195–96, 210–
   11; in Southeast Asia, 13–14, 16, 37, 38,
   43–44, 137; Tanimbar as, 170–73; Tikopia
   as, 107–10; Taroja as, 181, 182–83; uni-

linear society explained by, 39; Yap as, 191–
   92; Yurok as 20, 195, 212
Houston, Stephen, 219 n. 8
Howell, Signe, 105
Huelsbeck, David R., 81
Hugh-Jones, Stephen, 9, 13, 57, 58, 121, 215–
   16 n. 9, 218 n. 1; on language of house, 46–
   47
Hunting privileges, 200–201

Identity: with house (building), 16, 67, 124,
   177, 180–81, 195; with house (social organization), 18, 20, 27, 45, 73–74, 135, 136,
   157, 173
Immobility, 139, 149, 159, 173, 223 n. 14
Indonesia: ancestral altars In, 17; fetishized
   houses in, 31; gendered space in, 179; house
   societies in, 11, 16, 17, 37, 70; kinship systems in, 43, 181; marriage alliances in, 30.
   See also Tanimbar; Toraja

Japan, houses in, 26
Jewitt, John, 97
Jones, Chief Charles, 89
Joyce, Rosemary A., 19–20

Kamakau, Samuel, 217–18 n. 2
Kan, Sergei, 192
Karo Batak, 31
Kent, Susan, 178–79
King (eighteenth-century explorer), 82
Kinship, 15, 24; agriculture frames, 61; in Austronesia, 28; bilateral, 182; cognatic, 28, 29,
   60, 68; cousin, 60, 181, 216–17 n. 4; house
   (social organization) to explain, viii, 7, 22,
   23, 25, 27, 31, 34, 37, 39, 43–44, 50, 54–
   55, 59–60, 66, 74–75, 170, 173, 182, 190–
   94; in Indonesia, 43, 181; Lévi-Strauss on,
   viii, 2, 23, 27, 28, 31, 34, 46, 51, 54–55,
   216–17 n. 4; in Mesoamerica, 54–55; Nahua, 53, 59–60, 61, 62, 63–64, 66; Nuu-
   chah-nulth, 74, 75; practical versus official,
   22, 31; as process, 1, 2, 13; ritual, 56, 66;
   shared locality as basis of, 40; sibling, 37,
   43–44, 62, 63, 170, 173; as strategy, 31;
   Toraja, 182, 183; as veneer or substitute, 33,
   34; Yap, 191–92; Yurok, 195–96. *See also*
   Descent groups
Kipling, Rudyard, 134
Kirch, Patrick V., 18, 19, 110
Kirchhoff, Paul, 213 n. 3
Kis-jovak, H., 186

Kolb, Michael, 112
Kroeber, Alfred L., 20, 189; on Yurok, 24–25, 194–96, 198–99, 201
Kuper, Adam, 38
Kwakiutl, 24, 34, 74; house of, 25, 26, 49, 74

Leach, Edmund, 39, 222 n. 12
Lévi-Strauss, Claude, 11, 21; on architecture, 121; on between-house relations, 29–30, 32, 33; on continuity and memory, 121; on corporate groups, 29; on embryonic houses, 68; on fetishized house, 17, 22, 24, 30–31, 36, 37, 48, 56, 66–67, 137, 158; on hierarchy of houses, 9, 29–30, 33; on house (building), 135, 136, 137; on house as institution, 36, 37; house model of, 1, 3, 6–9, 10, 12, 15, 17, 20, 22, 23, 24, 26, 27, 28–29, 30–33, 34–39, 40, 41, 42–43, 47, 48, 51, 56–57, 67–68, 74, 103, 107, 135–36, 137, 141–42, 158, 162, 189–90, 213 n. 3; house model of critiqued, 10, 32, 34–35, 37, 38, 40, 47; on house societies, vii, ix, 23, 27–32, 55–56, 121, 181, 189, 190, 195, 210–11, 212, 213 nn. 1, 3; on Karo Batak, 31; on kinship, viii, 2, 8, 23, 27, 31, 34, 46, 51, 54–55, 216–17 n. 4; on Kwakiutl, 34, 74; on marriages, 30; on membership in house, 12, 29, 30; on social systems of Africa, 28; on transmittal of property, 66; on unity of oppositions in house, 31–32, 36, 41, 42, 64, 162; on villages, 31–32; on Yurok, 65, 194–95, 212
Lio, 105
Longhouse, 40

Macdonald, Charles, 36, 38, 40, 47
McKinnon, Susan, 13, 17, 42, 69–70, 105, 211
Malays, 38
Marriage alliances, 7, 8; endogamous or exogamous, 26, 37; fetishized, 24; hierarchies affected by, 30, 211; house (social organization) affected by, 9–10, 11, 12, 26, 30, 37, 43–44, 171, 195–96, 211; in Indonesia, 30, 171; of Nahua, 60; of Nuu-chah-nulth, 75
Marshall, Yvonne, 18–19, 50
Mathews, Peter, 209
Matrilineality, 193
Matrilocality, 61, 62–63
Mauss, Marcel, viii, 29, 214 nn. 2, 3
Maya, 137–60; altar of, 17, 139, 143, 144, 145, 146–47, 149, 151, 157, 159; ancestors venerated by, 17, 140, 141, 144–45, 146–

47, 149–50, 159; burials by, 140, 146, 147–49, 207, 208–9; on caves, 219–20 n. 9; in compounds, 141, 157; on containers, 146, 154, 158–59; cosmology of, 137, 139, 143, 144–46, 147, 150, 151–52, 153, 154, 158–59, 219–20 n. 9; creation text of, 154; cross or tree shrines of, 145–46, 151, 153, 154, 157; hierarchy of, 141, 150–51; house (building) of, 135, 137, 139, 143–46, 151–57, 158, 159; house (social organization) of, 141–42, 157, 220–21 n. 13; on immobility, 139, 149, 159; language of, 142, 155–56, 220–21 n. 13; miniature houses of, 153, 154, 158; modern, 149, 153; names of, 140, 142; ornaments of, 141, 204, 206–7, 210; outbuildings of, 140; as patrilinear, 141–42; peoples, 143, 144, 146, 147, 150, 151, 153, 154, 155, 157, 158; rituals of, 139, 144, 150, 154, 155–56, 219 n. 8, 219–20 n. 9; sites, 150, 151, 156, 158, 204, 206–7, 210; square as symbol for, 143, 145, 146, 154, 155, 156; sweat houses of, 150, 219 n. 8, 219–20 n. 9; wealth of, 19–20, 140, 150–51, 189
Maynard, Richard, 92
Meares, John, 83
Melanesia, 200
Mellaart, James, 126, 127
Memory, 121; of house (building), 124–26, 131, 177, 195, 196–97, 201–2; of house (social organization), 184–85, 189, 193–94, 201, 203–10; via oral narrative, 193–94
Mesoamerica, 54–55. See also Maya; Nahua
Missionaries, 88
Mixtec, 38, 70–71
Monaghan, John, 38, 70
Munn, Nancy, 200
Murphy, August, 98

Nahua, 58–72; age-stratified, 64; agriculture as basis of society of, 59, 61; house (building) of, 58–59, 67–68; house (social organization) of, 18, 59, 60–61, 64–68, 71; identity of, 67; kinship among, 53, 59–60, 61, 62, 63–64, 66, 68; labor exchange among, 62, 66, 71; marriage among, 60; as matrilocal, 61, 62–63; names of, 64–66; as patrilocal, 60, 61, 62, 63; religion of, 59, 67–68; transmission of wealth by, 66
Names: of ancestors, 140, 196, 222 n. 8; of house (building), 173, 175, 182–83, 195, 196–97, 201, 202; of house (social organi-

Names (*cont.*)
  zation), 65, 105, 142, 170–73, 191, 196,
    201, 202, 203; loaned and returned, 202;
    Maya, 140, 141; Nahua, 64–66; as property,
    173, 191, 202; recycled, 196; rituals for,
    202–3; Tanimbarese, 175, 222 n. 8; Tlingit,
    202; Toraja, 182–83; transmitted, 202; on
    Trobriand, 202; Yurok, 65, 201, 202, 203
Needham, Rodney, viii
Neolithic Europe, 16, 26, 116–34; house
  (building) in, 117, 123, 124–26, 129, 133;
  household units in, 121, 129; house
  societies in, 115–21; open versus closed settlements in, 117–19, 123, 124–26, 129,
  131, 133. See also Tells
Nootka. See Nuu-chah-nulth
Northwest Coast, 18–19, 24, 25, 26, 49. See
  also Kwakiutl; Nuu-chah-nulth
Nutini, Hugo, 61
Nuu-chah-nulth, 50; continuity of location of,
  76–77, 79; economic pressures on, 88–90,
  96, 97–101; eighteenth-century visitors on,
  82–84; hierarchy among, 81–82, 94–96, 97,
  102; house (building) of, 75, 76–77, 79, 81–
  82, 84, 90, 92–94, 96, 101, 102; house
  (social organization) of, 79–81, 84–88, 89,
  90, 92, 96, 97–102; as house society, 18–
  19, 73, 74; kinship among, 74, 75; marriage
  among, 75; political units among, 74; rituals
  of, 76, 94, 96–97, 102; settlement patterns
  of, 98–99, 100–101

Open settlements, 127, 129, 131, 132. See also
  Tells
Origin: concern for, 12, 13; myth, 12, 154,
  184–85; house, 16, 105, 177, 179, 182,
  184, 186–87
Ornaments, 203–10; as exchange valuable,
  203–5; history written on, 205, 206, 207,
  210; on house, 94–96, 102, 141, 161, 162,
  177, 180, 182, 185, 197; Maya, 141, 204,
  206–7, 210. See also Heirlooms

Palenque, 150, 151, 156
Parmentier, Richard, 189, 193–94
Patrilinearity, 27, 141–42
Patrilocality, 60, 61, 62, 63
Periphery, versus center, 13–14, 139, 156–57
Perpetuity, 48–49. See also Continuity
Placenta, burial of, 177, 180, 182
Plant growth metaphor, 162, 168, 169, 173
Polynesia, 104, 105–14; burials in, 112;

descent in, 110–11; house societies in, 19;
  language in 111–12; ritual deities in, 111;
  ritual posts in, 109, 111, 112; ritual spaces
  in, 110–12; temple complexes in, 103, 106,
  107–10
Potlatch, 97, 202; house, 76, 102
Porteous, Douglas, 133
Proskouriakoff, Tatiana, 210

Riedel, J. G. F., 169
Ritual: ancestors' role in, 149, 165, 167, 168–
  70, 173; architecture for, 106, 107–10, 111,
  112; in Austronesia, 104, 106; burial (see
  Burials); center versus periphery in, 13–14,
  139, 156–57; childbirth, 177, 180, 182, 291
  n. 8; continuity, 154–55; construction as,
  136, 183, 197; dance as, 198–99, 200, 201,
  202; dedication, 144, 154, 155–56; deities,
  111; destruction, 183–84; feeding, 155;
  house's (building) role in, 16, 17, 47, 67–68,
  76, 94, 102, 103, 104, 105–14, 135–36,
  139, 144, 147, 149, 150, 155, 157, 159,
  162, 163–68, 170, 174, 175, 177, 180, 182,
  185, 192, 195, 197, 198, 199, 202; for
  house (social organization), 10, 13–14, 17,
  19, 59, 88, 96–97, 105, 111, 157, 174, 202;
  kinship, 56, 66; landscape's role in, 199–
  200; language for, 111–12; Maya, 139, 140,
  144, 146, 147–49, 150, 154, 155–56, 207,
  208–9, 219 n. 8, 219–20 n. 9; naming, 202–
  3; Nuu-chah-nulth, 76, 94, 96–97, 102;
  origin house in, 105, 186–87; Polynesian,
  105–14; potlatch as, 76, 97, 102, 202;
  rebuilding, 115, 119–34; space, 110–12;
  specialist, 198–99, 200; sweat house in,
  150, 195, 197, 198, 199, 219 n. 8, 219–20
  n. 9; Tanimbarese, 165, 167, 168–70;
  Tlingit, 192, 202; Toraja, 182, 183–84, 186–
  87; valuables in, 185, 198, 203; Yurok, 195,
  197, 198–200, 201, 203
Robichaux, David, 61

Sabean, David W., 214–15 n. 5
Sahagún, Fr. Bernardino de, 153
Sandstrom, Alan, 18, 50
Sapir, Edward, 87
Scaling, 151–52
Schneider, David, 69, 189, 191–92, 210–11
Schrauwers, Albert, 44
Sedentism, 120
Sewell, William, 158
Shankland, David, 132

Sibling relationships, 37, 43–44, 62, 63, 170, 173
South Sulawesi, 10, 16, 44. *See also* Toraja
Space, 178–79; ritual, 110–12
Steadman, David, 113
Stevanović, Mirjana, 116, 124
Stuart, David, 220 n. 10
Sumatra, 31
Sweat houses: Maya, 150, 219 n. 8, 219–20 n. 9; Yurok, 195, 197, 198, 199

Taggart, James, 61, 63
Tanimbar, 70, 161–76; ancestor statue (tavu) of, 162, 163–70, 171, 173, 174–75, 221 n. 5, 222 n. 8; ancestor veneration of, 163–68, 169–70, 171, 174, 175; burials of, 180; heirloom valuables of, 171, 172–73, 174; hierarchy among, 162–63, 170–73; house (building) of, 163–68, 170, 172–73, 174, 175; house (social organization) of, 105, 170–73, 174, 223 n. 15; household head's role, 175–76; language of, 168–69, 172, 221 n. 5; marriage among, 171; names of, 105, 170–73, 175, 222 n. 8; plant metaphors of, 168, 169, 173; rituals of, 165, 167, 168–70, 180; sibling relationships among, 170, 173; village society of, 163
Tells: in Bulgaria, 132; continuity of, 120; and not-tells, 117–19, 123, 124–26, 127, 129, 131, 132, 133; as social formation, 119–20; in Turkey, 117, 126–27, 129, 132
Thomas, P., 179
Thompson, J. Eric, 153
Tikal, 205
Tikopia, 103, 107–10, 112
Tlingit, 192, 200, 202
Todorova, Henrietta, 119
To Pamona, 44
Toraja, 180, 181–88; ancestors of, 183, 184–85, 186–87; burials of, 182; heirloom valuables of, 184; hierarchy among, 182–83, 185–86; house (building) of, 182–84, 185–86, 187; as house society, 181, 182–83; kinship among, 181, 182, 183; names of, 182–83; oral history of, 185; origin houses of, 179, 182, 184, 186–87; origin myth of, 184–

85; outbuildings of, 183; rituals of, 182, 183–84, 186–87
Traube, Elizabeth C., 184
Tree. *See* Cross/tree symbolism
Tringham, Ruth, 16
Trobriand Islands, 202
Tukanoans, 215–16 n. 9
Turkey, tells in, 117, 126–27, 129, 132

Valuables. *See* House (building), wealth of; House (social organization), wealth of
Vancouver Island. *See* Nuu-chah-nulth
Village societies, 31–32, 129, 163
Vogt, Evon, 143, 151–52, 158

Walls, meaning of, 179
Waterman, T. T., 196–97
Waterson, Roxana, 16, 43, 51, 104, 121; on house as symbol, 137; on house as womb, 220–21 n. 13; on immobility, 223 n. 14; on Lévi-Strauss's model, 39, 48; on living house, 136
Webber, John, 82
Wickham, Chris, 185
Wilson, Peter J., 179
Wisdom, Charles, 143
Womb, house as, 179–80, 220–21 n. 13
van Wouden, F. A. E., viii

Yap, 69, 210–11; dwelling platform of, 191, 192, 194; as house society, 191–92; kinship among, 191–92
Yugoslavia. *See* Neolithic Europe
Yurok, 194–202; dance by, 198–99, 200, 201, 202; dead not spoken of, 196; hierarchy among, 198, 211; house (social organization) of, 25, 195, 198, 200–201, 202, 203–10; as house society, 20, 195, 212; kinship among, 195–96; landscape has meaning for, 199–200; Lévi-Strauss on, 65, 194–95, 212; named, 65, 201, 202, 203; oral traditions of, 198–99, 200; rituals of, 195, 197, 198–200, 201, 203; ritual specialists of, 198–99, 200; sweat houses of, 195, 197, 198, 199; wealth of, 198, 200–201, 203

Lightning Source UK Ltd.
Milton Keynes UK
UKHW010203270120
357609UK00012B/104